CAPITALIST DEVELOPMENT AND CLASS CAPACITIES

Recent Titles in
Contributions in Labor Studies

CAPITALIST DEVELOPMENT AND CLASS CAPACITIES

Marxist Theory and Union Organization

Jerry Lembcke

Contributions in Labor Studies, Number 25

Greenwood Press
New York • Westport, Connecticut • London

Library of Congress Cataloging-in-Publication Data

Lembcke, Jerry, 1943-
    Capitalist development and class capacities : Marxist theory and
union organization / Jerry Lembcke.
        p. cm. — (Contributions in labor studies, ISSN 0886-8239 ;
    no. 25)
    Bibliography: p.
    Includes index.
    ISBN 0-313-26209-8 (lib. bdg. : alk. paper)
    1. Trade-unions—United States—Organizing—History—20th century.
2. Capitalism—United States—History—20th century. 3. Socialism—
—United States—History—20th century. 4. Social classes—United
States—History—20th century. 5. Marxian sociology. 6. Marxian
economics. I. Title. II. Series
HD6490.07L46 1988
331.88'0973—dc19   87-37546

British Library Cataloguing in Publication Data is available.

Library of Congress Catalog Card Number: 87-37546
ISBN: 0-313-26209-8
ISSN: 0886-8239

First published in 1988

Greenwood Press, Inc.
88 Post Road West, Westport, Connecticut 06881

Printed in the United States of America

⊗

The paper used in this book complies with the
Permanent Paper Standard issued by the National
Information Standards Organization (Z39.48-1984).

10 9 8 7 6 5 4 3 2 1

Contents

Preface

This book attempts to advance the theoretical understanding of the U.S. labor movement. It builds on three rapidly developing theoretical areas—class formation, class capacities, and organizational studies—seeking to unify the advancements in these areas under the general theory of uneven and combined development. The essential argument of the book is that capitalist development begets working-class development. It is argued that the capacity of the working class to transform the social relations of production basic to capitalism are enhanced with the maturation of capitalism and that one facet of that increased capacity can be observed in the organizational forms of labor unions. Specifically, it is argued that the more proletarianized fractions of the working class give rise to union organizational forms that enhance the capacity of the working class to transform capitalist social relations. This book explores the question of organizational efficacy as a single proposition of a much larger theoretical problem bearing on working-class historical agency.

Chapter 1 establishes the demarcation between recent neo-Marxist theory and the theoretical position taken by this book. This chapter argues that the neo-Marxist work of the 1970s failed to break, in fundamental ways, with the basic philosophical, methodological, and ideological tenants of liberal pluralism. The assumption of the labor process literature that flowed in the wake of Harry Braverman's (1974) work, for example, has been that as workers become proletarianized, their capacity to struggle in their own behalf is diminished. The theoretical implications of the labor process studies is that Marx incorrectly identified a dialectical relationship between labor and capital; his aphorism that capitalism creates its own gravediggers was wrong. Translated into strategy for labor and the socialist movement, the labor process tradition has resulted in a dismissal of the working class as an agent for social change (e.g., Aronowitz 1983; Gorz 1982; Katznelson and Zolberg 1986).

Chapter 2 attempts to reconstruct the relationships between the development process, class formation, and organizational forms. It does this within the theoretical tradition of uneven and combined development. After reviewing the principles of this tradition, U.S. labor history through the formative years of the Congress of Industrial Organizations (CIO) is reconstructed in a way that the relationship between class structure, class formation, and organizational forms begins to emerge. Chapter 2 also begins the presentation of empirical data that constitutes the basis of this study. The concepts central to this study—class, class capacity, and the logic of collective action—are all rigorously operationalized in this chapter. Offe and Wiesenthal's (1980) point that organizational forms are class specific is central to the analysis. It is shown that union organization forms vary from most capitalist-like to most working-class-like, depending upon the level of proletarianization of the class fraction dominant in the organization. The most capitalist-like organizations emphasize the mobilization of financial resources and are governed by representation structures based on a per-capita logic, while the latter rely more on the mobilization of human resources and are based on a unit-rule logic of representation. Quantitative data are developed from a content analysis of the constitutions of the 27 unions comprising the CIO in the late 1930s.

Chapter 3 is comprised of three case studies: the International Woodworkers of America; the United Autoworkers; and Mine, Mill, and Smelter Workers. The purpose of the case studies is to show that the relationships between organizational, demographic, and industrial variables is not positivistic and static but rather dialectical. They are relationships that can be understood only as part of an historical process and they are relationships shaped by conscious decisions, made with strategical and tactical considerations in mind. By the end of Chapter 3 it is clear that there is a pattern to the organizational preferences of various working-class fractions. The chapter concludes:

> In each case it was the most proletarianized fractions of the work force that pursued representation forms tending to unit-rule. The least proletarianized fractions pursued per-capita forms of representation. Moreover, the arguments used in support of each form were very different. The supporters of unit-rule emphasized class solidarity and the need to build class power. The supporters of per-capita rule cited fiscal logic—"dollar democracy," in the words of one critic.

Chapter 4 extends the analysis to the level of international organizations. The example of the United States' recent withdrawal from the International Labor Organization (ILO) is used to illustrate the applicability of the analysis at this level. I examine the organizational history of U.S.-Canadian unions during the CIO era to show that varying degrees of internationalism within the unions is related to uneven class formation (proletarianization) and that that unevenness is transformed into a political logic through specific organizational forms.

Because this project began with the questions upon which Chapter 5 is based, the chapter has special etiological significance for the book. The role played by the Communist party (CP) in the CIO continues to be a virtual obsession with historians and sociologists. Conventionally framed, the questions focus on whether or not the CP made a difference and, if so, whether that difference was positive or negative. In *One Union in Wood: A Political History of the International Woodworkers of America* (Lembcke and Tattam, 1984) we answered both questions in the affirmative. One of those differences was observable in what sociologists would call the organizational behavior of communists. In the IWA we saw that communists were more democratic and that they advocated forms of organization that were different enough to be labeled "commie structures" by anticommunist CIO leaders like Adolph Germer. A content analysis of union documents (which, as nearly as I have been able to tell, no one else has done) quickly produced evidence that the CP in the IWA was not unique—the Communist party was a democratic influence in the CIO.

But was that because there was something special about the Communist party, per se? Or was there some more structural reason that could account for the range of organizational choices available and the choices made by the party's activists? It was the sociological literature on organizations that led me to a formulation of the questions in class terms and set me on the path to trying to explain working-class organizational variations through reference to the process of class formation. The arguments and data bearing on the conventional questions about union democracy are presented in this chapter, however, because I think it will help other scholars move beyond those questions to a class-based analysis more quickly than I did.

Chapter 6 recapitulates the central theoretical argument and empirical findings of the previous chapters and applies the conclusions to the conditions of the late twentieth century. The basic argument made is that working-class organizations are the links between uneven temporal and sectoral levels of development. The newest sectoral development in the U.S. political economy is the public sector. Yet, the power of the labor movement is based in private sector unions. In this way, a situation similar to that of the early twentieth century—when the new and fastest growing sector was the monopoly, mass industry sector while working-class power was based in the competitive sector —is being repeated. Now, as then, the unevenness within the working class is manifested in organizational imbalances that must be redressed if capitalism's contradictions are to be realized in working-class advances.

In general, this book argues for a restoration of the classical Marxist position linking the development process, class formation, and class capacities. In practical terms, it argues for a restoration of strategies and tactics premised upon a dialectical understanding of capitalism that sees the process of proletarianization as capacity-enhancing rather than capacity-eroding.

Acknowledgments

I am grateful to many people for their contributions to this book.

Carolyn Howe called my attention to the relevance of the "logics of collective action" literature to the historical material I was struggling to interpret. Carolyn also helped code and analyze the quantitative data in Chapter 2 and assisted in the preparation of the manuscript.

Mark Wardell encouraged me to develop the material on uneven development and provided helpful comments on early drafts. Julia Adams urged me to pursue the connection between class and organizational forms.

Lawrence University librarians Gretchen Bambrick and Kathleen Isaacson helped locate census data and archival materials that were the crucial sources for the study. The staff of the Wisconsin Historical Society Library in Madison was also invaluably helpful in locating union documents that provided the key data for this study. June Woods and Pat Bauer helped with the production of the tables and typing the manuscript. Christopher Gamsky helped proofread the last-minute drafts.

Much of the historical material on the International Woodworkers of America in Chapter 3 was developed with the help of Bill Tattam. Jeremy Egolf and Michael McDonough read and made helpful suggestions on various portions of the manuscript. I am grateful to Carolyn Howe, Michael Gordon, Rhonda Levine, Jay O'Brien, George Saunders, Ron Mason, and Marty Hart-Landsberg for their personal and intellectual companionship while I was working on this project.

CAPITALIST DEVELOPMENT AND CLASS CAPACITIES

1

From Organizational Democracy to Organizational Efficacy: Toward a Class Analysis of Union Organization

INTRODUCTION

As the crisis of U.S. capitalism deepens during the closing decades of the twentieth century, the need for the U.S. socialist movement to formulate strategy and tactics that will lead to a transformation of the national political economy becomes more pressing. Central to the discussion of an agenda for change has to be the role of the U.S. working class in a socialist transformation. This chapter begins with the recognition that the most influential organizations within the U.S. Left have relegated the working class to an increasingly marginalized role. The chapter reexamines the theoretical work on which the socialist movement is premising its strategical choices and attempts to reformulate the most important propositions.

There are two theoretical problems central to the question of the working class as the historical agent of socialism. One involves the relationship between capitalist development and class capacities. Two lines of argument on this question can be found within recent studies of the U.S. working class. The dominant position, taken by those associated with the New Left traditions of the 1960s and 1970s (Aronowitz 1973, 1983; Braverman 1974; Ehrenreich and Ehrenreich 1976; Marglin 1974) and supported by work done on the European working class (Aminzade 1984; Gorz 1982; Katznelson and Zolberg 1986), has contended that as capitalism developed, the economic, cultural, and political capacities of the working class to struggle for socialism were diminished. The alternative position, consistent with classical Marxist theory, argues that advancing proletarianization is a factor that enhances class capacities. The Marxist position has received some support from Gedicks' (1976) study of radicalism in the Finnish-American community, urban political economic studies (Tabb and Sawyers 1978), studies of Black working-class formation (Trotter 1985; Marable 1985), and from studies of working-class voting behavior by Hamilton (1972) and Szymanski (1978). The Marxist position, however, has remained vastly underdeveloped. There have been few attempts (Benenson 1985; Meiksins 1987) to critique the New Left position from a Marxist perspective.[1]

The second theoretical problem concerns the conceptualization of class capacities. Offe and Wiesenthal (1980) made clear that capitalist-class sources of power (accumulated capital) are distinct from producing-class(es) sources of power, but they collapsed both proletarians and petty bourgeois producers into the same category and called it "working class." Offe and Wiesenthal identified the "association" of individual producers as being the source of power indigenous to the producing class. However, their producing class is actually two classes —petty bourgeois and proletarian—and each has a distinct source of power. Petty bourgeois capacity is based upon the association of autonomous, individual producers while proletarian capacity is based upon the unity or collectivity of wage-earning workers.

The confusion left by Offe and Wiesenthal has allowed non-Marxist formulations of class capacities to continue to dominate the literature. These formulations have been drawn essentially from pluralist tradition. Within that tradition power is equated with individual sovereignty based upon the control of production. As a notion of *class* capacity, it is appropriate to the petty bourgeoisie under capitalism since petty bourgeois-class capacity is derived from control of production. But it is inappropriate as a conceptualization of working-class capacities. In this book I use the terms "association" and "collectivity" interchangeably to refer to the logic of working-class capacity, and refer to petty bourgeois or artisanal capacity as simply "control of production process."[2]

The two theoretical problems are linked because the relationship between the development process and class capacities largely depends on how one conceptualizes working-class capacities. If one accepts traditional pluralist notions of class capacity as applicable to the working class, then it is probably true that the capitalist development process erodes working-class capacities. If, however, the capacity of the working class is something other than an aggregation of sovereign individuals, a more dialectical relationship between development and working-class capacity can be established.

This chapter is a contribution to the development of a Marxist theory of working-class capacity. It proceeds by reviewing the historical and political context out of which New Left-era scholarship arose. It is then argued that in key respects the work of radicals failed to break with the political and theoretical problematic established by pluralist social theorists. Specifically, the relationship between class and organizational behavior formulated by Lipset et al. (1956) and the subsequent framing of the organizational question as one of "democracy" rather than class capacities has never been rejected.

Finally, the chapter moves to a reformulation of the union organizational question. It is argued that the organizational question can be more productively posed as a problem of class capacity, that is, a problem of organizational efficacy, not organizational democracy. Three bodies of literature are synthesized in this effort: the work in logics of collective action (e.g., Offe and Wiesenthal 1980; Lembcke and Howe 1986); studies of class formation (Gordon, Edwards, and Reich 1982) and class capacities (Therborn 1983); and organizational studies done within the "strategical choices" framework (Child 1972; Cornfield 1986). Following Therborn's (1983, 38) suggestion, this chapter replaces the conventional concern with static class properties and formal organizational structure with questions about the "capacities of a given class to act in relation to others and the form of organization and practice thereby developed." The chapter adopts Therborn's (p. 41) position that "the fundamental power resource available to the working class, therefore, is its *collectivity*: especially its capacity for unity through interlocking, mutually supportive and concerted practices [emphasis in original]."

This chapter takes the discussion beyond the current level of theoretical development by giving greater specificity to the notion of class capacities and linking the relationship between class formation and class capacities with the more abstract level of uneven historical and spatial development. In this chapter I argue that *working-class* capacity is a social-relational phenomenon that is observable as an *organizational* variable—that is, the essential "resource" mobilized in pursuit of working-class objectives is neither pecuniary, as it is for the capitalist class, nor control of production, as it is for the petty bourgeoisie, but rather organizational structure (see Figure 1.1). Therborn's notion of collectivity materializes, in other words, through organizational forms.

Moreover, some organizational forms maximize working-class collectivity while others frustrate or block it. The working class must not only consciously pursue an organizational form that advances collectivity, but it must also oppose attempts by the capitalist class to impose organizational forms that atomize the working class and must adopt organizational forms that mitigate the effects of uneven capitalist development. Uneven sectoral and regional development in the

Figure 1.1
Conceptual Dichotomies of Class and Class Capacities

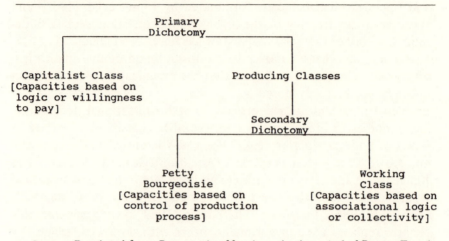

Source: Reprinted from *Recapturing Marxism: An Appraisal of Recent Trends in Sociological Theory*, Rhonda F. Levine and Jerry Lembcke, eds., 1987, with permission of Praeger.

United States has produced a working class that is unevenly formed: some sectors of the economy and some regions are highly unionized, for example, while others are not. How that structural unevenness manifests itself within the working class is an organizational question: Are the imbalances reproduced by the organizational choices made by the working class or are the strengths of one sector/region transmitted as a resource deployable in another? The struggle over organizational forms thus becomes an important dimension of the class struggle, and the study of class capacities becomes, in key respects, a study of the relationship between uneven development and organizational forms.

CAPITALIST DEVELOPMENT AND CLASS CAPACITIES

During the twentieth century the U.S. working class has been shaped by three trends. In the workplace the displacement of craft and skilled labor by mass production techniques has allowed the employment of large numbers of unskilled workers; culturally, the integration of diverse ethnic strains produced by the centralization of production facilities and the constant infusion of petty bourgeois ideology has precluded the development of a clear-cut working-class consciousness; politically, the increasing intervention of the state in the regulation and management of the economy has added to the complexity of class relations and complicated the formulation of working-class strategy and tactics.

The first of these trends, the deskilling or degradation of labor, has been the focus of most studies of the U.S. working class done during the past 15 years. The dominant thesis has been that as monopoly capitalist forms of work, community and political organization encroached upon earlier forms, the capacity of U.S. workers to struggle in their own interest was undermined. In a seminal piece, Katherine Stone (1975) argued that the source of power for steel workers in the late 1800s was their monopoly of skill and knowledge of the production process. The institution of mass production techniques and the separation of the knowledge of how steel was made from the workers themselves was the key to breaking worker control of the industry. Addressing the relationship between culture and class formation, Stanley Aronowitz argued in *False Promises* (1973) that a nascent labor radicalism based in the homogeneity of the native-born craft workers was blunted by the arrival in the United States of the polygloted, unskilled work force demanded by monopoly capitalism. More recently (1983) he has portrayed the "technical intelligentsia' as the modern day equivalent of the nineteenth century craft workers in terms of its ability to play a leading role in social change. The increasing role of the state in the management and regulation of the private economy has been emphasized by Piven and Cloward (1982) among others as a key to understanding the failure of U.S. workers to achieve socialist reforms in times of crisis.

There is no doubt that the rich historical detail provided by these studies has improved our understanding of an important dynamic of monopoly capitalism. But the theoretical implication of these studies is that the cutting edge of history lies at the interface between monopoly and competitive (or even precapitalist) forms of organization. As such, they lead to agendas for further research that elevate the central importance of the labor aristocracy and the petty bourgeoisie in the class struggle and to strategical thinking that is reactive and protectionist. The failure to identify the dialectical properties of the capitalist development process has produced a kind of static and unimaginative quality in the U.S. socialist movement that will at best be able to frustrate monopoly capitalism without being able to advance socialism. In short, the contemporary scholarship upon which many currents of the U.S. Left base their action has failed to identify the ways in which the capitalist development process produces the conditions for socialism and, by failing to do so, has failed to move the historic agenda to the stage of monopoly capitalism versus socialism.

The theoretical implication of these studies can best be appreciated against the backdrop of Marx and Engels' attempt to describe the capitalist development process as a dialectical process and therefore as an historical force whose long-term effect was to empower the working class. The Marxist assertion that capitalism would produce its own grave diggers is not supported either by the logic of the work-process analysts or by their empirical work. The practical consequences of these studies is that casting the working class in a central role for contemporary socialist strategies would be a mistake precisely because the degradation of work under capitalism has rendered the working class decreasingly capable of independent action. Consistent with these conclusions, many socialist organizations have targeted middle-class and "new working-class" segments of the population for their organizing activities.

While it is true that Marx and Engels did not provide the concentration of detail on the work process that has emerged in the last decade, it is nevertheless true that the corpus of their work contains a clear effort to identify the contradictory relationship between the development of class relations under capitalism and the development of working-class capacities.

The notion of proletarianization is based on the Marxist understanding of exploitation. Marx argued that the source of all profit lies in human labor, and that if the capitalist is to earn a profit it must come from the unequal distribution of returns on production. Because the capitalist controls the means of production and hence the sale and distribution of products, the capitalist returns less to the workers than what the worker actually produces. This is called exploitation, and the rate at which the capitalists extract surplus from the labor of their workers is called the rate of exploitation. Marx expressed this as the rate of exploitation: surplus/variable capital.

The capitalist is also in competition with other capitalists, both nationally and internationally. There is a constant pressure to produce for a lower selling price. This means getting more out of the productive process for the same or lower costs. It means workers will have to produce more without receiving a commensurate increase in wages, that is, an increase in the rate of exploitation. The first way to do this is to increase the ratio of constant capital (machinery and raw material) to variable capital (wages)—what Marx called the organic composition of capital. The second is to increase the scale of production—what Marx called the centralization of capital.

Proletarianization captures the human and social effects of capitalists' efforts to maintain an acceptable rate of exploitation. Increasing the organic composition of capital most directly effects workers by displacing their jobs through mechanization and automation; the quality of the remaining jobs is also diminished. Accident rates in manufacturing, for example, have increased as production processes have become more capital intensive. While Marx and Engels were by no means oblivious to or unconcerned about the dehumanizing effects of the proletarianization process, they also saw it as a contradictory process that would ultimately strengthen the working class. "All political economists of any standing," wrote Marx in *Capital* (1967, 447), "admit that the introduction of new machinery has a baneful effect on the workmen in the old handicrafts and manufactures." Early worker struggles were fueled by resistance to the brutal imposition of machine technology and their desire to return to previous forms of production. In the *Communist Manifesto* Marx noted that workers "direct their attacks not against the bourgeois conditions of production, but against the instruments of production themselves; they destroy imported wares that compete with their labour, they smash to pieces machinery, they set factories ablaze, they seek to restore by force the vanished status of the workman of the Middle Ages" (Marx and Engels 1972, 42). But in Marx's view, the past could not be restored and he characterized continuing efforts to do so as "utopian." Many of Marx's writings during the period of the First International were criticisms directed at followers of Michael Bakunin and Ferdinand Lassall, whose efforts to form associations of individual producers (cooperatives) as a hedge against capitalism he saw as an extension of the utopian tendency.

Marx and Engels saw in the emergence of capitalist production something far more profound than the radicalization of workers. Capitalism, "with all the miseries it imposes upon [workers] ... simultaneously engenders the material conditions and the social forms necessary for an economic reconstruction of society" (Marx and Engels 1972, 186). With the loss of individual control over production and the workplace, social individualism was broken down and the groundwork was laid for the collective struggle of workers for the social ownership and control of capital.

Marx and Engels did not write in any detail about the specifics of union organizational forms. It is clear from their general theory, however, that they viewed proletarianization as a favorable development for working-class capacities. Marx wrote,

> The real fruit of [workers'] battle lies, not in the immediate result, but in the ever expanding union of the workers. This union is helped on by the improved means of communication that are created by modern industry, and that places the workers of different localities in contact with one another. It was just this contact that was needed to centralize the numerous local struggles, all of the same character, into one national struggle between classes. . . . This organization of the proletarians into a class, and consequently into a political party, is continually being upset again by the competition between the workers themselves. But it ever rises up again, stronger, firmer, mightier [Marx 1967, 43].

Engels (1975, 418) emphasized the contradictory effects of the centralization of capital and labor in industrial cities:

> If the centralization of population stimulates and develops the property-holding class, it forces the development of workers yet more rapidly. The workers begin to feel as a class, as a whole; they begin to perceive that, though feeble as individuals, they form a power united. . . . The great cities have transformed the disease of the social body, which appears in *chronic* form in the country, into an *acute* one, and so made manifest its real nature and the means of curing it [emphasis added].

The processes of capitalist development proceeded unevenly, however, and that unevenness was reflected in the uneven development of the working class. "The more the factory system has taken possession of a branch of industry," noted Engels (1975, 529), "the more the working-men employed in it participate in the labour movement; the sharper the opposition between working-men and capitalists, the clearer the proletarian consciousness in the working-men." In locales and regions where technology lagged behind and the centralization of workers did not occur, the individualized precapitalist artisanal forms of production persisted. The "small masters" occupy a middle ground between "proletarian Chartism and shopkeepers' Radicalism," according to Engels.

Several points applicable to the general thesis of this chapter can be derived from the Marxist position as outlined here. First, it is absolutely clear that for Marx and Engels the proletarianization of labor attendant upon the development of capitalism entailed the simultaneous development of working-class capacities to transform the class relations of capitalism. Second, it is evident that the representation of individual economic and political rights under capitalism was, for them, not the principle objective of working-class organization. Rather, the objective was the empowerment of the working-class struggle. Finally, there emerges from the outline a working-class strategical agenda of unifying the broadest possible elements of the working class, including the unemployed and the marginally employed. This is the key point because in the context of current struggles it becomes the criterion by which we can specify the most efficacious form of union organization.

In the United States the culmination of capitalist development in the unionization and political mobilization of millions of industrial workers during the 1930s lent credibility to the Marxist thesis that the industrial proletariat would be a leading socialist force (Gordon, Edwards, and Reich 1982). During the 1930s working-class movements like the CIO became rallying points for not only workers but for many middle-class activists. As a consequence, the notion of proletarian agency was more than an academic issue at the outset of the Cold War—it was a material force to be reckoned with. In other words, the political context in which the post-war union democracy studies were done demanded that the credibility of the basic Marxist theory of capitalist development and class formation be challenged.

The CIO period is given special attention in this book because of its proximity to the current period. It is assumed that the events of those years, and their interpretation by historians and sociologists, laid the ground work upon which the present conditions developed. The following section is a critical review of the dominant scholarship on that era; in Chapter 6 I outline a structural interpretation that is based on the organizational analysis developed in the intervening chapters.

POST-WAR LABOR STUDIES

Prior to the late 1940s union organizational studies were the purview of labor historians, many of whom worked within a framework established by institutional economics. Most of these studies focused on the unions affiliated with the Congress of Industrial Organizations and emphasized the factional struggles between communists and non-communists within the unions. A major theme of these studies was that Communist Party influence was a detrimental influence in the unions. The issue of Communist Party influence was never discussed in terms of class capacities, however; rather, "democracy" was made the issue. In 1938, for example, Benjamin Stolberg wrote that the rank and file in the CIO was rebelling against the Party's "complete disregard of all union democracy" (Stolberg p. 155). Writing about the International Woodworkers of America in 1945, Vernon Jensen likewise counterpoised communist presence in the union to rank-and-file democracy.

Although the notion of democracy employed by the labor historians was very vague and under-theorized, it was framed in a way that had specific political implications. The assumption of the studies was that unions represented the material interests of their members against the interests of capital and that, generally speaking, unions that were controlled by their members were democratic; unions that were controlled by "outside" forces were considered undemocratic. In their accounts of the CIO, historians conventionally treated communist unionists as agents of foreign interests or "outsiders" and it was on this basis that they were considered an undemocratic influence.

Implicit in this approach to the question of democracy within unions was the understanding that the relationships between union and nonunion groups (including employers) and various factions within unions involved an element of power that was exercised in pursuit of group interests. Moreover, the careful documentation of the socioeconomic bases of the factions provided by these studies made it possible to account for organizational differences in class or class-fractional terms.

Framed in this way, union organizational studies were sure to remain politicized because it would always be possible to challenge, on empirical grounds, someone else's conclusions about what (or who) was or was not democratic. They were, in other words, asking promising questions and, although their own ideological biases prevented them from acknowledging the conclusions to which their data pointed, it was only a matter of time before someone else would. Moreover, the empirical evidence usually did not support the Cold War contentions that the communist movement was alien and antithetical to "democracy": Communists were indeed indigenous to the factories and communities they organized and, in case after case, it was the constitutional rights of communist unionists that had been violated by their opponents; the key actors in the purges of the late 1940s were often trade union professionals, leaders of liberal movements outside the unions, state agencies, and employers, not the rank and file (Levenstein 1981; Lembcke 1984a; Keeran 1980). In short, the logic behind the purges of the Cold War period was anything but democratic and the energy for them appeared to emanate from everywhere but the industrial working class. This framework left open the possibility that not only were industrial workers capable of democracy, but that non-working-class elements were quite capable of undemocratic behavior—possibilities that made the relationship between class and democracy a fit subject for study. In the context of the Cold War this framework was clearly too dangerous; a new framework that would depoliticize the questions of union democracy was needed. Liberal sociologists accommodated this agenda.

Sociology and Union Democracy

The most important of the union democracy studies was that of the International Typographical Union (ITU) published as *Union Democracy* in 1956 by S. M. Lipset, M. A. Trow, and J. S. Coleman. The authors viewed their study of the ITU as important for what could be learned that would be applicable to political processes in the larger society. They adopted the historians' definition of the analytical problem—the conditions favorable to union democracy—and used the ITU case as an exception to prove Michels' (1959) "iron law of oligarchy": In the absence of countervailing forces, individuals will seek to maximize their power and influence in organizations. They defined democracy as the "possibility that an official can be defeated for reelection" and concluded that the ITU was democratic by this criteria. It had been able to maintain its high level of democracy, moreover, because three conditions checked the natural human and organizational propensities toward oligarchy: The ITU was small, its members (printers) were relatively high status workers, and its governance system (the two-party structure) was pluralistic (Lipset et al. 1956, 452-53). Stated in theoretical terms, Lipset et al. found union democracy to be positively associated with political pluralism and the status of members, and negatively associated with size.

Radical Critiques of Union Democracy Studies

On its own terms—those of political pluralism—*Union Democracy* had a number of problems. In the first place, Lipset et al. conceptualized their dependent variable (union democracy) in a way that isolated it from social relations external to the union. By their definition, a union could be democratic even if its leadership positions were filled by a succession of persons having no connection with or interest in the union's members; and a union could be considered democratic without reference being made to the adequacy of its performance in representing worker interests. In short, neither the relationship of the leaders to the members nor the relationship of the union to the larger society were germane to the notion of union democracy as it was conceptualized by Lipset et al.

Lipset et al. assumed away the criticism of their narrow conceptualization by saying that a union that did not represent its members would not be able to hold their allegiance and would therefore cease to exist. Thus, a union that was democratic by their criteria was assumed also to be representative of worker interests in other social, economic, and political arenas. More recent research done by Valentine (1978), however, found little association between the level of union democracy (as defined by the pluralists) and the efficacy of unions as representatives of worker interests.

With the notion of democracy conceived as narrowly as it was, it was easy to demonstrate quantitative relationships between it and similarly narrow independent variables like size; but even a slightly broadened notion of democracy such as that employed by Faunce (1967) dissolved the certainty of the relationship. The narrowness of the conceptualization was typical of post-war "abstracted empiricism" that reduced its subject to psychological explanations and failed to relate sectors of society to one another. As a consequence, the ITU study led to conclusions that may or may not have been "true" but that had little "genuine relevance" and that functioned in a way that "eliminate[d] the great social problems and human issues of our time from inquiry" (Mills 1959, pp. 62, 73).

Few studies could have had less "genuine relevance" than did *Union Democracy*. Indeed, what is most remarkable about the ITU study is the absence of its authors' attention to the ideological issues and political factionalism that was tearing the North American union movement apart while they were doing their work. With whole internationals being expelled from the CIO, with the Canadian border being sealed to left-wing unionists, and with hundreds of union activists facing prosecution under various pieces of Cold War legislation, the question of governance structures *internal* to unions was hardly *the* issue. What *Union Democracy* did provide was a deflection of attention away from the real issues.

The main contribution of subsequent liberal and radical critiques of the ITU study was to move the questioning away from purely formalistic notions of union democracy into a framework that recognized the conflicting interests of union members and employers. Despite some attempts to reconceptualize the organizational problem in terms of social relations (e.g., "logics of collective action"), however, the term "union democracy" has generally been retained to refer to both formal organizational structure and representational efficacy. Moreover, the failure to question more fundamentally the pluralist assumptions of the union democracy studies has resulted in many of those assumptions being carried over into contemporary radical and neo-Marxist studies.

For activists, the confusion has meant that organizational theory has been essentially irrelevant. In the absence of any theory to guide practice, reform efforts have been sporadic and ad hoc; demands have been inconsistent from one reform effort to another and sometimes contradictory in light of the overall objectives of the union. It is safe to say that, while nearly everyone, incumbents and insurgents alike, lays claim to the plank of union democracy, it has become a purely normative expression with increasingly vague meaning.

TOWARD A MARXIST THEORY OF CLASS AND ORGANIZATION

Because radical sociologists never really focused their critique in a theoretical way, neither they, nor the reform movements they have influenced, have broken with the fundamental premises of pluralism. Specifically, (a) the definition of the organizational problem as one of "democracy" has never been questioned, and the relationship between class and organizational forms found in *Union Democracy* has never been criticized; (b) the assumptions made by the pluralists about the relationship between organizational size and organizational efficacy (efficacy understood for the moment to be "democracy") has not been reexamined; and (c) the ideological bias of Lipset et al. has not been subjected to an empirical critique.

Class and Organizational Behavior

Having no empirical base on which to stand, Lipset et al. dismissed the notion of proletarian democracy on philosophical grounds.

Aristotle . . . suggested that democracy can exist only in a society which is predominantly middle class. . . . that only in a wealthy society with a roughly equal distribution of income could one get a situation in which the mass of the population would intelligently participate in politics and develop the self-restraint necessary to avoid succumbing to the appeals of irresponsible demagogues. . . . Applying this proposition to trade-union government, we would expect to find democracy in organizations whose members have a relatively high income and more than average security [p. 14].

In other words, Lipset et al. theorized the relationship between class and organizational forms just the opposite from Marxist theory: The conditions for the most positive organizational developments are most favorable in industries and occupations in which working conditions most closely approximate those of middle-class occupations; those industries and occupations that are most working class, on the other hand, are least likely to produce a desirable form of unionism.

For Lipset et al., the organizational problem to be analyzed was focused by a pluralist notion of democracy—a "good" organization was a democratic organization. Their argument entailed the adoption of a philosophical notion of democracy consistent with Cartesian methodology and Rousseauan social philosophy. "In the Cartesian world . . . phenomena are the consequences of the coming together of individual atomistic bits, each with its own intrinsic properties, determining the behavior of the system as a whole. Lines of causality run from part to whole, from atom to molecule, from molecule to organism, from organism to collectivity" (Levins and Lewontin 1985, 1-2). Applied to human society, the Cartesian view held that the individual was ontologically prior to the whole and that, methodologically, one can understand society only by reducing it to the characteristics of its parts—individuals. Individualism, as a social philosophy, met the needs of an emergent capitalism and thus came to be the ruling ideology of the new ruling class.

Lipset et al. premised their analysis of organizational behavior on this Cartesian model. A democratic organization (a "good" organization) thus was one in which individual sovereignty was maximized. The authors never examined the historical correspondence between capitalism and Cartesian reductionism; nor did they acknowledge that organizational models based on individual sovereignty have an ideological bias that reflects a specific, bourgeois, class interest. Finally, there was no recognition in *Union Democracy* that a different organizational logic might be spawned by the interests and historical experience of the working class.

Post-war radical theory accepted this pluralist formulation. In *New Men of Power*, C. Wright Mills (1948, 267) described U.S. workers as "underdogs [who] lack the hardy self-confidence and capacity for indignation common to middle-class people." Through Mills' influence on the New Left, the same class bias was carried into later studies. Throughout the 1960s and 1970s the dominant theme of working-class studies (e.g., Braverman 1974; Ehrenreich and Ehrenreich 1976; Marglin 1974; Aronowitz 1973; Piven and Cloward 1982) was that monopoly capitalism undermined the capacity of the U.S. working class. Writing specifically about union organizational forms, Sam Friedman (1982, 254) noted about Teamster Local 208 that the local was exceptionally democratic and militant because of the high level of communication among truck drivers, their high levels of skill and craft identity, and their high pay—all of which were high-status characteristics Lipset said made printers more inclined toward democracy.

There are at least three important problems with this formulation. First, while there is undoubtedly the available empirical evidence to sustain a variety of positions on this question, the record is not nearly as clear-cut as the liberal and radical traditions have presented it. The argument will be made at greater length below that the CIO unions representing the more proletarianized workers were in fact the most democratic, even by pluralist standards. Second, the theory implies that capitalism deskills workers, and deskilled workers are less democratic. While the statement is in itself an indictment of capitalism that compels an understanding of how to transform the system, it also implies a logic of causation that is unidirectional and social relationships that are static. As such, it does not contain within it a theory of how change in the actual structure of capitalism might occur. It leads to strategies and tactics that are reactive and defensive rather than transformative. Friedman (1982, 262), for example, notes that "capitalism produces strong tendencies toward both union bureaucracy and work degradation" but concludes that "these tendencies need not be absolutely determinant. Workers can resist, and they can win major victories." While this formulation is an advance over that of pluralists who saw bureaucratization as inevitable, resistance, however successful, is not likely to be transformative. The weakness of analyses like Friedman's lies in their failure to identify the contradictory properties of the class struggle that can be built upon for the enhancement of working-class *offensive* capacities.

Finally, given the long-term trend for capitalism to *eliminate* the kind of job conditions characteristic of printers and truckers (highly skilled with a high level of control over the work process and high status in the society at large), the prospects for union democracy (or efficacious unionism understood in other ways) were dismal. Logically, this theory leads to the conclusion that capitalism itself erodes the conditions favorable to democracy, but liberals and radicals both evaded the implications of this conclusion. Alternatively, the relationship between worker status and union democracy could be the reverse of the way the authors hypothesized it; that is, that the greater the proletarianization, the greater the chances for organizational democracy. If, in addition, the dependent variable is conceptualized as an aspect of class capacity (organizational efficacy) rather than formal organizational democracy, the theoretical problem is opened to a vastly broader and more political set of considerations.

These possibilities ran counter to a fundamental class bias in both pluralist and radical scholarship, however, and, as a result, the propositions were never seriously explored. The emphasis of New Left historiography and the "work-process" studies of the radical economists, moreover, laid the ground work for the assertion of very conservative themes in writing of labor history. If it was craft and skilled workers who were on the cutting edge of history at the turn of the century, and if technical workers are there today, is it not then possible to interpret the CIO period in a way that places AFL unions and craft/ skilled workers at center stage? While most accounts of the period have always emphasized the role of unskilled workers, left-wing leaders, and community forms of organization, there has been a recent spate of books and articles that portend a rewriting of the period. David Brody (1975), for example, has downplayed the importance of working-class collective action to the period and Robert Zieger (1983) has produced an unblushingly sympathetic account of AFL business unionism. Their work is wholly consistent with New Left premises and the work of Cold War sociology.

In his critique of Braverman, Szymanski (1978, 50) argued that the popularity of the work-process studies "among professionals and intellectuals at the current time can probably also be explained by the fact that [Braverman] is speaking to our fears, needs and experiences, as well as those of skilled craftsmen. Our jobs are under considerable pressure to break up our traditional privileges and skills and relinquish control to managers, administrators and capitalists. . . . We very much fear losing our relative privileges and being proletarianized." The preoccupation of radical scholars during the 1970s with questions of *control* was a matter of self-interest consistent with their petty bourgeois position. With the demise of radical social movements, the deepening malaise of the labor movement, and intensifying academic repression of the 1970s, the class base for theoretical work and the class composition of theoreticians was increasingly bourgeoisified. The result has been a rightward drift toward neo-Weberian and neoclassical theory (Wright 1985; Elster 1985; Roemer 1982).

Size as an Organizational Determinant

The inverse relationship between size and organizational democracy (or efficacy) has remained one of the most commonly accepted tenets of organizational sociology. Even for Offe and Wiesenthal (1980, 81), who in other respects move organizational theory into promising new areas, size transcends the logic of class as an organizational determinant.

The theory that large size begets organizational oligarchy poses two problems for a Marxist analysis. First, it is based on an assumption derived from neoclassical economics (and, in turn, from the same philosophical premises discussed above) that if the cost to an individual for his or her voluntary association with the organization exceeds the benefits of association, then that person's association can only be maintained by organizational mechanisms that compel the association. The larger the organization, argues Mancur Olson, the higher the cost-benefit ratio for the individual:

> [in] small groups each of the members, or at least one of them, will find that his personal gain from having the collective good exceeds the total cost of providing some amount of that collective. . . . In such situations there is a presumption that the collective good will be provided. Such a situation will exist only when the benefit to the group from having the collective good exceeds the total cost by more than it exceeds the gain to one or more individuals in the group. Thus, in a very small group, where each member gets a substantial proportion of the total gain simply because there are few others in the group, a collective good can often be provided by the voluntary, self-interested action of the members of the group. . . . Even in the smallest groups, however, the collective good will not ordinarily be provided on an optimal scale. . . . This tendency toward suboptimality is due to the fact that a collective good is, by definition, such that other individuals in the group cannot be kept from consuming it once any individual in the group has provided it for himself. Since an individual member thus gets only part of the benefit of any expenditure he makes to obtain more of the collective good, he will discontinue his purchase of the collective good before the optimal amount for the group as a whole has been obtained. In addition, the amounts of the collective good that a member of the group receives free from other members will further reduce his incentive to provide more of that good at his own expense. Accordingly, the larger the group, the farther it will fall short of providing an optimal amount of a collective good [Olson 1980, 33].

Thus, contends Olson, the reluctance of union members to support their unions is "rational" and the explanation for conservative business union leadership lies in "the need for coercion implicit in attempts to provide collective goods to large groups" (pp. 71, 86).

The neoclassical argument holds up, however, only if two things are true. First, it is true if the cost-benefit analysis of participation is calculated in narrowly economic terms, that is, the cost in terms of dues-dollars, income lost due to strikes, et cetera, exceeds the income gained through improved wages and fringe benefits. If, however, participation in union affairs is viewed as a form of self-determination in one's work life, it ceases to be a "cost" at all. Likewise, if the notion of "benefits" is understood more broadly than immediate economic gain (e.g., the economic security that comes with having close friends to fall back on in old age as opposed to having to count on individual retirement savings), solidarity with fellow workers gained through union work has to be taken into account. This challenge to neoclassical reasoning is precisely what underlies the current questioning of the "prudent man" formula by which union pension funds have traditionally been invested in the private sector for maximum short-term profit rather than, for example, in low-income housing for union members or publicly owned enterprises that would ensure long-term social security and community stability (Rifkin and Barber 1978). Marxist theory (Lozovsky 1935) has always recognized that the representation of worker interests within the parameters of capitalism is only part of unions' *raison d'etre*; they are also the foundations upon which an edifice of revolutionary political and cultural institutions arises. Viewed in this broadest possible way, the satisfaction of workers' needs under capitalism becomes secondary to the logic of strategical efficacy in the struggle for the transformation to socialism.

The second necessary premise supporting the neoclassical argument is that the inverse relationship between organizational size and democracy holds only if workers' behavior conforms to neoclassical notions of rationality, that is, their primary motive is to maximize economic gain and minimize economic costs. If the neoclassical theory is correct, union members' enthusiasm for their unions should be greatest when economic returns are the most certain. But, in fact, during economic expansion of the post-World War II period U.S. workers benefited enormously economically while union membership and participation declined. It can be shown through detailed case studies (Lembcke and Tattam 1984) that the decline in union participation had virtually nothing to do with size and everything to do with class conflict. It was not the failure to negotiate lucrative contracts but rather the narrowing of union concerns to wages, hours, and working conditions at the expense of the broader social issues like civil rights and imperialism that discouraged workers in the postwar years.

The argument that workers conform to neoclassical rationality could be more a projection of a class-specific bourgeois ethic onto the working class than anything else. If the Marxist assumption that social conditions give rise to social consciousness is true, however, it is logical that the conditions of working-class existence would engender a different consciousness, and that one dimension of working-class formation is the displacement of individual consciousness by class consciousness. In the following section it will be argued that in the United States this process has proceeded very unevenly, with the result that one finds a range of consciousness among workers and that the internal power struggles in unions can be interpreted as struggles among class fractions rooted in very different material conditions. Specifically, it can be shown that those fractions that advocated an economistic agenda resembling neoclassical rationality were precisely the least proletarianized craft and skilled workers.

The second major problem with using size as an independent variable for organizational explanations is that in the context of the post-World War II trends—the increasing concentration and centralization of capital, the centralization of economic planning, and the internationalization of production—it offered no insights into the problem of increasing working-class capacities through union reforms. Firm sizes were increasing, bargaining units were getting larger and more geographically dispersed, and the work force more heterogeneous. Clearly, in order for unions to effectively represent worker interests, unions had to get larger but, as Lipset et al. posed the problem, the working class had to choose between organizational democracy and organizational efficacy.

There was the same ahistorical and static quality to the pluralists' proposition on size and organization as there was to their formulation of class and organization; for the most part, radical and neo-Marxist theory has made no attempt to retheorize the relationship. There has been no attempt, for example, to show that size becomes a determinant of organizational behavior only if allowed to do so. That is, how size is mediated by organizational forms such as representation structures, delegate selection rules, roll-call vote processes in conventions, and so on, will determine if and how size affects matters such as leadership selection and rank-and-file enthusiasm for the union, and most importantly, the union's capacity as an agent of social change.

It will be argued in the next section that the relationship of size to other organizational features cannot be separated from the relationship of class: For the capitalist class, size is positively related to class power but for the working class the relationship is more complex. How union size gets mediated is determined by the balance of political power within the organization (power derived, that is, from sources other than size), is not, in itself, a determining feature of organizational behavior. As Child (1972, 2) argued with respect to corporate organizations, the choice of organizational form is an "essentially political process, whereby power-holders within organizations decide upon courses of strategic action. This 'strategic choice' typically includes not only the establishment of structural forms but also the manipulation of the environmental features and the choice of relevant performance standards." In the study of labor unions the relationship between power holders, or leaders, and members of the organization, or rank and file, is especially critical. The historical data (Lembcke and Howe 1986) concurs with Child (1972) and Chandler (1962) that strategical choices made by organization leaders is a major source of organizational variation.

The Ideological Legacy of Pluralist and Radical Studies

In addition to the class bias in the conclusions of Lipset et al., there was a political bias associated with it. On the matter of political pluralism within unions, the authors argued (1956, 456-57) that a more pluralistic "pattern might have developed in a more clear-cut fashion than it has if a part of the left wing of the labor movement had not been captured by a totalitarian political movement, the Communist Party." "The Communists," they contended, "by refusing to play the democratic game, help to break or prevent the institutionalization of internal democratic procedures." Stated as a theoretical proposition, one would expect to find the least amount of internal democracy in those unions where communists had the most power.

In fact, neither the pluralist sociologists nor the Cold War historians made any attempt to empirically verify their claims about communist totalitarianism in unions. Lipset tried in a very curious way to base his claim on a single quote from Harry Bridges, president of the International Longshoremen's and Warehousemen's Union (ILWU) who was close to the Communist party. According to Lipset (1952, 60), Bridges used the following words to defend the Soviet Union at the 1947 ILWU convention: "What is totalitarianism? A country that has a totalitarian government operates like our union operates. There are no political parties. People are elected to govern the country based upon their records. . . . That is totalitarianism . . . if we started to divide up and run a Republican set of officers, a Democratic set, a Communist set and something else we would have one hell of a time." What Bridges meant was that a country where the working class was the ruling class would be denigrated as "totalitarian" by its detractors. But in the context of the Cold War, the word "totalitarian" was already too loaded with negative connotation, and Lipset was able to use the quote to denigrate not only communism but working-class organizational autonomy as well. He said, "Bridges believes that there is no class base for opposing political groups within the 'one-class' trade union." For Lipset, Bridges' words confirmed that "one-class" unions were a condition for totalitarianism, and since a union is by definition a one-class organization, all unions tended toward oligarchy. Moreover, the Communist Party's line on union organization during the 1930s emphasized the autonomy of industrial workers from multi-class organizational forms such as company unions (Keeran 1980). The strategy of industrial worker independence, which had proven enormously successful in the organizing drives that produced the CIO, was dismissed as totalitarian in Lipset's model. In keeping with his philosophical stand that only the middle class was capable of democracy, in other words, Lipset found that unions controlled solely by their own members were undemocratic. There was no empirical basis for such a conclusion, but in the McCarthyist climate of the 1950s it was sufficient for his purposes to be able to associate communists in U.S. unions with Soviet "totalitarianism" and let Cold War imaginations do the rest.

Unfortunately, New Left sociology never redressed the ideological assumptions of Lipset et al. If anything, Mills added fuel to the fire. Of communists in unions, he wrote, "Communist rule within unions they control is dictatorial: although they talk the language of democracy, they do not believe or practice democratic principles" (1948, 199-200). In *False Promises*, a book that influenced New Left-generation union activists more than any other, Stanley Aronowitz concluded that unions organized by the communists were conservative and "instruments for the disciplining and control of workers" (1973, 13-14).

In the revival of labor history during 1970s, virtually no attempt was made to see if the equation of communists and organizational authoritarianism held up empirically. In fact, it probably does not. A review of labor history and union constitutions reveals that in the unions such as the Mine, Mill and Smelter Workers and the International Woodworkers of America, which were headed by communist leadership, one finds the highest level of rank-and-file participation in leadership selection (Chapter 5). Moreover, the social base of these left-wing factions was most often the most proletarianized sector of

U.S. industries—according to the assumptions of Lipset et al. about democracy and the working class. Their implicit association of the communist movement with a working-class social base was correct, but rather than empirically testing the association between that connection and union democracy, they simply repeated the accepted Cold War assumptions about communist "totalitarianism" and used the equation in a way that supported their thesis that the working class was not an historical agent likely to advance social democracy.

SUMMARY AND CONCLUSIONS

The recent theoretical contributions of radical neo-Marxist scholars have had little impact on the practical work of labor union activists. This chapter has attempted to understand that failure as the failure of analysts to break with the assumptions and conclusions of pluralism.

It has been argued that a break with the pluralist tradition must be made in two very specific ways. First, it is necessary to reconsider the conventional assumptions about the direction in which capitalist development influences working-class capacity: Whether the organizational problem is conceptualized in the abstract pluralist sense, or in a relational sense as it is here, it can be shown that the more proletarianized fractions of the working class produce the most democratic and efficacious forms of organization. Secondly, as this chapter has argued, the conceptualization of class capacities as a matter of *control* of production needs to be reconsidered. That conceptualization, being consistent with the realities of petty bourgeois and professional work life, leads to strategies and tactics useful to that class but irrelevant to the working class. Theoretical work treating working-class capacities as a matter of control, for the most part, has not been translated into meaningful practice and, where it has, it tends to be reactive and protectionist rather than transformative.

This chapter has argued that the problem of working-class capacities is largely an organizational one—the manner in which the members of the class are associated for class struggle. Forms of organization that minimize competition among class members and maximize unity are considered to be capacity-enhancing or efficacious forms, while those that invite competition or attempt to substitute sources of power that are naturally more advantageous to the capitalist class (capital) or the petty bourgeoisie (control of production) are considered to erode capacity.

While a retheorizing of union organizations must have as its first objective the establishment of definitions and relationships that correspond logically and empirically to the world they purport to describe, it must be done with the recognition that the relationship between class and organizational form is not one of simple, unidirectional determinism. Union organizational form at any given moment represents a balance of class struggle; class, in other words, is a determinant in a structural rather than instrumental sense. Capital's ability to influence union leadership and organizational forms through economic, ideological, and legal means is an integral factor in the overall logic that shapes union organizations. Ultimately, the test of the theory has to be whether or not those who act on it in practice are able to produce the desired results. These are to represent the interests of union members within the parameters of capitalism and to increase the capacities of the working class to transform the class relations that define the capitalist order.

The next chapter begins an attempt to formulate a theory of organizational forms that advances beyond the pluralist theory critiqued above. What is needed is a theory that relates the internal logic of organizational forms to the social forces external to the organization. We need a structural understanding that enables us to see how class, understood in a relational and dialectical sense, is played out through the struggle over organizational forms. That struggle can only be observed and studied as an historical phenomenon, and the analytical framework provided by the Marxist theory of uneven development is the best tool we have for that task. Chapter 2 reviews the theory of uneven development and provides an interpretation of U.S. labor history consistent with that framework.

NOTES

1. Ellen Meiksins Wood in *The Retreat From Class* (1986) presents an interesting critique of these same aspects of New Left theory but she locates the source of the problem in the structuralist tradition rather than in the pluralist tradition as I have.

2. The lineage of the term "association" deserves more attention than given here. Sewell (1986) traces it to the resistance of French artisans to capitalism. "The idea of association," he says, "was for workers to establish 'associative' workshops in which they would be joint owners of the means of production. These workshops were to be capitalized initially by regular weekly contributions from the associates and would eventually expand to include the whole industry,

absorbing masters and workers alike into a unified trade community in which private property would be abolished" (1986, 61-2). In this sense, "association" was consistent with the utopian tradition criticized by Marx and Engels, and it designates something very different from the notion of "collectivity" that more appropriately designates the organizational logic indigenous to the proletariat. A reading of Sewell helps us see the impact on working-class studies of the French experience.

2

Historical Problems and Theoretical Advances in the Study of U.S. Working-Class Capacities

INTRODUCTION

Serious questions have been raised about the capacity of the U.S. labor movement to meet the challenges of a deepening economic crisis. Activists within the movement and interested academic scholars have increased their attention to the details of U.S. labor's last 50 years in an effort to understand better the current malaise. The history of the CIO period, roughly the years 1936 to 1955, have been given special attention because of their proximity to the current period; it is assumed, probably correctly so, that the events of those years laid the groundwork upon which the present situation developed.

Important as the CIO period is to our understanding of contemporary events, it has remained vastly under-theorized. Most accounts have been confined to as yet unresolved factual disputes and interpretations of the faction fights that tore the CIO apart in the late 1940s. For the most part, moreover, this interpretive work remains trapped in the thesis of American exceptionalism advanced by Fredrich Turner and adopted by Selig Perlman for a theory of the U.S. labor movement in 1928. Attempts by radicals to reformulate the central problem during the last 20 years have only managed to disassemble the historical body without reconstituting it in a way that advanced us theoretically. Thus we have numerous studies of the cultural and technological dimensions of U.S. labor history with great depth and intensity, but they have tended to fragment the subject and offer few strategical insights for activism in the current period.

In only a few recent works do we find a theoretical framework with the potential for deepening our understanding of the causal relationships that underlay the events themselves. One of the more promising works is Mike Davis's (1980) two-part essay on the U.S. working class. By periodizing history and keeping the analysis at the level of class forces, he is able to present his subject as a series of confrontations between labor and capital, with each juncture having a specific historical character. Struggles that determined the basic nature of bourgeois democratic institutions were decisive at one point; the influx of large numbers of European immigrants was the dominant influence during another period; the presence of "preemptive political repression," racism, and the ascent of U.S. imperialism held sway in still other periods. The class contradictions of each period reached crisis proportions in different arenas, and their resolution has had a cumulative effect that moved the struggle onto new planes at each point.

> Each major cycle of class struggle, economic crisis, and social restructuring in American history has finally been resolved through epochal tests of strength between capital and labour. The results of these historical collisions have been new structural forms that regulated the objective conditions for accumulation in the next period as well as the subjective capacities for class organization and consciousness [Davis 1980, 7].

Davis identifies three levels at which class forces were determining the CIO: (1) the international level that became increasingly defined during the post-World War II years by the rise of U.S. imperialism and the consolidation of socialism in Eastern Europe; (2) the domestic level of U.S. political economic crisis that had only been recessed by war-time production; (3) the struggle for control of the CIO between working-class socialist and communist movements, and a bureaucratic-professional trade union elite that was essentially petty bourgeois in class form.

Davis's essential thesis that each period of labor/capital relations is shaped by the previous period is sound and helps us avoid reductionist explanations. More structural than the most popular accounts of the CIO period, Davis's account nevertheless remains inadequate in two important respects.

First, movement from one level of class struggle to another is never adequately or satisfactorily explained. One must account for two important transitions. The first was the shift from community and shop-floor struggles that dominated from the turn of the century to the mid-1930s when class struggle at the level of the state became predominant. The second important transition occurred in the post-World War II years when developments on the international level superceded domestic contradictions in ways that were decisive for the CIO.

The second inadequacy in the thesis is that we get no structural explanation for the factional struggles that operated at his third level (above). Thus, Davis ultimately resorts to an idealist "Left's own fault" thesis to explain the decline of the CP's influence in the CIO.

His argument is that by supporting World War II the party incurred the disfavor of U.S. workers and lost its political base.

The remainder of this chapter pursues a deeper structural understanding of the CIO period through the use of the Marxist theories of uneven development and the concept of overdetermination. I begin with a summary of the theory of uneven development and then present a general overview of the spatial and temporal uneven development of the U.S. political economy. I argue that contradictions emanating from several different arenas of class conflict converged in the mid-1930s and again in the late 1940s to produce qualitative leaps (or ruptures) following which labor/capital relations proceeded in fundamentally different ways. Against this backdrop I then situate the pattern of uneven working-class formation, of which the organizational developments described in the following chapters are a manifestation, and argue that the organizational analysis presented in this book can be read as a specification of the class struggle at Davis's third level.

THE THEORY OF UNEVEN DEVELOPMENT

The theory of uneven development, as Neil Smith (1984) has noted, means many things to many people. Broadly speaking, there are three general, but by no means mutually exclusive, theoretical traditions that identify with the theory of uneven development.

One is the "permanentist" tradition (Lowy 1981), which has used the uneven development thesis as a basis for its theory of permanent revolution. Arising out of an attempt to understand how and why socialist revolution occurred in backward Russia before the more advanced capitalist nations of Europe, the theory dissented from the orthodox Marxist position of the Second International that world history proceeded through stages with socialism following capitalism. The Second International position held that socialism could only be achieved following the emergence of a proletariat within a fully mature capitalist society. Trotskyists use the history of the Russian Revolution to show that revolutions based in a peasantry but led by a proletariat in a noncapitalist social formation could be successful. From that position they argue that socialist revolutions can emerge from precapitalist social formations, by-passing the capitalist stage. The notion of "permanentism" is derived from the notion that revolutionary upheavals emanating from precapitalist formations need not follow the sequence of first achieving capitalist and bourgeois democratic forms, second, allowing the evolutionary maturation of social relations within the capitalist stage, and, third, proceeding on to the stage of socialism. The "pause" at the capitalist stage, in other words, can be eliminated, according to the Trotskyists, and the revolutionary process can thus be unbroken and permanent.

Although Trotskyists cite fragmentary references in the work of Marx and Engels to depict the uneven development thesis as consistent with the classics, the "permanentist" twist is clearly made in the period following the Russian Revolution by Trotsky and other critics of post-revolutionary developments. The thesis provided leverage for the criticism that by pausing to consolidate the Soviet Revolution, the impetus for world-wide revolution was lost and, as a consequence, the survival of the Soviet Union became more contingent on bureaucratic rationale. The thesis has also provided a beginning point for understanding the relationship between advanced capitalist nations and the Third World. For the most part, the Trotskyist tradition has conceptualized the unevenness of development in national units and therefore remained tangential to efforts to theorize class relations *within* advanced capitalist countries.

A second theoretical tradition within the uneven development framework is that represented by the literature on dependency theory and unequal exchange. While the Trotskyist theory of uneven and combined development is primarily a theory of revolution, the unequal exchange tradition mainly theorizes about the transfer of social surplus from underdeveloped to developed economies. Alain de Janvry (1981) traces the history of the unequal exchange model from the work of Marx and Engels, who anticipated that capitalism would recreate its patterns of growth in the less-developed regions. Rosa Luxemburg elaborated the thesis in her theory that capitalism was prone to a crisis of underconsumption. Capitalists, she argued, were driven by competition to invest in new technology, while labor was driven to maintain wage levels. The result was a dearth of capital goods and an excess of consumer goods that forced capital into precapitalist economies for cheap raw materials (to lower production costs) and new sales markets. The crisis of the center was thereby postponed at the expense of local economies in the underdeveloped regions. Once all the precapitalist economies were penetrated by capitalism, Luxemburg predicted that unevenness would diminish.

Lenin revised the thesis to argue that in the era of monopoly capital an over-supply of capital in the center can occur. The result is over-investment that drives down the rate of profit. This crisis is averted through the export of capital, industrial and financial, to the periphery. The model thus differs from Luxemburg's in that it is capital rather than consumer goods that is exported, but it agrees with Luxemburg that by the logic of the system, it will eventually accelerate the development of the periphery.

The watershed in the history of the unequal development tradition came in 1928 with Otto Kuusinen's claim that, "not only was capitalist penetration in the periphery under the aegis of imperialism a source of surplus extraction to the benefit of the center but it also created a bottleneck to industrialization and resulted in stagnation" (de Janvry 1981, 12). Paul Baran, Paul Sweezy, André Gunder Frank, and others associated with the dependency school developed the Kuusinenian thesis to the point that "the law of unequal development on a world scale [became] inverted relative to the formulations of Marx, Luxemburg, Lenin and Bukharin: unequal development is the development of the forces of production in the center and their underdevelopment in the periphery" (de Janvry, 13).

Samir Amin built on Baran and Sweezy's argument that state intervention to squander surplus value and manage labor-management conflict would permit sustained capital accumulation in the center. For Amin, the periphery functioned to expand capitalist markets, while destroying precapitalist markets, and increase the rate of profit. Within the periphery a duel economy operates in such a way that the growth sectors, with their short-lived "miracles," are concentrated in the capitalist production of exportables and luxuries, while the production of mass consumer goods remains noncapitalist and stagnant and that of capital goods is essentially nonexistent. And it is principally in the noncapitalist modes that the impoverished masses bear the social cost of unequal development" (de Janvry, 18). Although the dependency theorists were primarily attempting to understand the flow of social surplus between core and periphery, the theory of revolution implicit in their work is consistent with that of the Trotskyist model: socialist revolution is the only realistic strategical course for Third World revolutions.

A third theoretical tradition in the literature on uneven development emphasizes class formation. This tradition springs from Marx and Engels' propositions that (1) the geographic centralization of capital and labor necessary for economic efficiency had the contradictory effect of accelerating the formation of a revolutionary working class, and (2) that class formation proceeded unevenly. The unevenness was due to the fact that producers who were proletarianized in the early stages of capitalism developed socially in ways consistent with the terms of their struggles, for example, forming unions for the purpose of protecting the integrity of their craft traditions (see Chapter 1). Four things followed as a consequence of successful working-class protectionism. (1) Capital found it necessary to mechanize production and thereby make obsolete the skills of the craft workers. (2) Because the social relations and economic infrastructure of the early stage of capitalist development occupied a particular space, it was necessary that later development take place in a different space, that is, capital moves geographically at each successive stage of development. (3) The working class was saddled with social traditions and organizational forms that hindered its capacity to keep pace with capital's dynamism. Thus, unions refused to admit deskilled workers to their ranks and often adopted provincial and competitive attitudes toward workers outside their own areas. Where ethnic or religious differences overlaid geographic separations, class identifications were impaired even more. (4) Producers proletarianized at the latter stages of capitalist development did not have the albatross of past traditions and organizational forms encumbering their struggle. As a result, the most class-conscious workers and the unions most capable of pursuing a revolutionary course tended to be located in the most advanced industrial sectors and industrialized regions (Marx and Engels 1972; Engels 1975).

Expressed as a theory of class formation, the uneven development tradition thus becomes applicable to an analysis of class struggle internal to any one nation. It enables us to identify the barriers to class formation and thereby gain a more nuanced understanding of capitalism's contradictions. The chief advantage in the class formation interpretation of the theory over the surplus extraction interpretation is in the dialectical quality of the former. The surplus extraction version essentially holds that capitalist exploitation is a zero-sum game: The capitalist class develops (i.e., accumulates capital) only at the expense of the working class, which is underdeveloped (impoverished and incapacitated). Viewed in this way, change can only come from outside the system rather than from the contradictions inherent in capitalism itself. Strategical agendas following from such analyses have led in idealist directions. But such an interpretation can only be made if one assumes that the sources of power are the same for both classes. In other words, if one assumes that power for both classes is based on the mobilization of monetary resources, then the zero-sum formulation is correct—but undialectical. On the other hand, if one assumes that, although the process of extracting economic surplus from the working class might impoverish that class, it simultaneously develops it in political and organizational ways, then the dialectical relationship is restored. Viewed in this way one would expect to find working-class capacities to be the greatest in sectors and regions where exploitation is the greatest. This interpretation would be consistent with the basic theoretical propositions of this book.

Uneven development as a theory of class formation has not been widely utilized. Trotsky (1959, 7-9) alluded to it in explaining how it was that the seemingly backward Russian proletariat was able to skip over the epoch of craft-guilds and manufacture. The Russian working class, he argued, "did not arise gradually through the ages, carrying with itself the burden of the past as in England, but in leaps involving sharp changes of environment, ties, relations and a sharp break with the past." De Janvry (1981) uses a class formation version of uneven development from which to critique the surplus extraction tradition. Al Gedicks (1976) accounts for the existence of both radicalism and conservatism among North American Finnish workers through the uneven pace of proletarianization in nineteenth century Finland. A special issue of the *Review of Radical Political Economics* (Edel et al. 1978, 9) on "Uneven Regional Development" dealt only tangentially with the class formation question. Two recently written labor histories have identified characteristics of uneven development. Levenstein (1981. 59), for example, notes that in industries where AFL unionism preceded the CIO unions, the latter were likely to encounter stiffer opposition and be vulnerable to more intense factionalism. Abella (1973) likewise equated "older" and "richer" unions with conservatism in his study of communism and U.S.-Canadian labor relations in the CIO period. Clearly, the older, richer, more conservative unions during that period were also the AFL or former AFL affiliates. Neither Levenstein nor Abella, however, make any attempt to interpret these discoveries in a theoretical fashion. Two studies of U.S. working-class formation have employed uneven development schemes: Wardell and Johnson (1985) have examined the origins of class fractions within the United Mine Workers of America, and Lembcke and Tattam (1984) located the roots of divisions within the International Woodworkers of America in the uneven regional development of the lumber and wood products industry. Amy Bridges' (1986) analysis of class formation produces historical data useful for validating the uneven development model, but she does not make the connection between class formation and capitalist development.

By theorizing the problem of class capacities as one of class formation within the framework of uneven development, the conventional, idealistic renderings of U.S. labor history by the U.S. exceptionalist school and New Left historiography can be challenged. The next section attempts to sketch U.S. labor history within the framework of uneven development in a way that accounts for the dramatic advances of the 1930s and demonstrates the relationship between the larger historical project and the organizational study presented in the previous chapters.

U.S. LABOR IN THE 1930s:
A LEGACY OF UNEVEN DEVELOPMENT

The condition of the U.S. labor movement in the early 1930s was the culmination of several decades of uneven development in three arenas of class struggle.

Economic Organization

Organizationally, the development of U.S. unions had attempted to follow the transition of U.S. industry from craft-oriented production in small, decentralized units to production units based upon the employment of mass numbers of unskilled workers in highly centralized units. Early unionism, which had taken hold in the mid-nineteenth century when craft production dominated, followed craft lines in organizational structure. Thus, plumbers, mill wrights, carpenters, and mechanics would all be in separate unions though they worked for the same employer and in the same mill. Such a form of organization is commonly understood to have reinforced a narrowness of outlook that made unity across craft lines very difficult to achieve. It was, nonetheless, appropriate for the time, and the solidarity of craft workers became too great to contend with for capital (Brody, 1960). Subsequently, capitalists sought to dilute craft union power through the redivision and deskilling of labor, the substitution of mass production techniques for craft techniques, and the importation of a mass, unskilled labor force.

During the early twentieth century production shifted away from a craft form of organization to an industrial form. In most cases that shift entailed relocations that moved the geographic center of U.S. manufacturing westward. New production techniques and social relations could not be built on the already-occupied terrain of the premonopoly era. Thus, copper mining, for example, moved from a labor-intensive form of extraction used in the Michigan upper peninsula to a more capital-intensive form in the western states like Montana; at a later period it developed still more capital-intensive techniques and moved to the southwest. The wood products industry followed the same pattern and the steel industry left behind its eastern company towns for the Gary-Chicago region.

The craft unions, most of which were affiliated with the American Federation of Labor (AFL) adopted a protectionist posture toward the new developments and resolutely refused to organize the unskilled immigrant workers or to adapt their forms of organization to one that followed industrial lines. Thus, in an industry like hard-rock mining, workers who sought unionization had little choice except to pursue that objective outside the bounds of the established AFL unions. In 1905 the Western Federation of Miners, which had been struggling within the AFL, broke away and joined with other socialist, syndicalist, and industrial union organizations to form the Industrial Workers of the World (IWW). For reasons examined more fully below, the attempt of the IWW to fill the gap in organization was throttled by state intervention and developments on the level of international politics in the years following World War I.

By the early 1930s the gap between the numbers of workers organized in AFL craft unions and the total number of U.S. workers wanting and needing organization had widened. Moreover, the AFL had grown still more conservative in its ways. In the face of depression conditions it still refused to accommodate itself to an industrial form of organization; continued to look askance at unskilled, nonwhite workers (to say nothing of the unemployed, which it totally shunned); and resisted attempts to involve it in the political arena.

The U.S. labor movement's incapacity to act in defense of working-class interests at this point was thus a legacy of U.S. economic development. The early era of craft production had wrought craft forms of union organization; in the later era, craft unions, threatened with extinction by mass production techniques common to monopoly capital, sought to preserve themselves and the relative economic and social privileges of their members over the mass of unskilled immigrant industrial workers. The protectionism of the craft unions became, in turn, a fetter on the subsequent development of unionism. Moreover, for historical reasons as outlined above, the balance of power within the AFL was strongly skewed toward the eastern United States. While the eastern bias within the federation was a given, its effects could have been mitigated by a union organizational structure that took it into account. As it was, however, the protectionist wing of the labor movement was not inclined to counter-balance the inherited unevenness and, more often than not, adopted forms of organization that actually amplified the imbalances. Finally, the political orientation of the labor movement and the immigration pattern of the early twentieth century reinforced the unevenness of the economic structures.

Class Consciousness

The failure of the U.S. working class to congeal into a self-conscious political force has most often been understood as a cultural phenomenon. The argument is most often made that successive waves of immigrants produced communities separated by ethnic and religious identities. Moreover, the time lag between early and later arrivals permitted the first arrivals (descendants of colonial settlers and mid-nineteenth century Irish and German immigrants) to have acquired a "nativist" mentality that would not graciously accommodate the later arrivals. Protectionist attitudes toward jobs and community resources became predecessors to prejudice and racism. Finally, European class relations had matured by the late 1800s so that immigrants coming to North America during those decades were more likely to have experienced socialist movements and industrial union membership.

The nativist influence in the union movement had two important effects. First, the arrival of early waves of immigrants coincided with the days of craft unionism; the conservative propensities of one matched and reinforced those of the other. This combination of factors had produced, by the late 1800s, a stratum of northern European craft workers who controlled the unions and were protected by them. The convergence of cultural factors with economic and political conservatism yielded a profoundly conservative cohort of union leaders. The translation of this conservatism into political dominance within the union movement was an organizational phenomenon, however. The capacity of the conservative fraction, in other words, was largely determined by its ability to foist an organizational form on the union movement that would consolidate its hold on the movement's future. Subsequent challengers to this incumbent cohort would find it virtually futile to work within the confines of the AFL establishment. The first major split in the union movement was fostered by this tension and resulted in the formation of the Industrial Workers of the World (IWW) in 1905.

Secondly, nativism provided a foundation for a virulent antiforeign ideology that was stirred at times to counter the emergence of class-conscious radicalism (e.g., the Chicago Haymarket affair in 1886, the

Palmer raids after World War I, and anticommunism during the 1940s and 1950s). Antiforeign activity reached its peak during World War I as anti-Germanism and was then transferred to an anti-Bolshevik and anti-Soviet hysteria following the war. Nativism thus provided the material basis for the pervasive anticommunism that crystallized as a reaction to the Russian Revolution and organizations of unskilled, immigrant workers, particularly the IWW. The antiforeign and anti-communist campaign tore the IWW apart. Transient workers, some of whom were foreign born and inclined toward socialist politics and others who were native-born drifters imbued with a deep sense of personal independence and adventurism, had been especially attracted to the IWW. After 1920 the ideology of anticommunism, appealing as it was to the nativist sentiment of both native-born migrant workers in the IWW and native-born conservatism in AFL unions, aligned business unionists and erstwhile IWW radicals in a united front against communists. The October Revolution had created the opportunity for the communists to affiliate their trade union activities to the Red International of Labour Unions and thereby broaden the international base of their support. But divisions over affiliation with the international hardened the political lines in the IWW, and in 1924 it split.

The left wing's relationship with the mainstream labor movement was no more promising. Throughout the 1920s communists experimented with a variety of party formations and relationships with the AFL, but economic prosperity in the early 1920s and AFL reluctance to work with radicals limited Communist Party effectiveness. In the late 1920s the AFL drove communist activists from its ranks, ending the Party's attempts to influence the direction of the AFL by "boring from within."

Political Organization

The economic unevenness of U.S. industrial development and the consequent unevenness in working-class unionization had its counterpart in the political arena. From its very earliest years the AFL, under the leadership of Samuel Gompers, had stayed aloof from political involvements. In 1894 Gompers joined other conservative AFL leaders in opposing an 11-point "Political Programme" that called for AFL political action independent of the mainstream parties and support for the socialization of production. The preconvention referendum on the "programme" resulted in overwhelming rank-and-file endorsement of the proposal but the Gomperites managed to defeat it in convention. Socialists and delegates loyal to the rank-and-file mandate struck back by defeating Gompers in his bid for reelection (Foner, 1975, 289-94). The apoliticism of the AFL leadership, coupled with the narrow craft unionism so characteristic of the organization, gave unionism an essentially syndicalist flavor at the turn of the century.

The syndicalist character of the AFL was appropriate to an era when class struggle was waged at the point of production and bosses relied upon privately mustered armies to control their work forces. Even in instances where the struggle spilled over into the community, as it did with the Homestead, Pennsylvania steel works in 1892, the nature of the company town environment meant that the forms of control remained simple and direct (Edwards 1978). With the shift to larger scales of production and the employment of larger numbers of unskilled workers, new forms of control became necessary; the concentration of workers in company towns where class lines were visibly drawn and political control was direct was too explosive. The new mode would decentralize workers, let the "market" control the off-work life of workers, and encourage the development of the state as the primary control apparatus. At local levels, new company towns like Gary, Indiana supplanted the Homesteads of an earlier age (Greer 1979). But where the craft unions had been able to translate their control of the workplace into community power in instances like Homestead, their failure to transition to an industrial form of organization in the twentieth century meant a concomitant failure to adapt to the increasingly more central role played by the state.

The IWW partially filled the gap in industrial organizing but the anarchist influence in the organization made it, if anything, more opposed to political action than was the AFL. The success of the Bolshevik Revolution in Russia mobilized the right-wing business community and activated the repressive apparatus of the U.S. government for a campaign to crush communism. Straining to conceptualize its role in class terms at the level of the nation-state, the IWW was overtaken by events with a logic far more complex than its agenda for workplace revolution.

By the early 1920s it was apparent that capital had been able to outflank AFL-style craft unionism through mass production processes and outflank syndicalism common to both the AFL and IWW by elevating the struggle to a more global level, that is, to the level of state intervention in the class relations of private industry. Politically, therefore, the apolitical legacy of early AFL unionism was as crippling to the union movement in the early 1930s as was the failure to organize the unorganized. Workers who were organized into AFL unions were under a very conservative influence, while workers with the most serious grievances went begging for organized support.

The fragmentation and demoralization that marked the labor movement of the late 1920s masked other realities, however. Beneath the surface appearances was an undercurrent that would burst into being as the CIO in the mid-1930s. That rupture must be accounted for through reference to the same historical logic that had rendered the labor movement impotent by the eve of the Great Depression. It is in the dialectical opposites of the trends identified above that one can locate the explanation for the major events of the 1930s.

Overdetermination and the Post-World War I Years

The last section sketched the pre-1930s development of U.S. labor history through three major arenas of class struggle: economic, ideological, and political. It was argued that the conflicts emerging during the first decades of the twentieth century were resolved in the post-World War I years when capital resorted to state intervention in economic relations and the working class was unable to follow the struggle to that plane. The main obstacles to labor's ability to make that transition were (a) the apolitical and conservative tradition of the AFL and (b) the anarcho-syndicalism of the IWW. The threat of political crisis inherent in the post-war situation had been resolved on terms favorable to capital.

That resolution, however, contained contradictions that by the early 1930s would shift the balance of class struggle toward the working class. Essentially, the argument made below is that, whereas in the immediate post-war years the working class was *not* able to transition to a political form of struggle, it would be able to by the mid-1930s. Moreover, it was the victory of capital over labor following World War I that enhanced and empowered the working class a decade later.

The initial effect of state intervention against labor in the post-World War I years was to break up and scatter concentrations of working-class political and organizational power that had taken decades to build. By breaking up some combinations, however, the possibilities of recombination in ways more favorable to labor was opened. To take the most salient example, the communist faction within the IWW had seen the necessity for struggling around state power, but its ability to do so had been fettered by the lack of consensus on the question within the IWW. State repression of the IWW brought the question of state power to a head and hardened the factional lines within the IWW. The communist faction, with its political base among foreign-born workers, was much more vulnerable to repression; thus, it had little choice but to force the issue to the level of a split in the organization. In the absence of external pressure of state repression, it would never have been necessary to raise the issue to that level. The split having occurred, however, the possibility for recombination in new and more advanced forms was created. International uneven development, moreover, determined what form those recombinations would take.

In some respects, the Russian Revolution had propelled historical development in that part of the world far beyond that in the United States. By virtue of the Bolshevik victory, the communist faction of the IWW could now affiliate itself with the Red International under Bolshevik sponsorship. By doing so, the communists were able to turn a set-back into a tremendous advance. The fragmentation and scattering that initially resulted from state intervention against the IWW ultimately produced recombination and greater condensation.

There were other facets of that process that contributed to the concentration of working-class forces. First, the class struggle was immediately politicized by the state's intervention. Second, the vacuum for industrial unionism that had been partially filled by the IWW between 1905 and 1917 was reproduced with the state's suppression of the IWW; and since the trend in industry had continued toward economic concentration, the number of workers left beyond the pale of AFL interests was larger than ever. The vacuum in industrial unionism represented, on the one hand, the weakness of working-class organization but, on the other hand, it represented potential and opportunity. Where AFL craft unionism had bothered not to tread, there were no preexisting organizational barriers to overcome, no incumbent leadership to contend with, and no prior expectations on the part of workers for what unionism should or should not be. Thus, those entering the field had a clean slate upon which to write the strongest, most progressive form of union organization possible. The leadership vacuum created by the persecution of IWW leaders and deportation of many foreign-born leaders immediately after the war was soon filled by the purge of communists from the AFL and by communist IWW members who left with the 1924 split.

The communists had pursued a "boring from within" strategy during the early and mid-1920s, hoping to influence the AFL without breaking with it. But the AFL, in characteristically undialectical fashion, would not tolerate the communists and managed to isolate and purge them by the late 1920s. Freed from their own strategy ("boring from within") by circumstances not of their own choosing (AFL intransigence), communist cadre turned their energies toward building industrial unionism outside AFL ranks. Formed under the auspices of its Trade Union Unity League (TUUL), their organizations became the nuclei for the industrial unions that comprised the left wing of the CIO.

The purge of communists from the AFL also had the effect of weakening corporate liberalism, which was a mainstay of class politics during the 1920s. As an example, the labor education movement, which attempted to provide workers with a "gateway to the enjoyment of a larger life" through means other than economic struggle, depended for success on the AFL's ability to legitimize it as a surrogate for union militancy. AFL leaders like Matthew Woll dedicated themselves wholeheartedly to the effort. Many of the best labor educators, however, were communists (or at least fellow travelers) and by purging them, the AFL lost all chances to gain broad-based working-class support for its participation in corporate liberalism's reform programs. The failure of one of the schools was attributed directly to the AFL's inability to work with the IWWs and communists (Lembcke 1984b).

Finally, the impotency of the AFL shed of its radical elements gave capital almost unilateral control over wages and working conditions. With no checks on its capacity to drive wages down, capital created a crisis of overproduction/underconsumption unprecedented in the United States. The crisis deepened during the last half-decade of the 1920s, driving thousands of people out of work. Unemployment rose from a decade-low of 1.9 percent in 1926 to 4.4 percent in 1928, and 8.7 percent in 1930. By 1933 it had nearly tripled again to 24.9 percent—a total of 17 million people out of work. The AFL, having ignored the "unwashed" when they were employed, not surprisingly turned its back on the unemployed. As early as 1927 debates over a program for the unemployed began to divide the labor movement. In Portland, Oregon, for example, a proposal that the Central Labor Council survey the city's unemployed was defeated by conservatives who charged that the project was "communist inspired" (Lembcke, 1984b). It was, of course, the AFL's complete disregard for the unemployed that did force many laid-off workers to seek relief through organizations and activities sponsored by the Communist Party.

The locus of the contradictions noted above lies in capital's own post-World War I strategy. In the mid-1930s those contradictions

erupted in three main arenas of struggle. In the political arena, the
bankruptcy of AFL fealty to the two-party political establishment
and general apoliticism in regard to the effects of the depression de-
legitimized the AFL and traditional policy solutions to the crisis.
Thousands of workers were thereby forced to either break with Democratic and Republican party traditions and seek third-party alternatives
or press their demands within the Democratic party to the point where
the party had to make serious breaks with past practice. Several factors also converged to advance the ideological consciousness of U.S.
workers. First, the awareness of links between politics and economics
was broadened by depression conditions, economic policy debates,
and government suppression of early movements seeking redress of
economic hardship. Second, the intransigence of U.S. anti-Soviet
policy helped alienate thousands of workers (especially foreign-born
workers) at a time when the Communist Party was able to trade on
its association with the popular Russian Revolution. The Russian
Revolution also provided a model that stimulated thinking about
alternatives to capitalism, which was obviously not working. Coupled
with the presence of Communist Party cadre that was capable of giving leadership, the mass base of disaffected workers and bankrupted
farmers and the example of the successful Russian experiment was a
combination that expanded class consciousness and encouraged the
recognition of national and international dimensions of class politics.
In the economic arena the AFL's disregard for the unemployed and
industrial workers left an open field for communist organizers. The
vacuum in industrial organizing filled by the Left was the legacy of
uneven U.S. capitalist development and was the main contradiction
that accounts for the leap that U.S. labor made with the formation
of the CIO.

The key to understanding that break entails more than just recognizing the convergence of accumulated contradictions, however. The
vacuum in industrial unionism had existed since approximately 1900,
yet no break had occurred. The attempt by the IWW to fill the gap
had been defeated. Why did the break occur when it did in the 1930s?
The answer lies in the temporal juxtaposition of events flowing out
of political, ideological, and economic clusters of contradictions. Each
cluster had its own locus of contradictions that, to some extent, had
a logic of its own; but each also was reinforced at crucial moments
by the contradictions emanating from the other arenas. The contradiction of craft union narrowness, for example, was an objective condition that took a political form only when it resonated with immi-

gration patterns. The sequencing of events was also crucial. Prior to the successful Russian Revolution the class struggle in the United States remained under-politicized; the political repression following 1917 put events on a more political plane and set the stage for a struggle at the level of national politics in the 1930s. It is this converging and sequencing of events that overdetermines the situation and forces a rupture in the structure of class relations.

RETHEORIZING THE ORGANIZATIONAL PROBLEM

As we have seen, the effects of uneven development can be observed and studied in many ways. Methodologically speaking, this book treats organizational forms as the sediment of class formation. Working-class fractions take the form of organizations consistent with their needs at the moment of formation. Organizational forms are the mechanisms through which historically specific class characteristics are transmitted temporally and spatially. Even more to the point, organizational forms provide the *linkage between temporal and spatial unevenness* that enables us to see the relationship between those two dimensions of the phenomenon. As presented in Chapter 1, one of the central theoretical problems facing the working-class movement in the United States concerns the relationship between the capitalist development process and class capacities. Does proletarianization advance or retard the capacity of the working class as an historical agent in the transformation of capitalism? Contributions to the debate have generally lacked a rigorous enough operationalization of the key concepts to produce empirically testable propositions, and, for that reason, discussions of the problem have been vague, normative, and of little practical value.

This section attempts to put some substance in the notion of class capacities by focusing on one of its dimensions—the organizational capacity of the working class to act in a manner that transforms the basic class relations of capitalism. The importance of organizational forms can be understood within a theoretical framework established by Offe and Wiesenthal (1980, 76). They argue that "the positions of a group in the class structure . . . not only lead to differences in power that the organizations can acquire, but also lead to differences in the associational practices, or logics of collective action, by which organizations of capital and labor try to improve their respective position vis-a-vis each other." They contend further (p. 80) that the difference between capitalist and working-class forms of organization "lies in the fact that [the former] depends upon its ability to generate the members' 'willingness to pay' whereas the [latter] depends, in addition, on its ability to generate its members' 'willingness to act.'" Extended to an analysis of union organizations specifically, the Offe and Wiesenthal theory suggests that unions could be placed on a continuum ranging from those with more capitalist-like organizational practices (i.e., those that rely on the mobilization of financial resources to achieve their objectives) to those with more working-class-like associational practices (i.e., those that rely on mobilizing human resources).

Although Offe and Wiesenthal are not writing specifically about unions, the meaning for a definition of "union efficacy" would seem to be clear: A union functions in an efficacious manner if it is effective in advancing working-class interests against those of the capitalist class. Moreover, "interests" is understood in an explicitly relational and class-specific way: The objective of union activity is the enhancement of working-class capacities to transform the social relations of production under capitalism. While capitalists' organizational power lies in the merging of their capital or money resources, the real source of working-class power lies in the collective power of union members, which cannot be merged but only associated. Thus, it is only through the "collective deliberation" of members of the organization that the collective interest—to maximize associational power—can be optimized. In this model, then, the dependent variable is understood to be a dimension of class capacity that manifests itself through organizational forms.

The variable "organizational capacity of the working class" is operationalized as forms of labor union organization. Union organizational forms are found to vary along a continuum ranging from those organizations impelled toward increasingly class-wide organization to those organizations with forms that encourage narrow occupational identities. The main independent variable, proletarianization, will be operationalized quantitatively in this chapter and qualitatively in the next chapter. The theoretical objective is to demonstrate the positive association between proletarianization and increased working-class organizational capacities.

Proletarianization

Proletarianization manifests itself as a determinant of union organization in three ways. First, the social base from which union members are drawn has to be considered as primary. Those industries with the most proletarianized (Bridges 1986, 168, 186) work forces we would expect to find associated with unions having the most "associational" organizational practices. But a general and positive association of this type would be too superficial to stand alone as an indicator of organizational proletarianization. It might be the case, for example, that a union in an industry with a very proletarianized work force has a structure that precludes the rank-and-file members from exercising their influence. Second, in the case of the CIO unions it will be shown that the impetus for the pecuniary forms of organizational structure often came from the professionalized strata of the union bureaucracy. Thus, in class terms, it can be argued that loss of rank-and-file control of a union represents a shift in the class basis of control and that shift, in turn, manifests itself in organizational forms. In this sense the traditional pluralist criteria of union democracy are treated as independent variables, and we expect to find that those unions that are most democratic are also the ones with the highest levels of associational practices. Both of these quantifiable dimensions of proletarianization are examined in this section.

A third, more qualitative, operationalization is still necessary, however. The uneven historical development of a particular industry is responsible for a checkerboard pattern of class formation. Levels of technology may be very different due to the time period during which the industry started in different regions, and the working-class cultural and organizational forms related to immigration patterns leave very uneven legacies for subsequent efforts at unionization. Thus it is possible that in an industry like wood products, which was very proletarianized in general, there were sizable pockets of less-developed forms of production. These pockets, obscured by the quantitative generalizations made in this section, provided the social bases for a conservative element that in most cases supported the pecuniary forms of organization described above. This more qualitative dimension provides the grist for much of what is actually interesting about the factional struggles in CIO unions; they will be explored through three case studies in Chapter 3.

Social Base and Union Organization

Unions are membership organizations and for that reason the characteristics of the social base or population from which their memberships are drawn has to be considered as a primary influence on the organizational structures of unions. Union members are drawn or re-cruited from the population of workers in the industry represented by the particular union. A union in an industry with a highly prole-tarianized work force will be comprised of highly proletarianized workers; a less proletarianized industry would yield unions comprised of less proletarianized members.

Occupational classifications provided by the U.S. census can be interpreted as indicators of the skill level required to perform indus-trial tasks and thus can be seen as indicators of levels of proletarian-ization. Table 2.1 classifies industries according to the occupational categories that dominate each industry. In cases where any one occu-pational category is larger than the other two combined, the industry is classified under that category. An example would be the automobile industry whose 246,356 operatives would dominate any combination of craftsmen (144,788) and laborers (55,029). Cases marked with as-terisks, on the other hand, are those having no dominating occupation. In these cases the assumption has been made that some coalition would emerge to dominate the politics of the union and that coalition would be formed by occupationally-contiguous groups (i.e., either craftsmen and operatives or operatives and laborers but not laborers and crafts-men) and would be dominated by the group most likely to have the highest level of occupational consciousness (i.e., either craftsmen or laborers). Thus, unionism in the steel industry would be expected to reflect the dominating influence of the 338,077 craftsmen, even though there are slightly more operatives than craftsmen.

Table 2.1
Classification of Industries Organized by CIO-Affiliated Unions According to Occupation

Craftsmen-dominated	Operative-dominated	Laborer-dominated
Furniture*	Coal Mining	Lumber
Printing-Publishing	Meat Packing	Water Transport
Petro. Refining*	Textiles	
Blast Furnaces, steel, rolling mills & others*	Apparel	
	Rubber	
Electrical Machinery	Footwear	
	Leather	
	Glass	
	Metal Mining-Refining	
	Automobile	
	Street Railway and Bus Lines	

Source: U.S. Department of Commerce, Bureau of the Census. Sixteenth Cen-sus of the United States: 1940, Population, Vol. 3, The Labor Force; Part I, United States Summary, p. 233.

Membership Control

To operationalize the concept of membership control I will use an index of three components central to the relationship between union members and their leaders: the process by which leaders are selected, the formal provision for recall elections, and the extent of control that leaders have over the appointment of union staff workers.

Leadership Selection Process. Given that direct membership rule in large organizations is generally unfeasible, the most direct mechanism through which union members can effect control over their organizations is through the process of leadership selection (Edelstein and Warner 1976). I have identified three levels of control based upon this criterion. The highest level of control lies in the presence of direct membership referendum election of leaders. The next level is comprised of those unions that circumscribed their referenda elections with restrictions on who was eligible to run for office and/or had nomination processes that were so cumbersome as to mitigate the effect of rank-and-file influence. The lowest level of rank-and-file control in the leadership selection process is in those unions that elect leaders in convention, thus precluding direct membership votes on the matter.

Typical of the direct referenda provisions found in the constitutions I studied was that of the International Longshoremen's and Warehousemen's Union (ILWU). It specified that nominees, selected in convention, "shall be placed on a referendum ballot for a vote of the entire membership" (ILWU 1941, 7). In the ILWU case, the details of how the referendum was conducted were largely left to the locals while other unions, like the International Union of Mine, Mill and Smelter Workers (Mine-Mill 1939a), spelled out the procedure in greater detail.

At the second level we find the eligibility of candidates circumscribed in several ways. The Amalgamated Clothing Workers Union (ACWU) limited nominations to those who had been members or employees of the union for five or more years (ACWU 1940, 10). Several unions, including the United Auto Workers (UAW), United Mine Workers of America (UMWA), and after 1941 the International Woodworkers of America (IWA) had clauses forbidding members of the Communist party from running for office. The relevant clause in the IWA constitution was worded, "Any member accepting membership in the Communist Party shall be expelled from the International Woodworkers of America and is permanently debarred from holding office." (IWA 1941, 4).

Typical of those unions that had a very encumbered nomination process was the United Steelworkers of America (Steelworkers). The Steelworkers required that a candidate be nominated by 15 locals. Moreover, the nomination process took place outside the convention, which made it necessary for a potential candidate to have the communicative resources, free time, and mobility to influence the internal politics of 14 locals in addition to his/her own. The chances of that being a realistic possibility for anyone other than incumbents or professional staff would appear to have been slim. Finally, the entire process for nominations was initiated by the international office and had to be completed within 30 days (Steelworkers 1944, 20).

The third and lowest level of membership control over leadership selection was comprised of those unions in which members did not vote directly but rather exercised their will through convention delegates. The UAW elected leaders in this fashion from its inception and survived several attempts to change to a referendum process (UAW 1940, 239-47).

Of the 27 union constitutions surveyed for this study, 13 provided for referendum elections of officers while 14 elected officers in convention. In the index of membership control (Table 2.2) I have assigned values of +1, 0, and – 1 respectively to the highest, middle, and lowest levels of membership participation in the leadership selection process. In this and subsequent tables, scores are intended to indicate ordinal relationships only. A variety of approaches were considered for scoring the ordinal relationships but there was no significant difference between the present approach and others examined.

Recall Provisions. It is important that union members be able to maintain some control over the leaders they elect (Edelstein and Warner 1976). Without the power to remove leaders between regularly scheduled elections, it is conceivable that leaders elected under very democratic circumstances could consolidate their power to such an extent that democracy no longer prevailed by the next election. It is necessary, therefore, that in extreme circumstances the rank and file be able to exercise ultimate authority over leaders. The union constitutions we examined revealed three levels of provisions relevant to this mechanism of control. Those allowing the greatest amount of membership control were those easily implemented, direct recalls by referendum. Second were those recall provisions that required such a large number of petitioners to initiate the recall that it seems unlikely they could have been effective. Third were those unions that had no recall provisions at all.

Table 2.2
Level of Direct Membership or Leadership Control of Unions. Twenty-Seven CIO Unions, Ranked Approximately According to Size of International Membership

CIO Unions	I Referendum Elections			II Referendum Recall of Officers Procedures			III Power of Officers to Appoint Subordinates			IV
	yes (+1)	qual. (0)	no (−1)	yes (+1)	qual. (0)	no (−1)	none (+1)	limited (0)	extensive (−1)	Index (−3 to +3)
United Mine workers		x				x			x	−2
Steelworkers		x				x			x	−2
Textile Workers			x			x		x		−2
United Auto Workers			x			x		x		−2
International Ladies Garment Workers			x			x		x		−2
Amalgamated Clothing Workers		x				x			x	−2
United Electrical			x		x		x			0
Woodworkers	x			x			x			+3
Packinghouse Workers		x				x	x			+1
Oil Workers			x		x				x	−2
Transport Workers			x			x		x		−2
Typographical Workers	x					x	x			+1
Rubber Workers			x			x			x	−3
Mine-Mill	x			x				x		+2
Shoe Workers	x			x				x		+2
National Maritime	x					x		x		0
United Retail		x				x		x		−1
Fur			x		x		x			0
Office			x			x		x		−2
AFSCME			x		x			x		−1
International Longshoremen	x			x				x		+2
Marine and Ship			x		x		x			0
Flat Glass Workers	x					x		x		0
Furniture Workers			x			x	x			−1
Communication Workers	x					x		x		+1
Marine Engineers			x	x				x		0
Architects			x			x			x	−3

Source: Lembcke and Howe (1986). Compiled from union constitutions. See Bibliography.

In the first category were unions like the ILWU (1941, 14), which required a petition signed by 15 percent of the members to hold a recall election. Slightly more restrictive was Mine-Mill (1937, 12) in which it took 25 percent of the membership to initiate a recall. In the second category were unions like the United Electrical, Radio, and Machine Workers (UE), which provided for a recall of officers but which required three locals comprising at least 25 percent of the total international membership to endorse the action. For two reasons the UE's recall provision has to be considered a qualified form of rank-and-file recall. First, it required that the electoral apparatuses of three separate locals be mobilized for taking a vote and that campaigns for those votes be conducted by the parties favoring the recall. Such a level of formality was much less fluid than a simple petition campaign whereby individual members of any local could be solicited. Second, the fact that only the combination of the three largest locals could meet the 25 percent requirement meant that a recall situation would likely require more than three locals.

The third and lowest category of unions on the recall question are those that had no provisions for the participation of the membership in that process. Some, like the Amalgamated Clothing Workers Union (ACWU), provided for a trial procedure that began and ended with the General Executive Board (ACWU 1940, 25-26). The Steelworkers' constitution also provided for a trial procedure but it was applicable only to "members" and "local officers." No mention is made of inter-national-level officers. Several unions, like the Steelworkers, covered their trial procedures under the rubric of membership "discipline" rather than officer "recall." The difference in the two forms of wording probably reflects a difference in who the drafters of the language perceived to be the discipliners and who they perceived to be most likely in need of disciplining.

In Table 2.2 I have assigned the values +1, 0 and – 1 respectively to the highest, middle, and lowest levels of membership participation in the process of leadership recall.

Membership Control of Elected Officials. Lipset (1952, 60) has indicated the importance of rank-and-file control over union staff. How much license the top echelon leadership (as opposed to the rank and file or representative boards) has to hire, appoint, and dismiss union staff is an important determinant of the overall relationship between a union's membership and its elected officials. I divided my sample into three levels according to his criterion. At the highest level are those unions in which the elected executive boards or councils had almost total control over staff and the officers had virtually none. The second level are those unions that specified certain staff positions that were under the control of elected officers but that subjected the officers' decisions to final approval by the executive council. At the third level are those unions in which virtually unlimited power over staff rested with the officers.

Typical of the unions in the first level is the United Electrical, Radio, and Machine Workers (UE), which gave its top elected leaders almost no power over staff. Powers of the UE's general president were limited to presiding at meetings and conventions and coordinating the work of vice-presidents. The general president had no power to hire, appoint, or dismiss anyone; nor did the general secretary-treasurer or the director of organization have those powers. All powers of appointment in the UE rested with the General Executive Board, which consisted of vice-presidents elected from its districts (UE 1939a, 14-15).

A plurality of unions in my survey fell into the category of "limited" powers granted to officers. In Mine-Mill (1937, 13) the president could appoint some positions "with the approval of the Executive Board." The Steelworkers, Mine Workers, and Amalgamated Clothing Workers gave "extensive" powers to their officers. The Amalgamated constitution read, "The General President may employ and dismiss such representatives (subject, in the case of members of the General Executive Board who are employed as representatives, to the approval of the General Executive Board), organizers, administrative, technical and other employees as may be required. The General President shall fix the salaries of all persons employed by him" (ACWU 1940, 11-12).

A separate article of the ACWU constitution required the president to report his activities to the convention and General Executive Board for approval, but this provision appears to have been a general formalism, unrelated to the specific powers to hire, appoint, and dismiss staff. Moreover, the inclusion of the parenthetical stipulation that board members appointed to paid positions had to be approved by the board is strongly suggestive that other appointments did not require board approval. The United Mine Workers' president could "suspend or remove an International officer or appointed employee for insubordination for just and sufficient cause" (UMWA 1938, 18).

In my index of membership control I have assigned values of +1 to those unions that ceded very little authority to officers to control staff, 0 to those that ceded limited control, and − 1 to those unions in which the officers had extensive unaccountable control over staff.

Table 2.2 summarizes the data for the indicators for "membership control" from the 27 unions. An aggregate score is given for each union. The membership control variable reflects the degree of direct membership versus leadership control of the union. Column one shows the presence, qualified presence, or absence of referendum elections for officers in the union with scores of +1, 0, and - 1, respectively. Column two gives similar scores for the presence, qualified presence, or absence of procedures for recalling officers. Column three indicates the relative power of officers to appoint staff and other subordinates. An index of membership control is given for each union reflecting the aggregate score for each row.

The Logic of Collective Action in CIO Unions

Most studies of union organization have uncritically accepted pluralist assumptions about what is and what is not effectual union organization. Chief among the conventional criteria used to assess the character of unions is the presence or absence of constitutional provisions ensuring the right of individual union members to elect and maintain some control over their leaders. The assumption, in other words, is always that if "democracy" prevails, all else, including the union's capacity to represent worker interests, will follow. As was shown in Chapter 1, the assumption is not supported by the evidence.

This section attempts to redefine the union organization question as a relationship between levels of proletarianization and class capacities and presents an initial effort to identify empirically the nature of that relationship.

Democracy Versus Collectivity in CIO Unions

The Congress of Industrial Organizations (CIO) was formed during the mid-1930s as an alternative to the established unions affiliated with the American Federation of Labor (AFL). The AFL had proven itself incapable of meeting working-class needs in the face of depression conditions. Its affiliated unions had been formed during the mid-nineteenth century when craft production dominated; these unions followed craft lines of organizational structure. Thus, plumbers, mill wrights, carpenters, and mechanics were all in separate unions although they may have worked for the same employer. The craft form of organization is commonly understood to have reinforced a narrowness of outlook that made unity across craft lines very difficult to achieve.

During the early twentieth century production shifted away from a craft form of organization to an industrial form. AFL unions, however, did not keep pace. Instead, they adopted a protectionist posture toward the new developments and resolutely refused to organize the unskilled immigrant workers or to adapt their form of organization to one following industrial lines. Thus, in an industry like hard-rock mining, workers who sought unionization had little choice except to pursue it outside the bounds of the established AFL unions.

By the early 1930s the gap had widened between the numbers of workers organized in AFL craft unions and the total number of U.S. workers wanting and needing organization. Moreover, the AFL had only grown more conservative in its ways: in the face of depression conditions, it still refused to accommodate itself to an industrial form of organization; continued to look askance at unskilled, nonwhite workers (to say nothing of the unemployed); and resisted attempts to involve itself in political solutions to the depression.

Franklin D. Roosevelt took office in 1933, and one of his first acts was the passage of the National Industrial Recovery Act (NIRA). Section 7(A) of the NIRA stipulated that workers were allowed to bargain collectively through a union of their choice. With large numbers of workers now legally eligible for unionization, the AFL established industrial-type federal labor unions to take in many of those workers it had previously scorned. Non-AFL organizing efforts that had been on-going throughout the depression years, such as the Trade Union Unity League (TUUL) sponsored by the Communist party, were dissolved and activists were encouraged to take their energies and loyal followers into AFL-sponsored unions.

Workers began flocking to the AFL unions; worker-initiated strikes, occurring in unprecedented numbers, increased pressure on employers to recognize the unions. In 1933 775,000 workers joined unions; 900,000 went on strike. Over one million workers struck in 1934 and 1935.

The high point of the strike wave was the series of general strikes that swept the country during 1934. In Toledo, Minneapolis, and San Francisco left-wing union militants employed mass picket lines and sitdown strikes to shut down basic industry and transportation. Through the use of public forums, cultural activities, and community institutions (such as ethnic clubs) the essentially economic character of the struggle was broadened to a struggle that increasingly had the appearances of a class-based social movement. By 1935 it was clear that the revived workers' movement had objectives far more radical than could be supported by the AFL traditionalists.

With only 10 percent of the approximately 40 million workers unionized, the AFL balked at throwing its weight wholeheartedly behind an organizing drive. A minority group of AFL leaders, however, met on November 10, 1935 and constituted itself as the Committee for Industrial Organization—later to be named the Congress of Industrial Organizations. Attending that first meeting were representatives from the International Ladies Garment Workers Union, Mine-Mill, International Typographical Union, Amalgamated Clothing Workers, United Mine Workers, Hatters, Cap and Millinery Workers, Oil Workers, and the Textile Workers (Galensen 1960, 3-4). The CIO was the catalyst that propelled the movement for unionization to its climax. Within six months one million new members joined the CIO and within 18 months basic industry was organized.

From the available documents it appears that differences over such things as election and recall rules were minimal during the formative years of the CIO. Those CIO affiliates like the United Mine Workers of America (UMWA) and United Auto Workers (UAW), which had formerly been affiliated with the AFL, simply retained their old constitutional provisions. Others, such as the International Woodworkers of America (IWA) adopted the structures of the rank-and-file committees or caucuses that organized unions in their particular industries for the first time during the 1930s. After the CIO was formed its national office carried out its own organizing drives, and unions formed under its auspices, such as the United Steelworkers of America (USA), used the UMWA constitution as a pattern.

There were also some unique cases like the International Union of Mine, Mill, and Smelter Workers (Mine-Mill). Mine-Mill was originally organized by radicals as the Western Federation of Miners in 1893. It affiliated with the Industrial Workers of the World from 1905 to 1916 at which time it entered the AFL. The union all but died during the 1920s but radicals revived it in 1934 and took it into the CIO. In Chapter 3, where the case of Mine-Mill is examined in detail, it will be seen how that union's structure reflected its checkerboard historical evolution.

There were, then, very few struggles over the original formulation of rules governing leadership selection and accountability. There were also few struggles resulting from subsequent attempts to change the existing rules. Where those instances are found, such as in the United Electrical Workers (UE) in 1944 and the National Maritime Union (NMU) in 1947, they can be fully understood only in the context of fights between communist and noncommunist factions. These instances will be given special attention in Chapter 5.

In surveying union convention proceedings and archival collections of the CIO unions, however, one's attention is inevitably drawn to the record of fights over representation structures at the level of international conventions and international executive boards. As will be demonstrated below, these struggles had particular relevance for the control of organizing programs and, therefore, for the logic of collective action in CIO-affiliated unions.

Operationalizing "Logics of Collective Action"

Within the union tradition, the term given to the activities constituting collective action is "organizing." The policies that govern ways in which organizing activities are conducted—the ways in which union members, potential members, and community resources are assembled and mobilized for collective action—are made by bodies of delegates representing union members. Organizing policies at the most general level are set by international (U.S. and Canadian), national, and regional conventions; the policies are interpreted and executed by executive councils. Given the necessity for representative bodies to make such consequential decisions for the union as a whole, the structure by which policy decisions get made is extremely important. The structure by which union members are represented in this process reveals two different forms of decision making with regard to organizing questions. These forms of representation have strategical significance in reference to the class struggle (Child 1972; Cornfield 1986) and, in turn, reveal the two logics of collective action discussed above. One form, which I have called a "pecuniary logic," predicates representation of the quantity of members' contribution to the international union through the payment of per-capita dues. In this arrangement, the greater a unit's aggregate financial contribution, the greater that unit's representation in the decision-making process. This form, I argue, corresponds most closely to what Offe and Wiesenthal have called a capitalist logic of organization and is least strongly associated with proletarianized organization (Table 2.3).[1] The second representational form, which I have called an "associational logic," predicates representation on the potential quality of members' contribution to the international union through the extension of the union's scope of representation and power in the broadest way—that is, through the extensive organization of locals in different plants, communities, and regions. The "associational logic" of collective action emphasizes (a) the antagonistic relationship between the working class and the capitalist class and the need for organization to take place in order that the working class is advanced in that relationship; and (b) the perceived

Table 2.3
Frequency Distribution and Gamma on Proletarianization and Logic of Collective Action for CIO Unions

Logic of Collective Action	Highly Proletarianized	Moderately Highly Proletarianized	Indeterminant Class Identity	Moderately Lowly Proletarianized	Lowly Proletarianized	Total
Associational Logic	2	2	3	2	1	10
Mixed Logic	1	1	1	3	1	7
Pecuniary Logic	0	0	0	2	2	4
Total	3	3	4	7	4	21

Source: Reprinted from *Recapturing Marxism: An Appraisal of Recent Trends in Sociological Theory,* Rhonda F. Levine and Jerry Lembcke, eds., 1987, with permission of Praeger.

political and cultural contribution the potential members would make to the development of the union as a whole. In this arrangement, a unit whose aggregate ability to contribute financially is slight would be given a disproportionately greater influence in the decision-making process. This form, I argue, corresponds most closely to what Offe and Wiesenthal call a working-class logic of organization and is most strongly associated with unions with proletarianized memberships and high levels of rank-and-file control (Table 2.3).

The differences between pecuniary and associational logics of representation become apparent when we consider several issues familiar to union members.

The issue of representing laid-off workers. It is common practice for unions to disenfranchise fellow workers when they lose their jobs. If a worker is not working and cannot pay dues he/she is not entitled to representation, cannot vote, and cannot attend union meetings. As a result, workers in the greatest need of social and political support, and union locals hardest hit by plant closures, are cut off from collective support. Moreover, because the workers who have kept their jobs and remained in the union are in a position to broker the conditions under which laid-off workers will return to work, the danger exists that they could use the union power for protectionist purposes.

Representation of seasonal workers. In industries like logging and fishing, where employment is seasonally cyclical, representation of workers on strictly per-capita bases periodically disenfranchises them and the locals to which they belong. In certain West Coast CIO unions this was a perennial issue.

Representation of underemployed workers. Some unions have sliding dues scales that allow part-time workers who earn less than full-time workers to pay lower dues. Often, however, paying less than full dues means getting less than full representation. Workers traditionally hurt by discrimination—nonwhites and women—are most under-represented. This has been an issue in the American Federation of Teachers (AFT), for example, where supporters of the conservative leadership of Albert Shanker have attempted to undercut the political power of teaching assistants and para-professionals.

Representation in setting organizing policy and participation in organizing campaigns. In most respects this is the critical issue and the one dealt with at length in this book. Certain aspects of it need to be highlighted here, however. An axiom of successful unionization campaigns is that workers have to organize themselves; organizing cannot be done from the "outside." Even the most autocratic union leaders would pay lip service to the principle. The reasoning behind the principle is that organizing campaigns focusing on issues raised by the workers themselves and relying on organizers that the workers themselves know and respect will have greater resonance with workers. The level of trust and cohesiveness developed during the struggle *for* a union will carry over and add to the union's durability. Such an arrangement means that, in a sense, workers have to become participants in a parent union organization before they are actually dues-paying union members. In other words, if they are to be responsible for their own organization campaign, they have to have some autonomy in decision making (e.g., who to hire, what leaflets to print, tactical choices, and budgetary control) before they are actually financial contributors to the union.

Recently, some internationals (e.g., AFT and the UAW) have adopted a policy that the parent body "organizes" the local first, and then those who are "organized" become union members. Since the workers being organized are not union members during the organizing campaign (nor are they dues-payers), they are not allowed to participate in the organizing campaign. Needless to say, the enthusiasm of the unorganized for this model is underwhelming and the type of locals organized are forever dependent on the international for leadership and financial resources.

A corollary to this issue is how broad participation in organizing campaigns should be. Should only dues-paying members be allowed to make decisions on strategy and tactics even though the execution of those may involve and have consequences for family and community members? A vivid portrayal of the issue was made in the movie *Salt of the Earth* where a strike of Mine, Mill and Smelter Workers was won only when nonvoting women were allowed to participate in decision making. In a more recent example, striking Hormel workers in Austin Minnesota opened their meetings to spouses and community members.

In Chapter 3 the validity of using representational forms as an operationalization of Offe and Wiesenthal's logic of collective action will be established contextually through a review of the historical struggles occurring within CIO unions. Through a review of concrete struggles over union organizational questions it will be shown that the issues of individual sovereignty important to pluralist sociologists were of little importance to CIO unionists. What emerges from the review of those struggles is evidence that the concerns were not about individual rights as much as the consequences of certain representation structures for the collective interests of the workers involved. The pluralist framework thus appears to be something imposed on the reality of everyday struggle within the union movement rather than a model validated by that experience.

Index of Logic of Collective Action

For each of the 27 unions in my sample I examined their forms of representation for both conventions, where policy decisions are made, and executive councils, where decisions are interpreted and implemented. For executive council representation I assigned the value +1 to those cases like the UE and IWA where each local was allowed one vote on organizing questions and the value – 1 to those cases, like the Steelworkers, where each local was allowed a vote proportionate to its per-capita contribution.

For convention representation a slightly more complex formula was used. Votes at union conventions are taken in two ways: voice votes and roll call votes. In the case of voice votes the manner in which delegates are apportioned is crucial because the number of delegates voicing a nay or yea vote is a strong determinant of whether a motion passes or fails. Thus, for example, if each local were allotted one delegate, voice votes on questions concerning the distribution of resources for organizing purposes would not result in any one local having an advantage over another. The forms of delegate apportionment I have found are of two types. One type, (a), is a form of proportional representation such as that found in the Steelworkers (1944, 30) where each local got one delegate for each 100 members or major fraction thereof. Thus, a local with 100 members would get one delegate and have one voice vote, while a local with 1,000 members would have ten delegates and ten voice votes. The other form of representation, (b), was that found in the International Woodworkers of America (IWA) before 1941 (IWA 1941, 74) where each local got two delegates for the first 100 members and one for each additional 300 or major fraction thereof up to 1,000. Thus, a local with 100 members would get two delegates and have two voice votes, while a local with 1,000 members would have four delegates and four voice votes. The power differential between large and small locals is thus significantly different depending on which form of representation is used. In the case of the Steelworkers, it would take the united effort of 11 locals with fewer than 100 members to out-vote one large local, while in the IWA any three small locals would be sufficient to out-vote a large local. As will be demonstrated below in the review of the IWA case history, this difference had special relevance for decision making on organizing questions in the early years of the CIO.

The case of convention roll call votes is slightly different still. On a roll call vote each delegate's vote is recorded and weighted by some factor. In the case of the IWA, each delegate vote carried the weight of "one," which meant that the structure of the delegate selection process carried over into the roll call procedure. In other words, since delegates were apportioned in a way that diminished the relative power of large locals, the roll call procedure also diminished their power. The United Electrical, Radio and Machine Workers (UE), on the other hand, allotted three delegates to locals having 500 members or less and one additional delegate for each additional 500 members (UE 1939, 32). Thus, on voice votes small locals were relatively favored. But on roll call votes each local was allotted one vote for each 100 members or fraction thereof. Thus, at the 1939 convention the Lynn Massachusetts local, with 4,200 members, was entitled to 10 voice votes and 42 roll call votes, divided equally between the delegates. The Hartford Connecticut local with 400 members, on the other hand, was entitled to 3 voice votes and 4 roll call votes. The power differential between the Lynn and Hartford locals was a factor of 3.33 on voice votes and 10.5 on roll call votes (see Table 2.4).

On my index of Logic of Collective Action (Table 2.5) I have made the assumption that decision making at the executive council and convention levels exerts equal influence as determinants of organizing policies. Thus, they have each been given a value of $+/- 1$. Since the convention process breaks down into two parts, however, I have divided the weight of the convention influence, giving half to the delegate selection process and half to the roll call vote process. A $+1/2$

Table 2.4

Membership, Size, and Convention Representation for Two Locals, United Electrical Workers: 1939

	Size of Local	Number of Delegates	Number of Roll Call Votes	Ratio of Roll Call to Voice Vote
Lynn Local	4,200	10	42	4.2:1
Hartford Local	400	3	4	4:3
Power Differential Between Locals			10.5	3.33

Source: United Electrical Workers (1939b).

has been assigned to unions that apportioned delegates through a form of diminishing proportional representation, and a value of $-1/2$ was given to those in which forms of apportionment are strictly proportional to the per-capita size. I have also assigned $+1/2$ to unions in which a roll call voting procedure gave an advantage to small locals and a $-1/2$ to unions that conducted roll call votes on a strictly per-capita basis. The summation of these values for any one union falls between $+2$ and -2, with $+2$ representing those unions with a structure of decision making that best resembles my description of associational logic and a -2 resembling the logic I have called pecuniary logic, corresponding to Offe and Wiesenthal's working-class and capitalist logic, respectively.

Table 2.5 summarizes the aggregate data, presenting the position of the 27 unions on the various indicators of logic of collective action. An aggregate score is given for each union, based on the score for each of the three columns. Column 1 shows the logic for decision making on executive boards. An associational logic reflected in unit voting systems (one local-one vote) is given a score of $+1$; a pecuniary logic, indicated by per-capita voting systems (votes apportioned according to each local's per-capita contribution to the higher body) is given a score of -1. Columns 2 and 3 show the logic of decision making at conventions of the union as a whole. Column 2 refers to the way delegates are apportioned as representatives to the convention. Those with diminishing proportional representation are given a score of $+1/2$. Those with direct proportional representation are given a score of $-1/2$. Column 3 shows how representation works on roll call votes. Roll call votes giving each local one vote reflect an associational logic and are given a score of $+1/2$. Roll call votes that give each delegate a number of votes based on the local's per-capita financial contribution to the international reflect a pecuniary logic and are given a score of $-1/2$. The aggregate scores, shown in column 4, provide an index of the logic of collective action, with scores ranging from -2 to $+2$, reflecting variations on a continuum from a purely pecuniary logic to a purely associational logic.

SUMMARY AND ANALYSIS

Table 2.3 summarizes the data pertaining to my argument at this point. There is a clear increase in the strength of association between the class or class fractional character of a union organization (as measured by the occupational characteristics of the work force and

Table 2.5
Logic of Collective Action, Reflected by Decision-making Procedures at Executive Board Meetings and Annual Conventions. Twenty-Seven CIO Unions Ranked Approximately According to Size of International Membership

| | I Executive Board | | Conventions | | | | IV |
| | | | II Delegate Apportionment | | III Roll Call Votes | | |
CIO Unions	Associational Logic (unit vote) (+1)	Fiscal Logic (per cap) (-1)	Diminishing Proportional Representation (+½)	Direct Proportional Representation (-½)	Associational Logic (unit vote) (+½)	Fiscal Logic (per cap) (-½)	Index (-2 to +2)
United Mine Workers		x		x		x	-2
Steelworkers		x		x		x	-2
Textile Workers	x		x		x		+2
United Auto Workers		x	x			x	-1
International Ladies Garment Workers		x	x		x		0
Amalgamated Clothing Workers	x		x		x		+2
United Electrical	x		x			x	+1
Woodworkers	x		x		x		+2
Packinghouse Workers	x			x		x	0
Oil Workers		x	x			x	-1
Transport Workers	x			x		x	0

Union						Value
Typographical workers	x			x		+2
Rubber Workers	x	x	x		x	0
Mine-Mill	x	x	x		x	0
Shoe Workers	x	x		x	x	+1
National Maritime	x	x		x		+2
United Retail	x	x	x		x	0
Fur	x			x	x	+2
Office	x	x	x		x	0
AFSCME	x	x		x	x	+2
International Longshoremen	x	x	x		x	0
Marine and Ship	x	x	x		x	0
Flat Glass Workers	x	x		x		+2
Furniture Workers	x	x	x		x	0
Communication Workers	x	x	x		x	0
Marine Engineers	x	x		x	x	+2
Architects	x	x	x		x	0

Source: Compiled from union constitutions.

the level of membership control of the union) and the logic of decision making on questions related to organizing. Higher levels of proletarianization are associated with an associational logic of collective action, reflecting a desire to maximize the organizational capacity of the broadest spectrum of union members or potential union members. On the other hand, leadership-dominated unions with craft-oriented memberships tend to exhibit a higher degree of pecuniary logic, reflected in decision-making strategies that give primacy to the ability of locals to contribute financial resources to the higher body. The findings thus support the general thesis of Offe and Wiesenthal that there are two logics of collective action, the interpenetration of which influences working-class organizations.

The findings also raise challenges to other points made by Offe and Wiesenthal, however, and implicitly to some basic tenets of conventional organizational theory. Offe and Wiesenthal argue that trade unions have to be large in order to have sufficient power to advance the interests of their members within the class structure. But as unions become larger, they become more centralized and autocratic, thus undercutting their ability to mobilize their members for action. Consequently, according to Offe and Wiesenthal, unions tend to move from a logic of working-class collective action to a logic of capitalist-class collective action—as their size increases—substituting the mobilization of financial resources for human resources.

Historical studies of actual transitions in logics of collective action presented in the next chapter will reveal, however, that the transitions have more to do with the internal balance of power within unions and the strategical choices made by leadership coalitions than they do social ecology.

NOTE

1. The sample size for Table 2.3 is 21 rather than 27 because the occupational indicator used for the variable proletarianization is inapplicable to six of the industries. The following system was used to code unions for classification in Table 2.3:

Highly proletarianized	=	laborer dominated with membership control.
Moderately high	=	laborer dominated with indeterminant control; operative dominated with membership control.

Indeterminant class identity	= operative dominated with indeterminant control; laborer dominated with leadership control; craft dominated with membership control.
Moderately low	= craft dominated with indeterminant control; operative dominated with leadership control.
Low proletarianization	= craft dominated with leadership control.

3

Class Formation and Class Capacities: Case Studies of Three CIO Unions

INTRODUCTION

The first two chapters have argued in favor of the general theory that organizational forms are class specific. Those chapters adopted Offe and Wiesenthal's (1980) position that capitalist-class organizations seek to mobilize monetary resources in pursuit of their class objectives, while working-class organizations seek the mobilization of human resources. Applying this general theoretical framework to the case of CIO unions, it was argued that these contending logics of organization manifest themselves within unions as disagreements over how members should be represented in decision making on questions related to organizing policies. While recognizing that unions must in varying degrees mobilize both pecuniary and human resources, support was found for the general proposition that the unions associated with the more proletarianized occupations and high levels of rank-and-file control were also those unions that primarily sought the mobilization of human—as opposed to financial—resources.

This chapter seeks additional confirmation of the link between class fractions and organizational forms. By comparing case studies of the International Union of Mine, Mill and Smelter Workers (Mine-Mill), the United Auto Workers (UAW), and the International Wood-workers of America (IWA), it will be shown that the disagreements over formal organizational structure can be more fundamentally understood as disagreements over organizational strategy—that is, disagreements over whom (or what) to mobilize—and that the hypothesized relationships between particular class fractions and organizational forms are evident. Moreover, it becomes clear with these case studies that the questions of whom/what to organize/mobilize reflected the very different material realities of the contending factions. The arguments used in support of or in opposition to specific organizational forms suggest deep-seated cultural differences rooted in the uneven historical development of U.S. capitalism and the concomitant uneven formation of the working class. As a result, the disagreement over organizational questions often had strong regional overtones to them. Table 3.4 summarizes the important descriptive data of the case studies. The chapter concludes with a comparative analysis of the data.

Background to the Organizational Struggles

Disputes over representational forms in CIO unions began occurring around 1940 within the context of CIO President John L. Lewis's attempts to centralize his control of the CIO and rein in the power of communists working in the CIO affiliates. While Lewis was president of the CIO, he remained president of the United Mine Workers of America (UMWA), which was his home union and the source of his power within the CIO. Lewis's control of the UMWA's organizing program, in turn, derived from his control of the union's largest district council, District 12.[1] The UMWA Executive Board was made up of district presidents who voted the per-capita strength of their districts, and District 12 had most of the votes (Cary 1968, 64; Dubofsky and Van Tine 1977). Lewis's control of the organizing program meant that when new locals were established and new members were brought into the organization, they came under the influence of Lewis or his hand-picked lieutenants. Lorin Lee Cary (1968, 116) has argued that Lewis was able to extend this structure into the CIO: "Lewis' links with unorganized and organized workers consisted primarily of representatives, such as [Adolph] Germer, who counseled and directed the inexperienced. As the CIO accelerated its campaign to organize mass production workers, it institutionalized the role of advisor by creating organizing committees, each headed by a Lewis protege, usually from the UMWA."

Lewis began the process of centralizing control over the CIO at a mid-October 1939 joint session of the CIO Executive Board and the CIO's regional directors (Cary 1968, 127). Following that meeting, battles over representation structures commenced in the unions affiliated with the CIO. In all cases it was the more conservative factions with the closest ties to the CIO national office that fought for per-capita representation forms similar to the one that allowed Lewis to control the UMWA by controlling one large local or district. An examination of the IWA, UAW, and Mine-Mill cases makes it clear that control of the organizing programs was the real issue and that a pecuniary logic was the foremost organizational principle guiding the decisions of their leaders.

THE INTERNATIONAL WOODWORKERS OF AMERICA

The main purpose of this case history is to demonstrate the strong association between the class characteristics of a union—the level of membership control and level of proletarianization of its members—and the logic of collective action exhibited by the union. A secondary purpose is to show the political dynamic determining which leadership structure and logic of collective action ultimately prevailed.

Between 1937 and 1940 the International Woodworkers of America (IWA) had elected its top echelon leaders through annual referenda. For four consecutive years the membership had elected an administration headed by Harold Pritchett, a British-born, Canadian Communist. Under Pritchett's leadership members were represented on executive bodies by unit vote, with each local receiving one vote. In convention they were represented by delegates allotted according to a formula of diminishing proportional representation. On roll call votes each delegate got one vote. The conservatives in the union and the CIO national office generally disapproved of the left-wing character of the IWA's leadership but they were unable to unseat the latter under the existing constitutional forms of leadership selection and convention representation. The ensuing struggle to change the IWA constitution closely resembled the struggle over representation forms in the UAW and Mine-Mill examined below.

Following the 1939 convention, the Columbia River District Council (CRDC), the largest district in the international, withheld its percapita dues for the organizing program. The CRDC feared that new members brought in under the tutelage of left-wing organizers would only swell the ranks of Pritchett's supporters. The CRDC dues boycott threatened to bankrupt the international, which prompted CIO president John L. Lewis to extend financial assistance to the IWA—with strings attached. Lewis's terms were that the CIO national office, not the IWA leaders, would control the union's organizing program. While controversy would swirl around what the exact agreement was, one thing that was clear was that the CRDC dues boycott had dislodged control of the organizing program from the union's elected officials. It was the first of several measures the conservative CRDC would take to expunge the union's left wing by circumventing constitutional democracy (Lembcke and Tattam 1984).

The IWA case is important not only because the rank-and-file referendum elections offer solid evidence that union members did, in fact, support the communist Pritchett administration, but also because the union's left-wing leadership was ousted despite that broad-based membership support. It also allows us to locate the political roots of the factions that vied for control of the IWA in the social composition of the industry's work force, which was determined, in turn, by the industry's uneven historical development. Finally, it will be shown that the conflicts between contending forces were resolved in the early 1940s through the intervention of the state and an emerging bureaucratic stratum within the CIO. A critical dimension of that resolution was the change in the rules by which organizing policy was set. Those formal rule changes constituted a change from associational to pecuniary organizational logic.

Uneven Development of the Timber Industry

By 1900 the lumber industry had already established its reputation as a migratory industry. It had cut over the U.S. Northeast and maritime provinces of eastern Canada before moving into the Great Lakes states in the mid-1800s. In the next half-century it depleted some of the largest forests in North America before moving to the Pacific Northwest (Pike 1967, 1-51; Jensen 1945, 45; Stephenson 1915; Dunn 1977, 74, 182).

The earliest lumber mills in the Pacific Northwest were located along the lower Columbia River and along the lower reaches of the Willamette River near what is now Portland, Oregon. The earliest commercial mill was probably established by the Hudson Bay Company, six miles up the Columbia River from Fort Vancouver, in 1827. In the early 1840s, with a population in Oregon of just over 100, additional mills were established near the Willamette Falls (now Oregon City) and on the Tualatin Plains. With the arrival of 4,500 settlers "of comfortable means" in 1847, production for local consumption increased (Cox 1974, 9, 25).

Small mills also sprang up along the Oregon coast. Inland, loggers quickly cut the huge spruce and hemlock that could be easily felled into coastal tidewater and floated downstream to the mills. Coastwide shipment of lumber and logs, especially to San Francisco, provided a comfortable profit for these mills until the late 1890s. While some of these mills continued to cut for local building construction, many succumbed when newly developed deep-water steamship transportation began to serve larger mills on Washington's Puget Sound.

Lumber milling was a high-risk business. By the 1880s the industry was increasingly dominated by a few large firms backed by capital from California and the East. These big operations were attracted by the abundant timber and deep harbors in the Puget Sound area around Seattle that could accommodate steam powered vessels. Pope and Talbot established one of the most successful operations—Puget Mill Company—at Port Gamble, Washington in 1852. Port Gamble epitomized the company mill town, having been built by Pope and Talbot as a replica of the New England town where its company headquarters was located (Morgan 1955, 60-65). In 1858 the company built a second mill, "the biggest in the West." By 1880 Puget Company nearly dominated the Pacific Northwest, although other companies established large mills in the Grays Harbor (Aberdeen, Washington) area (Cox 1974, 118). The industry's later start in Washington enabled a qualitatively different development from that in Oregon. Table 3.1 shows that in 1880, when Washington's lumber industry had only a fraction of the number of mills in Oregon, its mills had 55 percent more capital. The arrival of Weyerhaeuser in 1900 would ensure that the capitalization of Washington's mills would remain high for several decades. Table 3.2 shows that in 1939 the rate of exploitation continued to be higher in Washington than Oregon.

The wood products industry got off to a later and less promising start in British Columbia. A British monopoly established the Alberni Mill Company in the 1860s. It eventually employed 700 workers but U.S. trade barriers kept the firm's lumber out of San Francisco, leaving it with insufficient markets and forcing it to close before 1870. Not until railroads punched west through the rugged Canadian Rockies in the late 1880s and opened the interior of British Columbia did the industry boom. By 1899 British Columbian lumber production had increased to 252,580 million board feet. Nevertheless, British Colum-

Table 3.1
Establishments and Capital in Oregon and Washington Lumber Industry, 1880.

	(1) Number of Establishments	(2) Capital	(3) Ratio Col 2/Col 1
Oregon	228	$1,577,875	6,920
Washington	37	$2,456,450	66,390

Source: Maxwell Reprint Company, *American Industry and Manufacturers in the 19th Century*, Vol. 8. (Elmsford, N.Y.: Maxwell Reprint Company).

Table 3.2

Wages in Manufacturing and Value Added for Lumber Industry, 1939

Region	(1) Manufacturing Wages	(2) Value Added	(3) Ratio Col 2/Col 1
Oregon	36,919,888	63,856,410	1.73
Washington	39,861,253	72,076,205	1.81

Source: U.S. Department of Commerce, Bureau of the Census. Sixteenth Census of the United States: 1940. Manufactures, 1939 Volume 3, pp. 850, 1050.

bia still lagged far behind Washington, which by the turn of the century was producing twice as much lumber as Oregon (Cox, 1974, 134).

This uneven regional development had two attendant features that shaped the political development of the industry's workers. The first was the immigration pattern that brought conservative, agrarian workers to the rich farmland of the lower Columbia River in the mid-nineteenth century while workers with industrial experience and socialist leanings were drawn to the big mills in northern Washington and British Columbia in the last decades of the nineteenth century. The second was the uneven development of unionization. In the lower Columbia River area, around Portland, Oregon, craft unionism had gained a foothold by the 1880s, while workers further north, especially in British Columbia, formed more advanced, industrial unions from the outset.

Social Cleavages in the Work Force

The influence of immigrants on the processes of class formation in the Pacific Northwest woods depended upon the nature of the experience specific immigrant groups brought with them and the time of their arrival.

Oregon had the earliest immigration but both Washington and British Columbia soon had larger numbers of immigrants. Oregon and Washington reached peak percentages of immigration in the last decade of the nineteenth century, while British Columbia continued to climb to an all-time high in 1920 when 53 percent of the provincial population was foreign born. Foreign-born workers made up nearly 50 percent of the laborers in Pacific Northwest mills in 1910 before the number of foreign born declined in the post-1920 period. (See tables in Lembcke 1984 for a summary of additional quantitative data.)

The largest immigrant groups to enter the industry in the North Pacific region were German, English, and Scandinavian. The heaviest German immigration to the northwest came in the middle and late nineteenth century. Many German immigrants came from agrarian and feudal backgrounds; they left Germany prior to the emergence of industrial unionism and settled in the Willamette Valley area of Oregon where they worked part time in small mills and farmed the cut-over timber land to supplement their income. These so-called "stump ranchers," while numerically significant in the Pacific Northwest and British Columbia, never expressed themselves in an ethnically identifiable bloc within the industry's unions (Kuczyniski 1967, 145).

The second major immigration group was British. Because the Industrial Revolution came earlier to Great Britain than to Germany, the British immigrants had greater experience with unionism and with working-class political organization. British immigrants to British Columbia arrived at a time when their experience could significantly aid the budding industrial union movement in the province's woods and mills (Phillips 1967, 25, 45-46).

The third major immigrant group, the Scandinavians, came in two waves. Like the Germans, those immigrating before 1890 were predominantly agrarian. Those who arrived later, however, were increasingly from industrial origins. The Swedish working-class movement was influenced by Marxist theory and "displayed a corresponding aversion to the capitalistic form of society" (Lindberg 1930, 135). Swedish capitalism, like capitalism everywhere in the late nineteenth century, was seeking expansion through imperialism, placing demands for compulsory military service on its working class. This, coupled with the general social instability inherent in capitalism, encouraged the emigration of class-conscious Swedish workers by the end of the century (Linberg 1930, 207-22). Like their English counterparts, this group of Scandinavians was able to play a prominent role in unionizing the timber industry.

Of all the ethnic groups that labored in the wood products industry and joined the IWA, Scandinavians were the most visibly active. With the notable exception of the international's first president, Harold Pritchett, who was born in England, most of the union's best organizers—Hjalmar Bergren, Ralph Nelson, Karly Larsen, Ernie Dalskog, Matt Savola, Ilmar Kouvinen—came from Scandinavian families.

Several leaders in the organizing of the IWA (including Dalskog, Savola, and Kouvinen) were Finnish. Studies done by Gedicks (1976), Blee and Gedicks (1980) and Howe (1985) locate the origins of Finnish radicalism historically in proletarian cultural forms arising from the mining camps and mill towns where Finns resided. The temperance and mutual aid societies and Finnish halls combatted "the ideology of individualism and the actual atomization of individual life" by incorporating entire families into activities that promoted collective solutions to individual problems (Howe 1985, 8).

These immigration patterns significantly influenced later developments within the IWA. First, the early settlement of German farmers in the lower Columbia River and Willamette River valleys was the foundation upon which the labor movement in the Portland area was built. These were the early workers who brought with them little industrial or socialist experience and came looking for opportunity as farmers. Work in the woods or mills was incidental to their primary goal of self-sufficiency. Also, they worked in mills that were small in comparison to those that were built later on Puget Sound or in British Columbia. Without the large concentration of capital that marked the late nineteenth century, and without large-scale industrialization, the conditions for radicalism and industrial unionism were absent.

Second, immigration came later to northern Washington and British Columbia, which meant that the newcomers brought with them a more advanced political attitude from their experience with industrial unions and socialist movements in England and Scandinavian countries. When they arrived, the concentration of production into larger units had already taken place. Thus, the social conditions were more favorable for industrial unionism and labor radicalism.

Immigration was, of course, only one factor that was affected by the uneven regional development of the industry. The evolution of the North American labor movement also contributed to the emerging political imbalance that would tear the IWA apart soon after its formation.

Organizational Development: Craft Versus Industrial Unions

The Portland, Oregon labor movement developed an early reputation for conservatism. One historian has noted that in the 1880s and 1890s "nowhere else in the North Pacific Region were labor leaders such models of restraint and caution as in Portland." The AFL was introduced to the region through Portland labor leaders in 1887 and for several years Portland stood alone in the vanguard of Samuel Gompers's "pure and simple unionism" (Schwantes 1978, 16).

A more radical union tradition was established in Washington and British Columbia. The coal mining communities of northern Washington and Vancouver Island attracted the attention of the Knights of Labor. Although some of the Knights gave expression to the anti-Chinese sentiment among railroad construction workers threatened by Chinese laborers, the left wing of the Knights shunned racial politics and provided a precedent for radical industrial unionism in the region. It was in this setting that the Industrial Workers of the World, formed in 1905, took root.

In 1917 the IWW formed the Lumber Workers Industrial Union, which led a war-time strike for the eight-hour day. Immediately a cry was raised by the employers and the government that the strike was hurting spruce production, essential to airplane production for World War I. The government responded by sending Lieutenant Colonel Brice Bisque to the northwest to stabilize the industry. Bisque granted the workers the eight-hour day and improved working conditions; but he closed the woods to labor organizers and union members and organized the Loyal Legion of Loggers and Lumbermen (the 4-L) with compulsory membership and a no-strike policy. The 4-L gained wide acceptance around the Portland area. Its headquarters was in Longview, Washington, just down the Columbia River from Portland, and many of its members hailed from the Willamette Valley running south from Portland. Twenty years later White Bloc leaders within the IWA would ply these same valleys seeking to enroll workers for the fight against the union's left-wing leadership (Dubofsky 1969, 413; Jensen 1945, 135).

The Russian Revolution produced new tensions within the ranks of lumber workers. The Communist Party, with its prestigious associations with the revolution, began to attract IWW members. In 1921 the IWW was invited to join the Communist Red International of Labor Unions, or the Profintern. The internal debate over affiliation tore the IWW apart and divided the IWW-affiliated lumber workers into two camps. Some, often Scandinavian immigrants with established residencies in the northwest, joined the new communist movement; others, often native-born midwesterners who migrated from camp to camp for work, followed James Rowan in forming the IWW "Emergency Program" headquartered in Portland. By the 1930s these two groups of erstwhile fellow workers were bitter enemies. The Scandinavian settlers in Washington and British Columbia would emerge as leaders of the Communist Party's National Lumber Workers Union, while the IWW holdouts would join ranks with the traditional trade union conservatives to make common cause against the communists.

The divisions surfaced during the 1935 lumber strike, the seminal event in the formation of the IWA. The Portland workers, in keeping with their traditional conservatism, were reluctant strike supporters, defending instead the AFL's attempts to settle the strike. The large Long-Bell and Weyerhaeuser locals down river from Portland were slow to join the strike. When the communist-led Northwest Joint Strike Committee broke with the AFL over how the strike should be conducted, the IWW issued a leaflet "declaring themselves neutral in 'this internal struggle within the corrupt A.F. of L.' " (Sparks 1935).

The Articulation of Class and Organizational Forces

It was the fractured social base of the working class in the north Pacific region (described above) that articulated with the intervention of the CIO's national office to oust the IWA's radical administration. An examination of that convergence enables us to see that the logic of collective action shifted from an associational logic to a pecuniary logic as the fractional basis of power shifted from leaders with a more proletarian social base to those with a more petty-bourgeois base. Second, we will see the implications of that shift for class relations in the industry. In the IWA case it is clear that the articulation of the historically-given social forces in the industry with the pecuniary logic of representation that prevailed after 1941 was a combination that had profoundly conservative implications.

Lewis appointed one of his best troubleshooters, Adolph Germer, to head the IWA's organizing program. Germer, according to Cary (1968, iv), "laboured incessantly to augment the authority of union leaders [and] hold the rank and file in line." When Germer arrived in Seattle, Washington in June 1940, he attached himself to conservative IWA leaders like Al Hartung, president of the CRDC, and immediately joined the battle over hiring organizers.

By August 9, 1940, Germer had received lists of recommended organizers from both conservative and left-wing factions. In consultation with Oregon CIO Director William Dalrymple and "one of the other boys in the Columbia River District," Germer ascertained that all but two of the names submitted by the international were "labeled" —a reference indicating some association with the Communist party (Germer 1940). On August 16 Germer informed international officers that he had no intention of submitting a list of proposed organizers to Harold Pritchett for his approval and that he had decided to interview five men from a list submitted by the CRDC.

On August 22, 1940, Harold Pritchett was deported to Canada, which effectively prevented him from exercising his duties as president. Soon after the deportation Germer began bringing in organizers from the east, all of whom were loyal acquaintances of his and none of whom had previous experience as workers or organizers in the industry. The international protested vigorously to the CIO but the protests were ignored. On September 9 Michael Widman, the CIO's director of organizing, assured Germer, "I have noted carefully our reports for the past few weeks [and] am wholeheartedly in accord with your actions to the smallest detail. . . . I can only suggest that you keep battling away at them. Your judgment seems sound and I know your experience will guide you in the best interests of all concerned" (Widman 1940). On February 20, 1941 the conservatives formed the CIO Woodworkers Organizing Committee and began publishing their own newspaper, *The Woodworker*. The committee, under the direction of Adolph Germer and headquartered in the Columbia River District Council, was funded by the CIO. Full CIO endorsement was given on March 15 when Germer was informed of:

a conference with Phil Murray . . . [where we] discussed . . . the organizational drive, that is to carry it on in the favorable places to our cause and by this method take [care] of the IWA problem in their next convention, as there isn't any way to take care of them under the CIO constitution, only in convention to kick them out. . . . With this Spokane and Willamette Valley organized, we should be able to take the COMRATS in the next convention in great style." [emphasis in original] ["Dick" 1941].

The committee's organizers set out to fill the IWA's ranks with members of their own political stripe. They found them in the Willamette Valley of Oregon. Running south from Portland for 100 miles to the Eugene/Springfield vicinity, the valley had long been a stronghold of conservatism. The lower reaches of the valley received the first Oregon Trail pioneer-farmers who settled small plots of land. The small sawmill-lumber industry that had matured in this area prior to the IWW era contrasted sharply with the heavily capitalized industry around Puget Sound, which received socialist Scandinavian workers at the turn of the century. The conservative political character of the Willamette Valley work force was established early, providing an opening for the conservative AFL in the Pacific Northwest (Lembcke 1984; Schwantes 1979).

The organizing victories in the Willamette Valley strengthened the conservative bloc and further polarized the union. By April 1, 1941,

Germer reported that the "breach between the two groups was beyond repair" (Germer 1941a). Locals aligned with the CIO Woodworkers Organizing Committee withdrew their support for the IWA and were suspended; the CIO stood behind the dissident faction, however, set up separate district councils to receive the suspended locals, and issued direct industrial union charters to them (Germer 1941a; Roley 1977).

In late July, 1941, Allan Haywood, CIO director of organization, called representatives of the two blocs to Washington and proposed constitutional changes giving the conservatives more power. Between 1937 and 1941 locals had been represented at international conventions on the basis of diminishing proportional representation, with two delegates for the first 100 members and one for each additional 300 or major fraction thereof up to 1,000 (IWA 1941, 74-75). Roll call votes prior to 1941 had been conducted on the basis of one vote per delegate, regardless of the size of the locals they represented. The same structure, called a "commie structure" by Germer (1941b), prevailed in locals led by the left wing. The changes proposed by Haywood allowed one delegate for each local up to 100 members, and one for each additional 300 members. Haywood's proposed roll call procedure allowed each delegate to vote a proportionate share of the membership of the local union he/she represented.

The proposal had very clear political implications. The existing structure of the one-unit, one-vote rule on roll call votes, which the left wing favored, empowered the smallest, poorest, and most recently organized locals. These were also the locals most likely to consist of loggers and unskilled workers who had traditionally been discriminated against by the craft-dominated AFL unions and who historically had been the most radical. This structure also ran counter to the popular business union expression that "those who pay the freight, drive the train." By implication, the one-unit, one-vote rule had challenged the logic of representation common to conservative, craft unions that gave the largest units the most power because their financial contribution was the greatest and replaced it with one where the smallest units, whose need was the greatest and whose political inclinations were most progressive, had at least equal power. The IWA conservatives, on the other hand, controlled the three largest locals in the international and the largest district council. By voting its membership strength on roll call votes, the CRDC could directly control almost one-fourth of the total votes. The proposed method of allocating delegates would give the conservative bloc three additional delegates while the British Columbia District, which was emerging as a left-wing power, would lose three delegates. Three Washington state left-wing strongholds—Bellingham, Sultan, and Everett—would lose delegates. Every local in the international would lose a delegate except for four, three of which were staunchly conservative and supportive of Germer (Lembcke 1978).

Between the Washington meeting and the IWA's October convention Germer campaigned for convention delegates sympathetic to the changes. The international resisted the changes but the CIO's control of the organizing funds made it a virtual captive union. After the first day of the 1941 convention Germer wrote in his diary, "The [conservatives] were clearly in control from the start. . . . Haywood saved the day for them by his membership roll call proposal" (Germer 1941c). By now Germer's organizing program was also paying dividends for the conservative bloc. When the 1941 convention met in Everett on October 8, 47 new locals had been added and 28 of them voted with the Columbia River District Council on the first roll call vote of the convention. No new locals had been added in British Columbia and three left-wing locals in northern Washington had ceased to operate during the year. The votes added to the conservative bloc by the organizing program, when coupled with the changes in the voting procedure, the deportation of Harold Pritchett, and the ideological effect of the CIO's anti-left crusade, gave the conservatives the clout needed to elect their slate of officers at the 1941 convention, implement the constitutional changes on representation, and pass a resolution banning Communist party members from leadership (IWA 1941).

Because of Harold Pritchett's deportation and other tensions between the British Columbian region and the Columbia River District Council, the constitutional changes made at the international level were never adopted by the Canadian region. As a result, we can assess the consequences of the changes described above by comparing the organizing results in the two regions following 1941. In the Pacific Northwest the IWA's membership never surpassed its 1941 level of 41,187. which was 41 percent of the industry's employment in that region. Shortly after World War II the percentage of the industry organized by the IWA began to drop until, by the mid-1980s, the survival of the union was in question. In British Columbia, meanwhile, the union grew from insignificance in 1941 to 39,725—91 percent of the industry—by 1971. In the IWA case, the correspondence between the logic of collective action and organizing results, then, is very strong.

By 1958 the more proletarianized Canadian district had sufficient power to change the basis of representation of the international executive board back to a unit form. Joe Morris, president of District One in Canada, argued in favor of the change: "There is no place in the Executive Board for the use or misuse of power. We want no part of it. We believe that the smallest Regional Council in the International Union has every bit as much right to exercise their voice and has every bit as much right to be heard as the big Councils have . . . we believe this is the very essence of democratic decision [making]" (IWA 1958, 80).

James Fadling, a White Bloc stalwart from southern Washington who was international president for a brief period during the 1940s, argued against the change. He referred to the 1941 struggle for proportional representation on roll call votes as the kind of "power plays we used to keep this International clean [of Communist influence]" (IWA 1958, 90).

Although the reinstatement of the unit vote in 1958 was unable to reverse the decline of the union in the United States, the debate tells us three things that are important. The logic of the debate had remained the same since 1941, indicating that the earlier disputes were not a fleeting phenomena attributable to an exceptional period of history. The social base or class fraction out of which the respective pro and con positions arose had remained constant, while the ideological affinities of the individuals representing those positions were somewhat different: Morris was as vehemently anticommunist as Fadling. The temporal and ideological transcendence of the organizational question suggests the presence of structural forces that have heretofore gone unrecognized.

THE CASE OF THE UNITED AUTO WORKERS

The case of the UAW reveals that struggles over organizational forms were not limited to small or geographically isolated unions, but they also occurred in a union that was probably more central than any other to the development of the labor movement in the post-war years. An examination of convention proceedings clearly shows that union members were aware of the relationship between forms of membership representation and the logic of organizing for collective action. The representation structures governing decision making over organizing programs were highly contested; it was struggles over these structures, rather than a logic inherent in the size of the union, that determined which form would prevail.

The United Automobile Workers Union (UAW) was formed in 1936 out of several predecessors that had been conducting organizing activities in the industry during the 1920s and early 1930s. The Auto Workers Union (AWU) was the oldest of the predecessors, having entered the AFL in 1891 as the International Union of Carriage and Wagon Workers. The union was comprised of mostly skilled tradesmen—painters, woodworkers, upholsterers, and sheet metal workers —who transferred their skills from the manufacture of horse-drawn vehicles to automobiles. The AWU was suspended from the AFL in 1918 for industrial unionism but continued, with Communist Party leadership, as the only union of significance in the auto industry during the 1920s (Keeran 1980, 32-43).

A second predecessor to the UAW was the Mechanics Educational Society of America (MESA). MESA was formed in 1933 by Matthew Smith, described by Keeran (p. 103) as an "English-born, independent socialist," to fight the declining wages and diminishing work conditions of highly-skilled tool and die makers. Communists also became prominent in MESA, although they never had a controlling influence (Keeran 1980, 103).

A third predecessor grew out of the AFL's efforts. When the National Industrial Recovery Act (NIRA) was passed on June 16, 1933, the AFL began efforts to establish a federal union for auto workers. The leader of the AFL's drive was William Collins, who was assigned the task by AFL President William Green. The AFL federal union concept was to temporarily enlist autoworkers in a generic AFL union and then later transfer those workers to appropriate craft unions (Keeran 1980, 100). In Cleveland, Ohio Wyndam Mortimer and other communists worked within the AFL federal unions to push for an international industrial union. The first UAW newspaper was published by Mortimer's group (Keeran 1980, 125).

In December 1934 the Communist Party dissolved the AWU and began concentrating efforts on building an industrial union for auto workers within the AFL. On August 25, 1935, delegates met in Detroit to form a new union. AFL President Green dominated the convention, forcing a standard AFL constitution on the union and appointing the new union's first president. The convention ended in a storm of protest over the AFL's heavy handedness; protest leaders carried their objections to the AFL's October convention in Atlantic City. At Atlantic City, John L. Lewis, president of the United Mine Workers, led other dissidents in a breakaway movement that would become the Congress of Industrial Organizations (CIO). The UAW met for a second time in April 1936 and emerged as an affiliate of the CIO. Three large MESA locals joined the UAW shortly after the 1936 convention (UAW 1935; Keeran 1980, 128-43).

The UAW carried with it the scars of its birth. Unlike the IWA, which had been formed by radicals in an industrial sector with virtually no previous union organizations, the prior presence of AFL-affiliated craft unions in the auto industry obstructed the path of UAW radicals (UAW 1935, 58). Moreover, although the masses of workers in the automobile manufacturing industry were unskilled and a high proportion of them were nonwhite, the membership of the UAW at its inception was overwhelmingly skilled and white. The first generation of union leadership, including many left-wing leaders (Lichtenstein 1982, 141), emerged from this social base. This problem was amplified by the industry's uneven regional development. The industry, of course, was centralized in the Detroit region, which meant that the UAW would almost inevitably become centered there. As indicated by the ratio between value added and wages (Table 3.3), Detroit's auto industry was also the least capital intensive. As a result, the industry's work force would have been the least proletarianized in Detroit and the surrounding area. In general terms, organizing activities conducted outside Detroit would have resulted in less-skilled, more proletarianized workers being brought into the union.

Finally, the base of the communist leadership initially lay in Ohio, and many of the UAW's first organizational activities (including its first newspaper) emanated from there. Operating with a unit-vote form of representation, the union rapidly expanded into the Detroit-

Table 3.3
Wages and Value Added in Manufacturing and Value Added for Automobile Industry, 1939.

Region	(1) Manufacturing Wages	(2) Value Added	(3) Ratio Col 2/Col 1
U.S. (Ex Mich.)	215,695,976	547,848,856	2.5
Michigan (Ex Detroit)	273,477,808	523,538,050	1.91
Detroit	155,730,837	247,982,669	1.59
Region/Aircraft			
U.S.	77,488,188	183,246,611	2.36
California	60,102,785	25,220,925	2.38

Source: U.S. Department of Commerce, Bureau of the Census. Sixteenth Census of the United States: 1940. *Manufactures*, 1939 Vol. 2, Part 2, pp. 540, 525.

Flint area where the industry was concentrated. The numbers of Detroit area workers brought into the UAW through the sit-down strikes of 1936 and 1937 were easily sufficient to dominate the union politically if representation was changed to a per-capita base. With the Detroit-Flint region organized, leaders there began a struggle to consolidate their power by changing the representation structure. Within a few years the capacity of locals located outside Michigan to influence the direction of the international had been severely diminished.

The UAW's constitution was revised at its 1937 convention in Milwaukee. The revisions were made in an atmosphere of great tension between the union's executive, Homer Martin, and the union's left wing. Keeran (1980, 194) notes that the substantive issues dividing the union entailed "questions of centralism versus localism and consolidation versus expansion." Debate over the provisions for convention representation became the lightning rod for those issues.

The constitution committee's majority proposed the following for Article VI, Section 4:

> Delegates to the International Convention shall be elected from the local unions of which they are members. Each local union shall have one vote for each 200 members or less and one additional vote for the next 300 members or major fraction thereof, and one additional vote for each additional 500 members or major fraction thereof, but no delegate shall have more than five votes [UAW 1937, 137].

The committee's minority proposed *delegate* strength be allocated the same as the majority indicated but that *votes* be allocated, as they had been, on a strictly proportional basis of one vote for each 100 members. As proposed by the committee majority, the article was a form of diminishing proportional representation that prevented large locals from fully translating their numerical superiority into political power. Walter Reuther from Detroit Local 174, which would soon be the largest in the international, was one of the first speakers to argue against the committee majority and in favor of strictly proportional representation as proposed by the committee minority:

> I do not agree with the idea that we want to try to penalize the big shops in order to take care of the small shops. . . . Under the set-up that is proposed by the Constitution Committee [majority], Dodge and Briggs Local would get 51 votes with 11 delegates. Under the proposal of the minority group they would have 50 delegates carrying 250 votes, based upon one vote for each 100 members [UAW 1937].

Supporting Reuther, Lloyd Jones from Detroit Local 2 argued that "if this proposal carries, 16 small local unions, paying in a total of

$1,377.00 could have one vote more than that Local Union which pays $33,750.00" (UAW 1937, 140).

Characterizing the statements of Reuther and Jones as "dollar democracy," delegate Carlstrom from Racine, Wisconsin Local 82 linked the representation question to the union's organizing priorities:

> the large plants, with one exception, are now organized. It is for the welfare of those large plants that are already organized, that I appeal to you to assist in making it possible to organize their small competing plants, because anything that would further the organization of the small competing plants would rebound not only to the benefit of the small locals, but more so to the large mass production locals [UAW 1937, 140].

After considerable discussion, the majority committee position was defeated and the minority position adopted (UAW 1937, 169-70).

In the aftermath of the 1937 convention action, the organizing activities of the UAW bogged down in ways very similar to those in the IWA. Two of the organizing drives effected were those at Ford and the West Coast aircraft industry. Although neither Ford nor the West Coast aircraft industry could be considered "small" shops, and the heart of Ford production facilities was in Dearborn, an industrial suburb of Detroit, each had special characteristics that distinguished it from the traditional center of the automobile industry where the UAW was based. Aircraft was geographically far removed from Detroit and, by comparison with auto, was a capital-intensive industry employing a low-skilled work force (Table 3.3). Ford's work force was black, with virtually no previous experience with unionism. Whatever UAW presence had been established in Ford and West Coast aircraft had been done by Communist Party members, making it likely that further support for membership recruitment in those plants would strengthen communist power within the union. For this combination of factors, the UAW leadership that was trying to consolidate its position during the late 1930s was concerned lest the addition of 80,000 Ford workers and several hundred thousand aircraft workers would destabilize the political balance of the union.

The Ford and Aircraft Organizing Drives

Organizing Ford began in earnest after a series of sit-down strikes early in 1937 had brought the General Motors empire into the UAW fold. In May 1937 the UAW began distributing leaflets at the Ford Rouge complex in Dearborn on Detroit's west side. On May 26 several UAW organizers, including Walter Reuther and Richard Frankensteen, were severely beaten by a Ford company goon squad. Using similar tactics and an ordinance passed by the Dearborn City Council that prohibited distribution of literature at the Rouge, Ford was able to keep his plant union free through the summer (Howe and Widwick 1949, 95-97).

In August 1937 the UAW convention passed a resolution for a one dollar assessment to fund the organizing drive at Ford. At the time the workers at Ford fell under the jurisdiction of the Detroit West Side Local, which was Reuther's Local 174. Reuther spoke in favor of the resolution (UAW 1937, 184-87; 1939, 102). The UAW was nearly destroyed by factionalism between the 1937 and 1939 conventions. The union's president, Homer Martin, had increasingly come under the influence of Jay Lovestone who had led a right-wing split from the Communist Party in 1928. The Martin-Lovestone UAW faction began attacking communists like Wyndam Mortimer, socialists like the Reuther brothers, and "pure and simple trade unionists" like Richard Frankensteen (Dubofsky and Van Tine 1977, 318). Martin was soon ousted and, although R. J. Thomas was his immediate successor, it was Walter Reuther who emerged from the fight as the heir to the future. During the same period the organizing drive at Ford stalled.

The problems at Ford conventionally have been understood to have been a by-product of the larger ideological and personal issues tearing at the UAW. Thus, according to these accounts, once Martin was removed from office and the CIO national office involved itself in the drive, the future of the Ford organizing campaign was secured (Howe and Widick 1949, 97). A rereading of the historical record produces a more complex picture, however.

In the midst of their fight with Homer Martin, the UAW socialists and communists also split; although they retained a common antipathy for Martin, they differed over the merits of an antifascist collective security agreement uniting the United States and European countries against Nazi Germany. In April 1938 the communists withdrew their support from Victor Reuther, who was a candidate for vice-president of the Michigan CIO. "Following this," wrote Keeran (1980, 196), "Walter and Victor Reuther and other Socialists began to build their own faction in the UAW." It was this split that tied up the Ford organizing campaign.

In August 1938 Local 600 was established for Ford workers. For the first time the organization of Ford workers had a measure of autonomy from Reuther's Local 174. At the 1939 convention, however, it was reported that the dues assessment supporting the Ford campaign had gone largely uncollected and that Reuther's local was one of the most delinquent. Strife between Reuther and others in the anti-Martin alliance was cited by convention delegates as a major factor in frustrating the union's effort at Ford. Geschwender (1977, 52-53) hints that there may have been a racial motive for the Reuther faction's reluctance to organize Ford's black workers. Certainly the strong base that communists had within the community of Ford's black workers was cause for concern on the part of the Reuther faction. The Ford drive finally got underway again in the summer of 1940, but only after the officers of the newly-formed Ford Local 600 had vacated their offices and the local was placed in receivership with responsibility for the organizing drive placed in the hands of a UAW-National CIO joint committee. Michael Widman was appointed by the CIO to head the Ford campaign (UAW 1941, 600).

While the documentation of the Ford case is not as clear-cut as that for the IWA, the outlines of a similar pattern can be discerned: A large local with a traditionally conservative base withholds its financial support for organizing activities until it is able to gain greater leverage in the control of the organizing program. For the UAW, that outline appears somewhat sharper in light of events occurring during 1940-41 involving the West Coast aircraft workers.

Aircraft workers were part of the UAW jurisdiction because as production for World War II geared up, much of the nation's automobile capacity was converted to aircraft production. Thus, many auto workers, some of whom were UAW members, were working in aircraft plants by the 1940s (Howe and Widick 1949, 108).

UAW organizing in West Coast aircraft began in 1940 when Wyndham Mortimer was assigned to the UAW regional office in southern California. As described later by Mortimer (1971, 167-68), the industry "extended from San Diego California, north to Seattle Washington, with the heaviest concentration in the Los Angeles area. With a potential membership of 150,000, this huge body of workers was almost completely without a union of any kind." Although the International Association of Machinists (IAM) held a few sweetheart contracts with the manufacturers, few workers were actually members of the IAM. "The most noticeable thing about the air craft workers," recalled Mortimer, "was their youth. Shift change resembled a high school dismissal." The companies had enticed young people to California "through false promises and advertising. The aim was to flood California with a huge surplus of unemployed and potential workers who would be driven by poverty to work for a pittance." Many workers were employed for 50 cents an hour.

Mortimer began publishing *Aircraft Organizer*, and early in 1940 the UAW won a representation election supervised by the National Labor Relations Board (NLRB) at the Vultee aircraft plant. On August 6, 1940, it was certified as the bargaining agent for all Vultee production workers. The union struck Vultee for a week in November 1940 before getting a contract that "smash[ed] the 50 cent minimum in the aircraft industry" (Prickett 1981, 218; Mortimer 1971, 168). The UAW also won representation at North American and began negotiating a contract for 6,000 workers on April 16, 1941. From June 5 to June 9 the union struck North American. The strike was opposed from the beginning by leaders of the UAW and CIO, as well as the U.S. government. Consultations between President Roosevelt and CIO President Phil Murray produced a decision to force the strikers back to work. When Mortimer, Lew Michener, and other UAW leaders on the scene at the North American plant refused to go along with the back-to-work movement, UAW Vice-President Richard Frankensteen fired them. On July 9, 2,500 federal troops ended the strike with fixed bayonets and the blessing of the UAW and CIO. As a consequence, the UAW lost the aircraft industry to the IAM, thus altering the course of its own history and probably that of the CIO.

Why did the top leadership of the UAW and CIO abandon the West Coast aircraft industry? Most historical accounts of the incident have focused on the significance of the communist presence in the UAW's aircraft campaign. Max Kampelman (1957, 25-26), for example, attributed the strikes at Vultee and North American almost solely to Communist Party agitation. The motive for the communist-led strikes, according to these accounts, was to cripple the country's defense capability. Accordingly, UAW leaders like Reuther acted out of a sense of national urgency and loyalty by joining the CIO and the Roosevelt administration in ending the strike. Writing more recently, Prickett (1981) and Keeran (1980) have convincingly refuted the argument that the strikes were "caused" by communists. They point that the workers' grievances and desires for unionization were reasons enough to have motivated the strike action. But these more recent versions fail to address the question of why, then, the UAW and CIO leaders withheld support for the strike. If the communist presence at North American was so minimal a threat to national defense, what then was the reason? Did the national leaderships of the UAW and CIO simply misread the situation, or was the communist issue a smoke-screen for more fundamental issues?

One explanation that has not been pursued is that the leadership of the UAW, Walter Reuther in particular, feared the emergence of a power base that would pose a challenge to its own in Detroit. In other words, the Detroit-based leaders feared the potential political power of large numbers of West Coast aircraft workers not under their wing. The political threat of the aircraft workers may have also appeared more ominous because of the perceived status differential between the more skilled workers in Local 174 and the unskilled youths who populated the California aircraft plants.

Reuther's split with the communists (see above) was the beginning of his own quest for power within the UAW; realistically, the only quarter from which opposition to him would come would be the union's communist-led left wing. When the aircraft drive was killed, so too was a potential base of political opposition to Walter Reuther. As Mortimer recalled (1971, 177), "it was apparent that [UAW President] R. J. Thomas and Richard T. Frankensteen and other people in the international office were apprehensive about our success, worried about the publicity that comes with success. If I succeeded in organizing 200,000 aircraft workers, as indeed it seemed I might now do, they could only see me as a dangerous threat to their jobs."

The CIO leadership had its own reasons for fearing the success of the aircraft campaign. Beginning with John L. Lewis and continuing under Phil Murray, the CIO began the attempt to consolidate its gains and rein-in the left-wing field workers who had built many of its affiliates (Cary 1968, 116). At least three of its affiliates based in the western states posed serious problems to this agenda of the CIO: the International Woodworkers of America; the International Union of Mine, Mill and Smelter Workers (discussed in this section); and the International Longshoremen's and Warehousemen's Union (ILWU). The ILWU was a particular problem for the CIO because its president, Harry Bridges, was also West Coast CIO director and closely associated with the communists. Bridges, moreover, was very popular inside and outside the trade union movement. Had West Coast aircraft been organized into a CIO union, the hand of the CIO's left wing would have been definitely strengthened. Beyond the strictly political and ideological issues embedded in the issue, it is hard to say how other dimensions of regionalism may have played a role. Workers in western states have often been perceived as prone to radicalism (Dubofsky 1966); this, plus even less tangible apprehensions about social and cultural unknowns, may have also been unsettling to union leaders from eastern or midwestern backgrounds.

The 1941 UAW Convention

The controversy over the North American strike was fully aired at the 1941 UAW convention. The convention was a marathon affair lasting 12 days; the verbatim proceedings run over 800 printed pages. The proceedings are important to our analysis in two ways. First, they provide support for the thesis that beneath the ideological issues lay an important power struggle. Second, since the future of the West Coast aircraft workers vis-à-vis the UAW was still not confirmed, the manner in which that was done shows how the convention representation structure passed in 1937 became a factor.

In essence, there were two issues regarding the aircraft campaign that came before the convention. The first was the matter of punishing the communist leaders who allegedly encouraged an unauthorized strike at North American. The second was the question of the autonomy of the West Coast region and other regions, such as Ohio, that were experiencing growth in aircraft employment. The resolutions pertaining to the issues were the province of the convention's grievance committee. On the fifth day of the convention the committee submitted a resolution (a) commending the CIO and UAW officers for their handling of the strike, and (b) placing the West Coast region "under direction of the International Executive Board until such time as the Board feels the Region can properly administer its own affairs" (UAW 1941, 246). The resolution made no mention of punishment for the strike leaders.

Victor Reuther spoke in opposition to the resolution and established the tactic that the Reuther faction would follow in the coming days. He argued (UAW 1941, 249) that the region should be allowed to retain its autonomy but that certain individuals should be barred from elected office. The position taken by Reuther was a smart one in terms of the convention's politics. It could not be construed as regionally biased since it advocated retention of West Coast autonomy. Yet, by eliminating certain individuals from leadership it ensured that aircraft workers would be brought into the UAW under terms (and leadership) to the liking of Reuther. In actual fact, it meant that the aircraft industry on the West Coast would never be organized by the UAW, which, given the internal political realities of the UAW, was also acceptable to the Reuthers.

Walter Reuther spoke at length on the resolution and named Lew Michener, who had been the UAW's West Coast director and an international board member, as the person who should be barred from office. He supported Victor's move to have the committee bring a different resolution to the floor but modified the proposal to "permit the International Executive Board to ,supervise [the work of the region] and to see to it that from now on all the money spent out there is spent for building a union" (UAW 1941, 254). After lengthy debate, the resolution was referred back to committee as moved by the Reuther brothers (p. 268).

On the eighth day of the convention the grievance committee returned with a majority report, a minority report, and a super-minority report. The super-minority report took the softest line: There should be no executive board administration of region 6, and Michener should only be barred from the international board for one year. The minority position took the hard line: The region should be administered by the international and Michener should be expelled from the union. The majority report took the middle ground: The executive board should "see that the affairs of Region 6 are so conducted as to build the UAW-CIO on a responsible democratic and American trade union basis"; Michener "shall be barred from holding either elective or appointive office in the International Union or any subordinate body" for one year. The majority position would have prevented Michener from being elected or *hired* by the UAW.

As the debate proceeded it became apparent that those delegates who supported the strike action at North American and the leadership of Lew Michener could only choose between the lesser of evils. As Everett Francis from Local 581 put it, "it is very difficult for me to decide whether I am for either one [of the reports] or not. I have not been convinced the brother from California is guilty of any offense so far [but] it is very possible that in order to save him from the wolves I will have to go for the super-minority report" (UAW 1941, 418-19).

Walter Reuther spoke in favor of the majority report:

I am opposed to the report by the super-minority committee . . . because I know that two weeks after this convention adjourns there will be pressure committees, and telegrams and letters putting pressure on President Thomas to put [Michener] back on the payroll as an organizer. I don't want Michener on the payroll . . . [nor do I] want to hang Michener. That is why I am opposed to [the minority report] . . . . Brother Michener ought to go back into the shop for a year and work. I think it will do him a lot of good. I say vote for the majority report" (UAW 1941, 420).

When Lew Michener spoke in his own defense he raised what he thought was the real issue: Reuther had accused him of attempting to form a "western federation of automobile and aircraft workers" as a separate division within the UAW, but that it was Reuther's ambition for power, not his own, that was the source of problems (UAW 1941, 441). Reuther did not respond to the charge so it is difficult to confirm or disconfirm if he was, in fact, directly motivated by a desire to consolidate his power through the organizing program. However, coupled with similar allegations related to the organization of aircraft workers in Ohio (UAW 1941, 634-36) and Reuther's support for constitutional reforms that put executive board voting on a per-capita basis, giving the Detroit locals the same power they had in convention, the interpretation of the North American strike given by Michener deserves further consideration.

Prior to the 1941 convention all votes on the UAW executive board had been decided by a simple majority vote. As a result, all regions, regardless of their financial contribution to the union, had equal influence in setting organizing priorities and disbursing money for organizing activities. At the 1941 convention a resolution was introduced to amend the constitution to read, "Each member of the International Executive Board shall have one vote for each 1,000 members or major fraction thereof represented by him in his region [and that] the International President and International Secretary Treasurer shall each carry the same number of votes, which shall be equal to the largest number of votes carried by an individual member of the Executive Board" (UAW 1941, 600). The amendment clearly put more power in the hands of large locals, and the method of allocating votes to the international officers added to the centralization of power.

Speaking in favor of the change, Victor Reuther contended that the old system constituted "taxation without representation." He defended the formula for officer votes as "customary procedure" and cited the UMWA constitution as a precedent (UAW, 1941:600, 612). Opponents of the measure argued against it but based their arguments neither on the principles of democracy, per se, nor on financial (pecuniary) logic, but rather on the fact that *the change would adversely affect the union's organizing program.* The opposition reasoned that the changes would allow the most powerful locals to control the organizing program. They feared that the large locals would simply organize in their own bailiwicks in order to build their membership numbers and their voting power. Areas needing to be organized, on the other hand, would not have the power to command the necessary resources to do the job. Moreover, the large locals would hesitate to "risk" their own resources in organizing ventures that were less than certain winners. As a result, workers who were already marginalized because they were in small shops or outlying geographic areas would become more marginalized due to the perpetuation of their non-union status. The point was made succinctly by delegate Delbert Rose: "The point is that if a Board Member has 50 votes by having 50,000 members in his region, he may team up with another Board Member of the same strength on the Board and put the organizer's staff in their region and continue to gain power, instead of sending them into the weaker regions where we need organizing" (UAW 1941, 614). Another delegate cited previous experience with the per-capita system of representation: "I found that in regions where organization was needed worst they received the lowest budget to operate on" (UAW 1941, 621). Nat Ganley, a communist delegate, pointed out that the amendment seemed to equate per-capita strength with quality in decision making: "I for the life of me cannot see why [on] an Executive Board . . . that one individual should have more voting strength than the other individual on that Board. Either they have a convincing policy . . . or [their policy should be defeated] by a simple democratic majority within that Board" (UAW 1941, 617). Despite these objections, the amendment passed the 1941 convention.

The partisan nature of the aircraft issue was made explicit later in the convention when the Reuther group argued for lowering the number of executive board members from the Ohio region from three to two. Delegates opposing the move pointed out that Ohio would soon see the largest concentration of the aircraft industry in the country and that the Detroit-based leadership was afraid board members from Ohio would not support the existing UAW and CIO leadership (UAW 1941, 634-36).

In retrospect, it seems clear that the constitutional changes made in 1941 contributed to the consolidation of Reuther's power. At that time Reuther's opposition was geographically dispersed and the key to his future was to keep it that way. The struggles over UAW organizational structure can thus be interpreted as attempts by Reuther's faction to prevent its opposition from building a power base that would rival its own.

It is more difficult to assess the effect the changed strategy had on the UAW's capacity vis-à-vis employers. The UAW was already a very large and diverse union in a large and growing industry. Production for the military kept employment high during the war, and the post-war conversion to an automobile-based economy ensured that the industry would grow and, therefore, that the UAW would have fertile conditions for organizing. Workers' collective bargaining rights, moreover, were often guaranteed and protected by war-time government contracts. Ford Motor Company, for example, came to terms with the union, in part, to ensure defense orders (Galenson 1960, 182). The fact that the UAW grew during the war years is not evidence in itself that it was not hurt by the changes made in 1941. Rather, the conditions under which workers were brought into the union were of a type that did not require the politicization of the workers nor their own participation in a struggle for union rights. Lichtenstein (1982, 80-81) quotes a UAW official calling war-time recruits " 'mere labor conscripts' who lacked the 'do or die' spirit of the union's formative years." As a result, when the industry began to abandon Detroit during the 1960s and 1970s, the union struggled to keep pace and did so only by signing what critics would call sweetheart contracts with large auto employers. In places like Lordstown Ohio the union was able to represent workers in return for enforcing speedups in highly automated plants (Aronowitz 1973). In 1985 the union cast itself in the role of labor contractor when it signed a contract with General Motors' new Saturn operation even before the plant site was announced or a work force assembled. The theoretical point to be made with the UAW case is that the logic of collective action was expressed as forms of representation in making decisions on organizing policies. Once control of the UAW's organizing program shifted from the membership to CIO officials and even government agencies, the mobilization of rank-and-file workers to achieve union objectives seemingly became less important. The union became dependent on the government and the maintenance of good relations with employers for survival.

Summarizing the UAW Case

While the consequences of the 1941 changes for the UAW's organizing program were less immediate than for the IWA, the case does not invalidate the basic thesis. Under certain historical conditions pecuniary logic can indeed increase dues-paying membership. U.S. world dominance that enabled an energy-intensive form of transportation like the automobile to reign supreme also made business unionism feasible in the auto industry. The industry was willing to abide union recognition and high wages in return for labor peace. As long as the UAW could maintain that peace and was willing to "give back" when hard times returned, it could survive and even grow. It fought its battles in board rooms and in Congress, not on the picket line; it mobilized lawyers, economists, and lobbyists rather than workers.

But those conditions were exceptional rather than the general rule of class relations under capitalism. The real test of the UAW's 1941 changes will come when the industry can no longer afford the union and the union no longer has concessions to make. When the UAW runs out of give-backs and no longer has the financial wherewithal to fight on legal and legislative fronts, will it be able to mobilize the resources of its membership to hold its position in the industry?

For this study, the most significant feature of the UAW case is in the record of debate over representation structures. Convention delegates like Delbert Rose were conscious of the connections between representation structures and the capacity of the union to maximize its power vis-a-vis employers. What thus remained an apparent *objective* reality in the IWA case clearly manifested itself as a *subjective* reality in the awareness of UAW members. Moreover, the fact that per-capita representation appeared to one group of workers to be "democracy" while to another group it appeared to be "dollar democracy" indicates that two distinctively different cultural frameworks were being used. That the distinctions correspond to the distinctions between pecuniary and associational logic made here confirms the validity not only of the theoretical distinction but that forms of representation are a valid indicator of more structural logics of collective action.

THE MINE, MILL, AND SMELTER WORKERS UNION

The case of Mine-Mill provides evidence for three of the propositions basic to my overall argument. First, I find additional contextual evidence that the battles over representational forms were really disputes over strategies and tactics of organizing. Second, the affinity of the international for fiscal or per-capita representation structure even when the union was very small suggests that size is not the definitive variable determining logic of collective action. Finally, the Mine-Mill case shows even more clearly than either the IWA or UAW cases how fiscal logic translated into political leverage and was used by an old craft-dominated local located in Butte, Montana to block the international's organizing activities.

This history of struggles over Mine-Mill's organizing program is inseparable from the histories of the copper industry and unionism in Butte, Montana, which for many years was the center of copper mining in the United States. The Butte Workingmen's Union was organized on June 13, 1878. In 1893, as an affiliate of the Western Federation of Miners (WFM) it became known as Butte Miners' Union No. 1, the

WFM's first local. The WFM affiliated with the American Federation of Labor (AFL) for one year around 1896 but otherwise remained independent until it joined with other socialist and anarchist organizations to form the Industrial Workers of the World (IWW) in 1905 (Jensen 1950, 289).

As part of the WFM, the Butte Miners local stayed affiliated with the IWW until 1908; in 1911 it received a charter from the AFL as the International Union of Mine, Mill and Smelter Workers. Mine-Mill competed with the IWW for the jurisdiction over copper miners during the years surrounding World War I, and following its unsuccessful organizing drive in Arizona it declined to a paper organization during the 1920s.

Mine-Mill was revived when 2,300 miners in Butte joined in 1933. Four locals attended the 1933 convention: Butte Miners' Union No. 1, Great Falls No. 16, Butte Stationary Engineers' No. 83, and Anaconda No. 17. The 1934 convention drew 25 locals and 55 delegates plus five officers. In November 1935 Mine-Mill joined seven other unions in leaving the AFL to form the Congress of Industrial Organizations (CIO). Following Reid Robinson's election as Mine-Mill president in 1936, the union leadership became increasingly identified with the communist movement and by the mid-1940s Mine-Mill had over 100,000 members. In 1949 it was one of the unions expelled from the CIO for being "communist dominated" (Jensen 1954, 52, 281).

During the 1930s and 1940s Mine-Mill established a reputation as one of the most democratic affiliates of the CIO. In addition to maintaining referendum and recall election procedures, Mine-Mill maintained strict rank-and-file control of its organizing program. Its organizing staff was basically its executive board members elected from each of its eight districts (Mine-Mill 1939a, 8, 17; 1940a, 387). There were two strengths in this system. First, the performance of organizers was subject to the close scrutiny of the members who elected them; organizers were expected to perform well as organizers first, and as union administrators in other respects second. If they did not perform well as organizers they could be voted out of office and out of the job. In order to be elected they had to be from the districts where they were expected to organize. Thus, they were part of the community and cultural milieu in which they had to work. In conformity with the principle that organizing cannot be done well, if at all, from the "outside," the organic link between these organizers and the workers they were organizing made them very effective. Under this arrangement the chances of a professional staff arising with interests antagonistic to those of the rank and file were minimal.

Controversy over Mine-Mill's organizing program flared in 1939 when it embarked on an expanded organizing campaign that stretched the limits of the internal supply of organizers and the budget to pay their salaries. The international, under the leadership of Reid Robinson, sought the approval of a per-capita dues assessment to support the organizing drive and provide for the training of additional rank-and-file organizers. The large Butte local blocked the passage of the dues proposal, forcing the union to curtail its organizing activities.

In retrospect, it appears that by blocking the union's organizing program, Butte delivered a decisive blow to the future of unionism in the North American metal mining industry. At the time Mine-Mill had jurisdiction over not only the copper industry but also the gold, silver, lead, zinc, and nickle industries. Its jurisdiction included refining as well as mining and extended to processed metals industries such as brass; but most important was that Mine-Mill laid claim to the iron ore industry. Had Mine-Mill, under Reid Robinson's left-wing leadership, been able to realize its potential for growth and defend its terrain from attack by the conservative United Steelworkers, the outcome of the CIO period of labor history would have been quite different. Thus, it is essential that we understand the intersection of social and organizational forces converging on Mine-Mill in 1940.

Vernon Jensen (1954, 52-54) attempted to account for Butte's opposition as personal and ideological phenomena. Robinson was from Butte and his family, including his father, had been Mine-Mill activists for years. The Butte locals, according to Jensen, recognized that Robinson had gravitated toward the Communist Party since his election, and they were afraid that by funding a Robinson-led organizing program they would also be furthering the interests of the communist movement within the CIO. Moreover, because Robinson was a Butte "favorite son" who had achieved prominence within the national CIO movement, there was a certain amount of disgruntlement that he was betraying the allegiance of his home town.

Jensen was probably correct, as far as he went. But the personal and ideological differences between Butte and Robinson were only surface manifestations of deeper material realities tearing at Mine-Mill. We need to know more about the historical conditions that set Butte apart from other regions of the hard-rock mining industry and the structural forces that were shaping the choices made by Robinson.

Social Conservatism

There were three features conditioning Mine-Mill's revival during the 1930s that are of theoretical importance. First, the rebuilding effort was dominated by conservative forces in the Butte Montana area. Despite the fact that Butte has often been associated with labor radicalism (specifically the IWW), and despite the eventual tie between Reid Robinson and the communists in the CIO, the social base upon which Butte unionism grew was conservative. There were three dimensions to that conservatism.

The Legacy of Craft-Dominated Production

That legacy stemmed from the origins of the Butte mining industry in late nineteenth century technologies. Early hard-rock mining required skilled workers to sink shafts, shore mine shafts with timber, and operate the steam-powered equipment used for hoisting, pumping, and ventilation systems. "In the early days the miners and mine owners were hardly distinguishable. They could speak to each other on the streets and discourse in language common to both" (Jensen 1950, 9). Gradually, however, skills were removed from the workers and became the "property" of an emerging engineering profession. "The engineer stepped in more prominently and the skilled miner faded out. In his place came an unskilled or, at best, a semiskilled miner" (Jensen 1950, 9; Stone 1975; Noble 1977). While these changes occurred in Butte, their effects, particularly on class relations, would always be mediated by the structures left in place by the previous period of technological and social development. Copper mining areas such as Arizona, on the other hand, opened up later with production techniques that utilized unskilled immigrant labor from the outset.

The Dominant Influence of Craft Unionism

This was a legacy that derived from the crafts' domination of the production process. Craft unions, affiliated with the AFL, were entrenched in the Butte area by the time industrial unionism, represented by the IWW, appeared. Employer paternalism still held sway in Butte during the late 1800s. "Employers," according to Vernon Jensen (1950, 290), "were solicitous of workers and catered to them, and this accounts for some of the numerical strength of unionism, yet the 'copper kings' by their solicitude kept union men divided." There was "a union for every occupation and no job for any man unless he was in a union" (p. 292). Battles between copper kings Marcus Daly of the Anaconda-based Amalgamated Company and William A. Clark, a financier and politician based in Butte, for the control of mineral-rich western Montana were fought out in the electoral arena, which meant that workers were curried for votes as well as for labor. "The truth," wrote Jensen, "is that the leadership of these unions was very conservative and was probably controlled or influenced by the company" (p. 299). The Butte locals affiliated with the WFM actually opposed affiliation with the IWW in 1905 and continued their oppositionist posture until the WFM left the IWW in 1916 and joined the AFL as Mine-Mill. The most conservative of the Butte locals, Engineers Local No. 83, survived until the 1930s and provided the leadership that revived Mine-Mill.

The Influence of the Church

The final dimension of the conservative social base of Butte's unionism was the overwhelmingly Irish Catholic work force. Davis (1980) has explained that the Roman Catholic church played a central role as a mediator for Irish workers arriving in a predominantly protestant and often hostile nation. Because the struggle for Irish independence from Britain always had religious overtones, the tie between Irish workers and the church in the United States reproduced strong Irish nationalism and Catholic religiosity at the expense of class identity. Moreover, the end of Southern slavery was perceived as a threat to Irish job rights in the North and this often forced Irish Catholics into political coalitions with reactionary Southern democrats. Finally, the capacity of the church to influence developments in the political arena depended on its ability to deliver the working-class vote to Democratic party politicians. As a result, the church not only availed itself of trade union organizations as vehicles that could mobilize the vote, but aided the formation of unions. Church support of trade union activity was contingent, however, on the union's staying within the bounds of liberal democracy. This meant that worker grievances were channeled into electoral politics and the church became an important ingredient in "machine" politics that bonded labor to the Democratic party. The intertwining of Butte, Montana's labor history with Butte's local political brokers is a classic illustration of the Irish Catholic experience. It also helps explain why the same community of workers would reject industrial unionism, represented by the syndicalist IWW in 1916, and yet embrace it in the 1930s after it had been legitimized by the passage of the Wagner Act and the creation of the CIO.

Technology and the Production Process

This fundamentally conservative social base influencing the rebuilding of Mine-Mill in the mid-1930s articulated with a second structural feature of the industry in ways that amplified the conservative influence. The largest numbers of existing hard-rock miners who had been associated with Mine-Mill were located in the Butte, Montana area; yet new production techniques were allowing the industry to move to new regions. This meant that the existing strength of Mine-Mill was based on past realities while its future strength lay in its capacity to move with the industry by organizing the new regions. The political strength of the conservative Butte workers within Mine-Mill, coupled with Mine-Mill's organizational structure, would undercut that capacity, however.

Arizona was a late-arriving competitor in the copper mining industry. In 1889 it was the third leading producer, behind Montana and Michigan; by 1919 it was the leading copper mining state in the country (U.S. Department of Interior 1890, 155; U.S. Department of Commerce 1940, 383). Jensen (1950, 354-55) attributes the lateness of its development to control exercised over the land by Apache Indians, the expansion of demand for copper, and the development of new technology and mining techniques.

> The traditional methods of underground mining gave way to shrinkage stopping, sublevel caving and block caving. With these methods the ore was broken in huge quantities and sent down shutes by gravity to waiting cars below. No special effort was made to separate mineral from waste within the mine, [a task that required the discriminating eye of skilled miners]. This task was done by new type milling equipment on the surface [Jensen 1950, 8-9].

The new and decidedly more capital-intensive mining techniques were disproportionately introduced in Arizona. In 1919 Montana and Arizona copper industries both had aggregate horsepower-per-worker ratings of 11; by 1939 Arizona's rating had risen to 36.2 and Montana's to 23.6 (U.S. Department of Commerce 1940, 383).

The new mining techniques called for a different type of labor force; the skilled hard-rock miner was displaced by semiskilled or unskilled workers. In 1889, 79 percent of Arizona's copper mining work was classified "laborers" or "boys" as compared with 54 percent of Montana's. But it was more than skill level that separated this new fraction of the mining work force from the Butte miners. The Arizona operations were filled with immigrant Mexican labor that was "without property and dependent solely upon the industry for a livelihood" (Jensen 1950, 9). In most respects, then, the work force of the Arizona copper industry appears to have been more proletarianized than the miners concentrated around Butte, Montana.

The Organizational Structure of Mine-Mill

Mine-Mill's organizing problem was further complicated by a third feature, which was that the formal structures by which decisions on organizing policies were made allowed Butte to dominate. The situation, briefly put, was that the Butte locals had the money to support the organizing activities of Mine-Mill, but they also had the political power to tie up the funds; by preventing additional locals from being established and large numbers of less-skilled workers into the union, its own conservative dominance of the international could be secured.

The problems with Mine-Mill's organizing program that surfaced in 1939 had appeared previously in the union's history. Tensions over who would pay to organize whom were part of the story behind the union's (then the Western Federation of Miners) departure from the IWW and subsequent decline during the 1920s. Jensen (1950, 246) explains that the IWW wanted to concentrate organizing efforts in the western states while the WFM leaders wanted to organize in places like Missouri, Minnesota, and Michigan.

Between 1915 and 1917 the IWW and Mine-Mill conducted competing organizing campaigns in Arizona, but an attempt by the WFM leadership to pass an assessment to fund the drive failed. From the available records it is not possible to say with certainty what role the Butte locals played in the struggle to pass the assessment but, given the numerical superiority of Butte in the WFM, it is hard to imagine that it would have failed if Butte had supported it. It is also not possible to assess how important a role race and ethnicity played. Dubofsky (1969, 169-70), however, describes the Arizona work force as "a notorious polyglot" made up of "Americans, East Europeans, Mexicans of American and foreign birth, Spanish-born workers, and even some American Indians, who were mixed together in a contankerous, divided, and discounted labor army." Sensitive to these conditions, IWW organizers like the famed Frank Little, himself a Native American, stressed the IWW's openness to workers regardless of creed, color, nationality, or skill level. The IWW employed Spanish-speaking organizers and distributed a Spanish-language edition of its paper. Whether Mine-Mill's failure in Arizona at that time can be attributed to fiscal conservatism, ethnic and craft chauvinism, or combinations entailing both cannot be known for certain. What is known is that with the failed organizing drive in Arizona, the union almost dissolved during the 1920s and Arizona remained unorganized.

When Mine-Mill revived in 1933 the constitutional provisions previously governing it continued in force. Locals had always been represented at convention on the basis of one delegate for each 100 members. On roll call votes each local was entitled to as many votes as it was allowed delegates. Thus, a local with 500 members would be allowed five delegates and five votes in a roll call situation. A single delegate could vote a maximum of five votes. Thus, a local of 500 members could send one delegate who could cast all five votes in a roll call situation. On voice votes, however, that local would be penalizing itself. Two delegates from Great Falls, Montana introduced a resolution to the 1933 convention that would have put representation on the following basis: "Each Local Union shall be entitled to one vote for the charter, and one vote for each one hundred (100) members or fraction thereof until one thousand (1,000) membership is attained, and one vote for each one thousand (1,000) members after the first one thousand (1,000) members" (Mine-Mill 1933, 20).

Had the resolution passed, the voting power of Butte would have been drastically reduced. Butte Miners Local No. 1, for example, had approximately 5,000 members by 1940. Under the original constitution, the local was thus entitled to 50 votes and at least ten delegates in convention. (As explained below, by tradition the union would have allowed Butte to divide its 50 votes among 50 delegates, thus giving Butte an enormous advantage in voice votes). The amended constitution would have given the local only 15 votes and three delegates. The resolution was withdrawn the next day, however, with no discussion on it recorded (Mine-Mill 1933, 26).

Nearly as important as the formal provisions for convention participation was the tradition that a local could send as many delegates to convention as it could afford, and on voice votes everyone was allowed to vote. On roll call votes, the votes alloted to a particular local could be divided into fractions, each fraction voted by a delegate. Thus, for example, at the 1940 convention in the Silverton, Colorado Local No. 26 divided its alloted one vote between two delegates; each voted ½ vote. Exactly how this informal structure affected decision making on organizing questions is not clear from the records, but its implications were made clear when delegates debated a resolution that would have changed it at the 1940 convention. The resolution to prohibit delegates casting fractions of one vote was introduced by the Wallace, Idaho local, one of the smallest locals in the union. Speaking in favor of the change, Angelo Verdu pointed out that under the present rules,

> the strongest Local in the International, which is Butte Miners Union, No. 1, could send 300 delegates to this convention—and they have money enough

to do it—and carry every question before this convention on a "yea or nay"'
vote. . . . They have very good lungs and are very good speakers, and have
been able to convince delegates of the convention on numerous occasions.
. . . I believe that most of those small Locals, who have less than 100 men
. . . are not in a position to send any more than 100 delegates [Mine-Mill
1940a, 427].

Delegates from Butte defended the status quo although the arguments
they used were a kind of modified version of the strictly fiscal reasoning employed in the IWA case. Reid Robinson, for example, alluded
to the fiscal logic in arguing that if a local could afford to send more
delegates, it should be allowed to do so; but he also contended that
there was some advantage for small locals in being able to get more
people experienced for leadership if they were allowed to send additional delegates. Eventually the structure worked against Robinson
because at the 1943 convention the Butte delegation was part of an
attempt to force him to resign. The convention was held in Butte and
the local packed the convention with 24 delegates, giving each delegate 2 17/24 votes on roll calls (Mine-Mill 1943, 361-87).

Mine-Mill was divided into seven districts (District 8, Ontario and
Quebec, was added by 1937) and the executive board was comprised
of one representative from each district and three officers. The 1934
constitution specified no provision for roll call votes at the executive
board level so it is presumed that each board member had one vote
(Mine-Mill 1934).

Decisions on matters relating to the organizing program were basically made in convention and by the executive board. In convention,
the large locals in the Butte area had a considerable advantage but
the one-district, one-vote rule for executive board voting evened out
the distribution of power. The problem was that, while decisions to
move ahead with organizing would pass in convention and executive
board, decisions to *fund* organizing activities required constitutional
amendments. Those amendments, passed in convention, had to be ratified by rank-and-file referendum, which meant that the huge voting
power of Butte was decisive.

In the years following Mine-Mill's revival, the union's organizing
activities were carried on mainly in the Naugatuck Valley in Connecticut. Known as "Brass Valley," the major employer in the area was a
subsidiary of Anaconda Copper Company. The valley was noted for
its conservative workers, and Mine-Mill's organizing program there
began when Tom Brown was still president of Mine-Mill. The Butte
local supported the expenditure of funds for the organizing drive and

in 1943 the Brass Valley locals joined Butte in trying to oust Robinson (Jensen 1954, 44, 55; Mine-Mill 1936, 122; Mine-Mill 1943, 361-
87).

By 1939 Brass Valley was organized and the union's attention turned
to organizing other regions. The 1939 convention was divided on the
merits of a per-capita dues increase to support an expanded organizing
program, but a resolution to raise the per-capita tax to 75 cents (the
increase going to support organizing activities) passed the convention
and was submitted to the rank and file. The referendum was held during October 1939. The November 6 edition of the union's paper reported that the referendum had passed by a vote of 7,008 to 5,720
and promised a detailed report on the tally in the next weekly issue
(Mine-Mill 1939b, 8). The next report appeared in a December 4 story
about a canvas of all balloting having been ordered by the international
president because Anaconda Local No. 117 claimed that its totals for
"yes" and "no" votes had been reversed. Thus, instead of 777 votes
in favor of the amendment and 153 opposed, as had been entered on
the local's notarized report to the international, the local now claimed
the vote was the reverse.

On November 27, three days after the canvassing committee began
its work, Butte Miners Union Local No. 1 "raised questions about
the votes of several locals, suggesting that some of [the locals voting]
may not have been eligible to vote" (Mine-Mill 1939c, 8). Butte al-
leged that several locals had filed their voting returns after the one-
week deadline designated for voting and that some locals allowed
newly acquired members to vote even though the new members had
not yet paid dues (Mine-Mill 1940a, 429-40). As a result of the claims
of Anaconda and Butte, the international executive board, feeling
that the credibility of the referendum's passage was now jeopardized,
declared it defeated. On January 22, 1940 the board levied a one dollar
special "assessment" to temporarily cover organizing costs and initiated a petition campaign to have another referendum on the dues increase (Mine-Mill 1940b, 1).

The "assessment" for organizing purposes had always been a controversial policy in Mine-Mill because it meant that board members
voting on a one-district, one-vote basis could set organizing policy
and raise the money to execute the plans. Thus, the ability of the
larger western Montana locals to block organizing programs by block
voting their per-capita strength could be circumvented. Given the representational structures of Mine-Mill, in other words, the decision to
raise funds through an executive board-levied assessment in lieu of a

referendum raising the per-capita dues represented the momentary triumph of associational organizational logic over fiscal logic.

The key to the success of Mine-Mill's future, however, rested on a more permanent source of income that could only be provided by a per-capita dues increase. The international campaigned relentlessly for the referendum during the first three months of 1940. In the April vote that would have put the international's organizing program on solid footing, the voting power of Butte was decisive. Butte Miners Local No. 1 voted against it 4,268 to 642; Anaconda Local No. 117 nixed it by 1,244 to 164. Of 11 Montana locals, only one in East Helena voted for the referendum.

The public record of the 1940 Mine-Mill referendum (Mine-Mill 1940a) gives us a rare opportunity to assess the consequences of a union following one form of decision-making logic over another. Had the referendum been on a unit basis, it would have passed with 82 locals voting for it and 42 against it. Moreover, the locals (and locales) most *needing* the resources for organizing would have been able to command their availability. The situation in Arizona best illustrates the point. Although Arizona had become the leading producer of copper, Mine-Mill had established only three locals with a combined membership of less than 300. Wages for Anglo miners in Arizona were 80 to 90 percent of Butte miners; wages for Mexican miners were about 60 percent of Butte wages (Mine-Mill, *CIO News* 1939d, 12). The Arizona locals voted overwhelmingly for the referendum but to little avail. In the weeks following the vote, the international laid off 20 organizers.

The eloquence of A. B. Lind's analysis of Mine-Mill's 1940 referendum is worth quoting at length because it accurately identifies the structural context of uneven historical development in which the referendum incident was set, and because it reveals the high level of awareness that some rank-and-file unionists had of the long-term dynamics of U.S. capitalism and the historical implications of their own strategical choices. Speaking to the 1940 convention as a delegate from the Wallace, Idaho local, Lind offered the following post-mortem on two failed per-capita referendums:

> I have noticed during the last two referendum elections [that] the local unions which defeated the increase in per capita were unions that are well established; that had been organized a long time, and are under either closed shop agreements or checkoff, and they have probably not got much to worry about.
>
> I notice also that in a majority of the small struggling locals [they] see right before them the problem of organization so strong that they were

willing to sacrifice part of the local revenue in order to . . . provide men in the field to organize for them. I wonder if those large locals are justified in their attitude of security? I wonder just how secure they are? . . . Suppose that the Anaconda Company and the other large copper companies decide that now is the time to smash this union. . . . They could afford to shut the hill at Butte tight, throw every single man out of work, and tell them, "When you boys are willing to go back to work without a union and with a dollar and a half a day reduction in pay, we will open Butte up again and mine. . . ." Sooner or later, after a certain number of years of starvation, as long as the market remains slack they can draw their copper from Arizona, South America, and other places, and supply the market.

And when the boys in Butte have either starved or have largely left the country [the company] can ship a bunch of sheep herders in there and open up Butte, then they can go back to Arizona and say to the boys there, "When you boys are willing to go back to work without your union and with a reduction in pay, we will open Arizona up. . . ."

These well established locals have reached their limit. They cannot get any further. They cannot get better conditions or hours until the smaller camps are organized. The only way [that organizing activity] can be financed is through all the camps, not just the small struggling camps. . . . It must be done throughout the entire International. When large established locals realize that fact, that they are not as secure as they think . . . they will be willing to finance the organization of our entire industry [Mine-Mill 1940a, 302].

Stymied by Butte's conservatism, the Robinson leadership of Mine-Mill had two choices: (1) it could let the organizing program die and, possibly, the future of Mine-Mill with it; (2) it could go outside the international for financial help. Following the second course of action, Robinson had two choices: he could (a) turn to the CIO national office and accept organizers selected, paid, and controlled by it, or (b) turn to other unions that, for ideological reasons, would be not only sympathetic to Mine-Mill's dilemma, but supportive of Robinson's left-wing objectives. Going outside the union meant, in either case, sacrificing the principle of hiring organizers only from the ranks of the union. The higher principle was that involving the future of the union, which only left Robinson the choice of who to turn to for help.

Events occurring between the spring of 1940, when the Mine-Mill referendum on the organizing assessment was defeated, and the spring of 1941 helped Robinson make his choice. In February 1941 Robinson served on a three-member panel formed by the CIO national office to conduct a hearing into the activities of Adolph Germer, an organizer assigned by the CIO to the International Woodworkers of America. Germer was a national office appointee to the IWA's organizing program following the blockage of organizing funds by that union's largest and most conservative district council (see the IWA case presented above). The IWA's dilemma, in other words, had been an exact parallel of that now faced by Mine-Mill. The 12-day hearing on Germer's activities in the IWA revealed that he provided a conduit for material resources and organizational expertise flowing from the national office to the conservative faction that eventually was able to unseat the communist leadership of the IWA. In the wake of that transition, the IWA's organizing program remained under the control of the CIO national office for over ten years, and during that period the union never grew beyond its 1941 level (except in Canada, where it remained independent from the CIO).

Robinson apparently saw in the Germer-IWA episode a preview of Mine-Mill's future. Accepting funding assistance from the CIO national office meant that Mine-Mill's traditional rank-and-file control of the organizing program would be relinquished; CIO control would be a foot in the door of the union's internal affairs that would never be removed. Robinson opted to accept help from other CIO unions that had communist leadership.

Robinson's choice would subsequently be interpreted as evidence of his fidelity to "outside forces"—that is, the Communist Party (Jensen 1954, 52-54). But in light of Cary's (1968) characterization of Germer as part of a stratum of rising professional bureaucrats who sought to dampen rank-and-file initiative, it would seem that the objective logic of Robinson's actions was to maximize the future of membership control of the organizing program in face of conditions that threatened to destroy it altogether. Moreover, given the history of the late 1940s, which was characterized by large-scale purges of communists from the union movement, Mine-Mill's capacity to resist those Cold War influences (while unions like the IWA totally succumbed) has to be attributed in part to the fact that Robinson's choices in the early 1940s insulated it from the conservative upper echelons of the CIO bureaucracy.

DISCUSSION OF DATA WITHIN A COMPARATIVE FRAMEWORK

By comparing the case studies presented above (Table 3.4), it is possible to eliminate certain variables as being decisive determinants of logic of collective action.

Table 3.4
Characteristics of Class Fractions and Their Organizational Preferences

Historical and Social Characteristics	IWA Faction Supporting Unit Rule	IWA Faction Supporting Per-capita Rule	UAW Faction Supporting Unit Rule	UAW Faction Supporting Per-capita Rule	Mine-Mill Faction Supporting Unit Rule	Mine-Mill Faction Supporting Per-capita Rule
Period of Formation	Late 1800s	Mid-1800s	n/a	n/a	Early 1900s	Late 1800s
Geographic Region	No. Washington/B.C.	Oregon/So. Washington	Non-Detroit	Detroit	Southwest	Western Montana
Industrial Form						
Size	Large Mills	Small Mills	Large Plants	Small Plants	n/a	n/a
Technology	Mechanized	Skilled Crafts	Mechanized	Skilled Crafts	Mechanized	Skilled Crafts
Social Ecology	Large Mill Towns	Rural; Small Towns	n/a	n/a	n/a	n/a
Social Characteristics						
Ethnic/Racial	Scandinavian	German; English	Black	White	Mexican; E. European	Irish
Demographic	Foreign Born	Native Born	Foreign Born	Native Born	Foreign Born	Native Born
Economic Base	Wage Labor	Farm/Factory	n/a	n/a	n/a	n/a
Consciousness	Proletarian Socialist	Frontier Individual	Proletarian Socialist	Liberal Reformist	Proletarian Socialist	Frontier individual
Organizational Legacy	IWW; CP; CIO	AFL; SP; 4L	IWW; CP; CIO	AFL; SP	IWW; CP; CIO	AFL

n/a = instances where the factions were not differentiated by that characteristic.

Industrial Characteristics

In Chapter 2 the general association between the level of proletarianization of whole industries and logic of collective action was
established. At such a level of generality, however, one could dismiss
that association as spuriously related to the general characteristics of
the industry (Kerr and Siegel 1954). One way of controlling for industrial characteristics (Smelser 1976) is to do intraindustry comparisons. Each of the unions examined above was in a different industry.
Within each union, however, we found factions that favored unit-rule
forms of representation and factions that favored per-capita forms.
Thus, it is safe to conclude that it was not the properties of any one
industry, per se, that accounted for the organizational choices of its
members. Moreover, we find the same associations between class
fractional characteristics and organizational choices at the micro level
of comparison as at the macro level, which lends support to the overall thesis.

Ideological Influences

CIO officials often attributed the unit-rule form of representation
to the presence of Communist party activists, for example, Adolph
Germer referred to unit rule as a "Commie Structure." Currently,
moreover, it is common to associate various organizational practices
to the ideological proclivities of union leaders, for example, unions
follow bureaucratic practices because left-wing influences have been
suppressed. In the cases studied here, however, there emerges little
evidence that ideology and representational forms were linked. The
IWA's communist faction, for example, supported unit rule while
Reid Robinson, communist leader of Mine-Mill, did not. Within the
IWA case, the Canadian District supported unit rule under both communist leadership and anticommunist leadership. What is constant in
all the cases is that the factions favoring unit rule are based in the
most proletarian fractions of their respective industries. Thus class,
rather than the ideology of leaders, would seem to be the more valid
determinant of representation structures.

In Chapter 5 the question of political affiliation and organizational
preferences will be taken up at greater length. While there is strong
evidence that the communists were more democratic in pluralist terms,
for example, many of the unions with Communist party influence
had referendum elections, it is less clear that they appreciated the

strategical significance of the representation structures discussed here. Suffice it to say that there does not appear to have been a "party line" on modes of representation within unions, although Chapter 4 will point out that within international bodies such as the United Nations, communist countries usually favor a unit form of representation (Galenson 1981).

Size and Bureaucratic Logic

Pluralists (Lipset et al. 1956) as well as neo-Marxists (Offe and Wiesenthal 1980) have generally held that as unions become large and their role as collective bargaining agents institutionalized, they need to evolve more complex administrative structures and amass greater financial resources. Essentially a functionalist argument, this position would view the advent of pecuniary-oriented representation structures as a mechanical occurrence related to organizational maturation.

The three case studies provide strong evidence against the functionalist position. Mine-Mill was the only union entering the CIO period with per-capita rule and it was the smallest union. The IWA and UAW both began with unit rule and switched. In the IWA case the impetus for that change came from dissident factions that sought power (rather than from those in power); the change was accomplished only with the support of forces (i.e., the CIO national office) from outside the organization. Moreover, at an even later date (1958), and at a time when the union was even larger, it switched back. Similarly, in the case of the UAW the impetus came from within the union (although one would suspect the same CIO involvement in the changes as was found in the IWA) but not from incumbents. Rather, it was initiated by those (the Reuther faction) who *sought* power and pursued the changes as a *tactical* maneuver. It would appear that the representation structures with a fiscal logic are as much a *vehicle* by which conservative bureaucratic elements arrive at power as they are mechanisms for the maintenance of power. They also appear to be a key mechanism through which size is related to organizational ossification. While pecuniary representation forms do not necessarily appear as unions become larger, it is true that in the presence of each other, pecuniary forms and large size tend to have a lethal effect on organizing activities.

In conclusion, it would appear that representation structures have a somewhat independent relationship to both size and bureaucracies, and that their specific form is more explainable through reference to the tactical and strategic choices made by contending class fractions.

The Effect

It could be argued that the ways in which workers are represented in decisions on organizing policies is a valid indicator of class-based collective action only if they have distinguishable results. In other words, do unit forms of representation better serve working-class interests than per-capita forms?

The IWA and UAW cases provide strong evidence that unit forms of representation stimulate organizing. The internal comparison of the IWA's Pacific Northwest and British Columbian Districts is particularly compelling. The Mine-Mill case is valuable as an exception that proves the rule. For a brief period Mine-Mill grew with a per-capita form of representation. It grew, however, in ways that were contradictory, so that by the mid-1940s it again stagnated and the Connecticut region, which accounted for much of its growth in the late 1930s, turned into an enormous impediment to additional growth. Moreover, Mine-Mill survived as long as it did only because Reid Robinson was able to circumvent both the obstructionism of the Butte local and the disruptive intervention of the CIO national office. Mine-Mill grew and survived, in other words, despite its own fiscal organizational logic, not because of it.

It would be a mistake, however, to base the validity of this analysis solely on the record of union performance under various forms of representation. Representation forms are only one of a multitude of variables to be taken into account. They are important mediating structures and at specific historical junctures they may be decisive. In a case like the UAW, which grew for several years during and after World War II, the indecisiveness of the organizational variable does not mean that it ceased to be a factor. The logic connecting class forces with organization forms and organizational behavior was present, if not dominant.

CONCLUSION

From the three case studies examined in this chapter it is clearly established that there was a pattern to organizational preferences of working-class fractions. In each case it was the most proletarianized fractions of the work force that pursued representation forms tending to unit rule. The least proletarianized fractions pursued per-capita forms of representation. Moreover, the arguments used in support of each form were very different. The supporters of unit rule emphasized class solidarity and the need to build class power. The supporters of per-capita rule cited fiscal reasons—"dollar democracy," in the words of one critic.

The arguments used represent more than the rhetorical choices of convention delegates. Rather, they are expressions of different senti- ments or value systems, based in the lived experience of different class fractions. In many ways the crux of the argument made here rests on the connections between class fractions, the *reasons* given by mem- bers of those fractions for their organizational preferences, and the actual correspondence between the dominance of certain organiza- tional forms and the dominance of certain class fractions.

NOTE

1. Although the UMWA is not examined as one of the case studies in this sec- tion, a cursory look at the relevant data supports the basic theoretical argument of this book. Lewis, by most accounts, maintained one of the all-time most auto- cratic union regimes. The base of his power was in the traditional Appalachian coal fields of Kentucky, West Virginia, and Ohio. The average horsepower per 100 miners in these states was 703 in 1939 while in Illinois, the state from which anti-Lewis movements perennially arose, the horsepower rating was 1,647.

4

Class Capacities and Labor Internationalism: The Case of the CIO-CCL Unions

INTRODUCTION

The first three chapters have sought support for the theory that union organizational forms have a class or class fractional specificity to them and argued that the ways by which group interests are represented in union organizations have significant political consequences. The proposition that the most efficacious forms of union organization arise out of the most proletarianized fractions of the working class was supported by quantified evidence and an historical/comparative study of three CIO unions.

This chapter examines the implication of different organizational forms for unionization at international levels. Extending the basic model established in previous chapters, it finds evidence that the most proletarianized fractions support organizational activities that unify workers of different nations and enhance their capacity to act in a solidary fashion against capital. The chapter loses some symmetry with the previous chapters because with the important exception of representation at the International Labor Organization (ILO), the question of representational forms arose in ways less specific than the unit versus per-capita forms used as operationalizations in Chapters 2 and 3. The chapter is introduced with the ILO struggle in order to show the logical connection between the analytical model developed in previous chapters and international struggles, and to highlight several points central to the theoretical argument of this book.

Class Capacities and Internationalism

Marx and Engels saw the progressive collectivization of the working class manifesting itself initially in the trade union movement and then in the formation of working-class political parties. As capitalism matured it would increasingly seek global arenas for the recruitment of workers (market expansion), which would have the effect of dissolving first local and regional boundaries and eventually national boundaries. The internationalization of capitalist production would make the common interests in different countries clearer to the workers themselves and thus elevate working-class collectivity to an international level.

The dynamic identified by Marx and Engels was an important one, for as Goran Therborn (1983, 41) has argued, "the extent to which the public practices of the working class are coextensive with the territorial range of the supreme political power which the class must confront" is a key determinant of which class will hold sway at a given historical moment. In other words, there is a sense in which the history of class relations under capitalism can be understood as a series of flanking actions, with the capitalist class first attempting to expand its geographical options and then attempting to block working-class efforts to keep pace. The discrepancy between the theory of international proletarianization and the historical record of continuing working-class nationalism can thus be interpreted as an indicator of the balance of class forces at any historical juncture rather than a static condition endemic to the social order. Specifically, the absence of an internationalist working-class consciousness can be interpreted, within this framework, as a *result* of blocked organizational capacities rather than a *cause* of nationalistic trade union practices.

U.S. Labor and the ILO

In 1977 the United States withdrew from the International Labor Organization (ILO) over precisely the kind of organizational questions examined in previous chapters. The ILO carries out training and educational programs related to the organization of unions, occupational safety and health, social security, and human rights. Many of its programs are designed to help workers in developing countries organize and administer unions. Countries are represented at the ILO on a unique tripartite basis: two delegates selected from government, one delegate from management, and one from labor. The U.S. labor delegation is selected by the AFL-CIO. Each country gets essentially four votes, regardless of its size or financial contribution. Debates over this structure prior to the U.S. departure followed classic lines of argument. The United States contended that "the principles of universal suffrage could not be simply transposed from the level of individuals to the level of States." Thus, the United States should have representation rights consistent with "the size of [its] active population [and] financial support." Representatives of less-developed nations argued that " 'there was no justification for those who paid more to have more rights than others.' " As more Third World nations severed their dependent relations with European and North American colonialism during the 1960s and 1970s, they became voting members of the ILO, making it more difficult for the United States to win important votes on questions of economic development. Moreover, the United States contended that countries with working-class-controlled governments (i.e., socialist countries) shifted the balance of power in the direction of working-class interests. Failing to get the reforms it wanted, the United States withdrew (Galenson 1981, 18-19, 93-103).

In 1984 the United States withdrew from the United Nations Educational, Scientific, and Cultural Organization (UNESCO) for the same reasons. UNESCO practices a form of voting that gave each country the same vote, regardless of its size or financial contribution, and this allegedly allowed Soviet Bloc and Third World countries to regularly out-vote the United States. The conservative Heritage Foundation, which advocated the withdrawal, argued that the United States, which paid 80 percent of UNESCO's budget, should return "only if reforms included proportional voting" (*New York Times* 1984).

The scenario played out at the ILO in 1977 can be understood within a Marxist, class struggle framework; it is also a conflict between organizational logics writ large on an international scale. Just as the organizational capacity of any of the unions discussed in Chapter 3 was enhanced by unit forms of representation, and just as capital collaborated with the least proletarianized elements in those unions to enforce per-capita representation forms and thereby block working-class unity, the U.S. delegation to the ILO, with the full complicity of the AFL-CIO, sought structures that would allow the larger size and wealth of developed countries to dominate. By tying representation rights to financial contributions, U.S. capital hoped to ensure that its dollars went into programs benefitting the international interests of U.S. capital and simultaneously blocked the increasing unity of Third World countries. The struggle over the rules for representation was essentially a struggle over organizational mechanisms that would determine which class interests would prevail with the ILO.

What culminated in the U.S. withdrawal from the ILO was a century-long struggle between those elements in the U.S. union movement that have traditionally pursued strength through increasing international working-class unity and those elements that have tied their futures to the fortunes of U.S. capital and allowed the unions to be used as yet another arm of U.S. imperialism. The context for the ILO struggle was set during the CIO years when some U.S. unions made the first serious attempt to pursue an authentically international strategy with regard to Canadian workers. By looking at the international dimension of the CIO period, two things central to the thesis of this book stand out: (1) that those unions that were the most internationalist bore the brunt of capital's post-war antilabor crusade, while those that were most nationalist were simultaneously assisted; (2) that the strongest internationalist sentiments emanated from the most proletarianized industrial sectors.

BACKGROUND TO THE CIO-CCL CASE

The CIO was formed in November 1935 when seven unions were suspended from the American Federation of Labor (AFL) for industrial unionism. All of the suspended unions had Canadian affiliates, which made the CIO an "international" body from the outset. The number of CIO affiliates soon increased when unions such as the United Auto Workers and International Woodworkers joined. All of the major unions in this "second generation" of CIO affiliates also had Canadian locals, and it was in this cohort of affiliates that conflicts over the international question would be fought the most intensely. The Canadian Congress of Labour (CIO-CCL) was formed on August 18, 1940, out of a merger of the Canadian Committee for Industrial Organization and the All-Canadian Congress of Labour.

The unions affiliated with the CIO-CCL fell into three categories. The seven unions that broke away from the AFL to form the CIO in 1935 had Canadian affiliates and the autocratic and colonialist organizational structures characteristic of TLC-AFL unions. This meant that the Canadian locals and districts had little autonomy. In terms of leadership selection, for example, Crispo (1967, 72) found that, typically, the top officers in Canadian AFL unions were appointees of the international president. This first generation of CIO affiliates, those that broke away from the AFL, differed little, if at all, from the remaining AFL unions in their relations with Canadian unions. The international president of the Textile Workers Union of America, for example, continued to select the Canadian leadership after it left the AFL.

The second group of CIO unions were those industrial union groups that had never achieved autonomy (i.e., charters independent of established craft unions) within the AFL. Some of those, like the UAW, modified AFL constitutions and adopted provisions covering Canadian affiliates a few years after joining the CIO. In the UAW the relationship between the international office and the Canadian units was forged in the heat of organizing struggles and factional battles for control of the union. The UAW's presence in Canada began in the wake of the sit-down strikes that swept the Flint and Detroit auto plants in 1936. An independent communist group had been organizing in General Motor's Oshawa, Ontario plant for about 18 months when it decided to strike on February 15, 1937. According to Abella (1973, 9), "Allen Griffiths, a [member of the Cooperative Commonwealth Federation, a social democratic group] and opponent of the [communist] group took it upon himself to phone the UAW office in Detroit for help." Hugh Thompson, UAW representative from Detroit, arrived within the day, signed up 250 workers for the UAW, and talked them into going back to work. The next day Thompson rented an office and set up UAW Local 222. Charlie Millard, a CCF member, was elected president of the local and on March 26 Millard was appointed a full-time CIO organizer (Abella 1973, 9-10). In one stroke the leadership of the Canadian industrial union movement in the auto industry had thus been snatched from the communists and Canadian autonomy with the movement compromised. Millard was soon accused of spending more time in Detroit than organizing in Canada. In 1939 he was ousted as UAW leader in Canada, only to be hired by the CIO as its Canadian representative. In August 1940 Millard became head of the newly-formed Canadian Congress of Labour (Abella 1973, 33, 37).

While the CCL was taking shape, events in steel were following a path similar to that taken by auto. Millard collaborated with Phil Murray, head of the Steelworkers Organizing Committee (SWOC) in the United States, to purge the communist Ontario executive faction of the Canadian SWOC. The communist group had maintained a model form of union democracy (including referendum elections) until it was purged in April 1941. As had been the case with the UAW, the purge was coordinated from the United States and left the Canadian Steelworkers movement in the hands of leaders too weak to chart an independent course. It never achieved autonomy within the international, and throughout the 1940s it served as a staging ground for purges and raids in other CCL unions (Abella 1973, 61-63).

The third group of CIO-CCL unions included those that were formed outside the structure of the AFL. Two of those unions, the IWA and Mine-Mill, were targets of extraordinary state interference on international issues; they, together with the UE whose U.S.-Canadian relations were also disrupted by state activity, were notably the unions whose Canadian affiliates had the greatest autonomy from U.S.-based international offices. Crispo (1967, 55) points out that only the United Electrical Workers (UE) and Mine-Mill permitted separate Canadian constitutions. Abella (1973) found the Canadian UE to have more autonomy than any other CCL union. The IWA was probably the most exceptional. Its first international president, Harold Pritchett, was Canadian—the only Canadian to ever head a CIO union. In other respects as well, the Canadian IWA had a high level of self-determination. A review of the IWA and Mine-Mill cases makes it clearer how the importance of their internationalism manifested itself.

THE TACTICAL IMPORTANCE OF THE U.S.-CANADIAN BORDER

The tactical importance of the U.S.-Canadian border has to be considered from both the standpoint of capital's design for an international investment strategy extending well into the post-World War II years and the standpoint of the factional struggles within CIO unions.

The importance of Canada for U.S. capital can clearly be seen in the light of post-World War II development. Between 1950 and 1960 U.S. foreign investments abroad grew by $20 billion, of which $7.6 billion or 38 percent occurred in one country—Canada. In mining and smelting, more than 50 percent of the growth in U.S. foreign investments went into Canada (U.S. Department of Commerce 1977, 870). While U.S. direct investment abroad decreased during the early 1980s, it continued to increase in Canada, making that country critical to U.S. investment strategies of the late twentieth century. With $120 billion being exchanged during 1984, the U.S. and Canada have "by far the world's richest trading relationship" (*New York Times* 1985).

Theoretically, one advantage capital gains through internationalization is access to larger numbers of workers. The increase in competition between workers of different countries acts to lower wages. To the extent that workers can meet capital's internationalization with their own form of international cooperation, however, the effect of capital's move is mitigated. Thus, it behooves capital to internationalize and at the same time be able to block labor's attempt to follow suit. We would thus expect to find historical evidence that U.S. capital did, in fact, attempt to block U.S.-Canadian internationalism. Moreover, we would expect to find that those unions with the most efficacious forms of international organization would be the ones singled out for attack. The cases of the International Woodworkers of America (IWA) and International Union of Mine, Mill and Smelter Workers (Mine-Mill) are useful for illustrating how the international issues were played out within the labor movement.

In the IWA case, the union was divided by issues with international dimensions from the outset. Loggers and sawmill workers of the Pacific Northwest and British Columbia had gone unorganized following the demise of the Industrial Workers of the World (IWW) in the 1920s. The onset of the depression in the 1930s spawned two new efforts to complete the task. One was conducted by the communist National Lumber Workers Union (NLWU), an affiliate of the Trade Union Unity League (TUUL); the other was that of the Sawmill and Timber Workers Union, AFL, which was a federal union (i.e., a quasi-industrial union administered by the AFL). In 1935, in the midst of a strike that put 20,000 to 30,000 workers on the picket lines, the Communist Party dropped its efforts to organize the NLWU, a dual union, and joined forces with those workers in the Sawmill and Timber Workers Union who were dissatisfied with the way their leadership was conducting the strike. When the strike failed, the disenchanted lumber workers formed the Federation of Woodworkers in Portland, Oregon in September 1936. Less than a year later, on July 19, 1937, in Tacoma, Washington, Federation delegates voted 385 to 71 to affiliate with the Congress of Industrial Organizations (CIO). A previous referendum among Federation members favored an exodus from the AFL by a 16,754 to 5,306 vote.

Almost immediately the newly-named International Woodworkers of America (IWA) split into two factions. Harold Pritchett, from Vancouver, British Columbia, was elected the first president. The leaders of the Portland-based Columbia River District Council (CRDC), who had been opposed to the break with the AFL on the grounds that it was premature, claimed that Pritchett was more concerned with left-wing politics than he was with the improvement of wages, hours, and working conditions. But to the dismay of the CRDC, a rank-and-file referendum following the convention ratified the election of Pritchett and executive officers who supported him. The Pritchett administration would be reelected by rank-and-file referendum during each of the next three years.

In 1938 the House Un-American Activities Committee, chaired by Representative Martin Dies (Democrat, Texas) raised questions about the role of foreign-born unionists in the CIO. Two of the most important figures investigated by the Dies Committee were Harry Bridges of the International Longshoremen and Warehousemen's Union (ILWU) and Harold Pritchett, president of the IWA. Captain John Keegan of the Portland Police Bureau testified before the committee that Pritchett was a Canadian communist who "was down in Oregon during the last election campaign trying to advise people how to vote." Both Bridges and Pritchett, according to Keegan, were merely "working under the guise of labor leaders but in reality they were communists" whose "real purpose was to overthrow the U.S. government by force and violence" (U.S. Congress 1939, 2014-15, 2910-11).

At the IWA's 1938 convention, a faction from the union's Columbia River District Council, based in Portland, Oregon, made an issue of Pritchett's politics by counterposing communism and Americanism. They urged delegates to support a resolution affirming the union's loyalty to the United States. The vote lost, but during each of the next three years the same faction renewed its attack on Pritchett and communism.

The opposition to Pritchett came from a powerful minority faction based in the Columbia River District Council (CRDC) in and around Portland, Oregon. The lumber industry had established itself there prior to the era of monopoly capitalism and industrial unionism. The combination of small family-owned mills, craft unionism, and conservative German immigrants left a legacy of labor conservatism that lingers to the present. Moreover, the breakup of the IWW had made bitter anticommunists out of erstwhile anarcho-syndicalists; it was they, among others, who first opposed the movement to break with the AFL and "go CIO" and then later shaped the opposition to Pritchett's leadership.

This formidable opposition notwithstanding, it is likely that the political course on which Pritchett's administration had set the IWA would have remained steady if rank-and-file referendums had continued to be the decisive determinant of the union's future. But such was not to be the case. In 1940 Pritchett was deported and forced to resign his presidency. He was the first Canadian to be president of a CIO union—and the last.

One of the strengths of the left-wing position within the CIO-CCL unions was its internationalism: Thwarted by the repressive apparatus of any one nation state (e.g., the United States), the Left could regroup in Canada and, in instances where the Canadian locals had full political rights within the international, the Left could conceivably build a power base in Canada sufficient to control an international headquartered in the United States. The strategy to outflank the legal jurisdiction of the United States required, at a minimum, a strong political base in Canadian locals, Canadian self-determination within the internationals, and a sufficient amount of freedom to conduct business across the border.

The Pritchett faction pursued this strategy vigorously during the early 1940s. Pritchett's deportation in 1940 made it impossible for him to carry out the responsibilities of the international presidency and he had to resign. Immediately he joined the organizing drive underway to build the British Columbia District into a power bloc that would be able to influence policy in the international. Beginning with Vancouver Island in 1940, hundreds of loggers were brought into the British Columbia District Council. With the island organized, the large sawmill complexes in and around the city of Vancouver were targeted. By the end of World War II the British Columbia District had grown from near nothing to 30,000 (Bergren 1966).

South of the border the Columbia River District Council still provided the backbone of the anticommunist movement but its membership growth had stagnated during the war. In 1946, on the strength of the left-wing Canadian vote, two communists—Karly Larsen from Washington and Ed Laux from Oregon—were elected to international offices. A communist from British Columbia, Jack Greenall, was elected an international trustee. In each case, the communists had unseated staunch anticommunist incumbents in the rank-and-file referendum. Clearly, the strategy to operate from a Canadian political base had proven effective for the Left, and clearly the issue of nationalism was moot as far as the rank and file was concerned. The representation structure giving Canadian members full voting rights meant that the superior organizing results of communists working in Canada would be translated into political gains at the international level (Lembcke 1978, 190).

Developments in the International Union of Mine, Mill and Smelter Workers (Mine-Mill) closely paralleled those in the IWA. In 1940 Reid Robinson from Butte, Montana, was elected president with Communist Party support. At the time, Mine-Mill was struggling to survive. Some of Mine-Mill's first organizing successes after Robinson's election were in Connecticut's Naugatuck Valley ("Brass Valley"). The workers in Brass Valley were noted for their conservatism and by the

1941 Mine-Mill convention their presence in the union had shifted the political balance against Robinson (Jensen 1954, 55-56). Organizing gains in Canada, however, would soon offset the influence of Connecticut, and by the late 1940s the Canadian District would be the mainstays of Robinson's support.

Mine-Mill's future in Canada was dismal in the early 1940s. The Canadian District had been dissolved in 1939 and many Mine-Mill leaders wanted to abandon all interest in Canada (Abella 1973, 87). Robinson, however, reopened the campaign. On November 18, 1941, gold miners at Kirkland Lake, Ontario struck for recognition against the advice of the Canadian Congress of Labour, at the time controlled by the social democratic Cooperative Commonwealth Federation (CCF). The strike was lost and the CCL leadership encouraged Mine-Mill to leave the country (Abella 1973, 90). But Mine-Mill, with 500 Canadian members, persevered and organized International Nickel Company (INCO), a feat the CCL had warned could not be done. Within months Local 598 in Sudbury was the largest in the international. At the 1942 convention the Canadian District was reestablished and during the next two years, 1943 and 1944, 32 Canadian locals would be chartered. The local at Trail in British Columbia, joined the Sudbury local as one of the largest in the international (Mine-Mill 1943, 1946).

The Canadian locals became unwavering stalwarts of the left-wing bloc, giving Robinson the critical political base he needed to survive. In the union elections following the 1942 convention the Connecticut District ran John Driscoll as a candidate against Robinson. The results of the rank-and-file referendum were controversial. The polling booths for some Connecticut locals were located on company premises and the executive board refused to count those ballots. While Robinson's opponents conceded he would have won even with the contested ballots (Jensen 1954, 101), the election of a board member from Connecticut District 6 was possibly affected by the ruling. The Connecticut locals threatened to secede from the international, at which point the national CIO stepped in. Philip Murray appointed Robert J. Davidson, a regional CIO director from Cincinnati, as administrator of District 6.

At the 1943 convention a resolution was submitted asking Robinson to resign and proposing that the national CIO take over the Mine-Mill organizing program. The resolution was referred to the executive board so as to not divide the convention, and the board debated it for three days while the convention was in session. Finally, it was agreed that "if during the year any problems confronting the International Union cannot be resolved harmoniously within the Executive Board, the Board would call upon Philip Murray of the CIO for his advice and council" (Jensen 1954, 112). According to Irving Abella (1973, 91), "it was only the support of the strong Canadian delegation led by Bob Carlin which allowed Robinson to continue as President."

In 1943 all the Canadian delegates voted with Robinson's bloc, and at several junctures during the mid-1940s Canadian board members and convention delegates cast the decisive votes against the anticommunist bloc. At the 1946 convention a notion to make Communist Party members ineligible to hold union office was defeated by 24 votes with the Canadian delegates casting more than the decisive number against the measure (Mine-Mill 1946, 374-425).

Robinson was reelected following the 1946 convention, which rekindled the secessionist movement in Connecticut. Robinson then resigned and Maurice Travis became president. A CIO committee investigating the trouble in Mine-Mill demanded, in turn, that Travis resign because he was "continuously dealing with representatives of the Communist party in shaping the policy of the union" (Abella 1973, 93). Travis resigned and John Clark became president. Clark was supported by Robinson, who became a vice-president, and by Travis, who became secretary treasurer, so the communist influence was not seriously damaged by the turmoil. The mounting anticommunism within the CIO leadership and the United States generally, however, meant that the international political base of Mine-Mill's leadership was becoming a more significant factor in the union's future.

State Intervention Against Labor Internationalism

Throughout the 1940s the U.S.-Canadian border had remained technically "open" to all union organizers, a fact that added to the viability of the communists' international strategy. Nevertheless, the outlines of serious impediments to that strategy were evident all along. Major figures like Harold Pritchett from the IWA and Reid Robinson from Mine-Mill were the subjects of deportation proceedings during the early 1940s. More problematic was the conduct of executive council meetings, conventions, and planning meetings at which representation from both sides of the border was necessary. Frequently, Canadian communists would be stopped at the border and denied permission to attend union functions. On occasion, communists from the United States would be denied entrance to Canada. A typical incident would involve the detention of a communist executive board member who was on his way to Seattle or Portland for a meeting. A noncommunist and nonelected individual from Canada would appear at the meeting and demand the right to represent the Canadian membership. In one specific incident occurring on June 28, 1948, Bert Melsness, a left-wing IWA board member from British Columbia, was stopped at the border. Al Hartung, a leader of the anticommunist bloc from Oregon, argued that Ray Eddie should be allowed to take Melsness's place. "Maybe Brother Eddie is of a different political belief," said Hartung, "but at least he is a member from the [British Columbia] District" (IWA 1948, 4). Still, the border was never completely closed to communists, although it played an increasingly important role in the calculations of both blocs by 1946.

After 1946 the situation changed radically. The passage of the Taft-Hartley Act in 1947 signaled a counter-attack by U.S. capital on the gains made by the labor movement during the 1930s. Taft-Hartley stripped labor of many rights it had won with passage of the 1935 Wagner Act. It gave employers the right to enjoin labor from striking, established a 60-day cooling-off period during which strikes were forbidden, outlawed mass picketing, denied unions the right to contribute to political campaigns, and abolished closed shops. Most importantly, however, the law required all union officers to take oaths that they were not members of the Communist Party. Failure to do so disqualified the union involved from recognition by the National Labor Relations Board. At the time, James Fadling was IWA president. Fadling, a native of Oklahoma, had been a member of the White Bloc since the early faction fights in the Southwest Washington District. When the international executive board met on July 22, 1947 to consider the Taft-Hartley Act, President Fadling recommended that the "union go on record to comply with the NLRB certification provisions" of the act. Left-wing board members Karly Larsen, Ilmar Kouvinen, and Ernie Dalskog all spoke against Fadling's recommendation. Dalskog, who was from British Columbia, argued that the IWA should defy the law. "But at the same time," he added, "we must strengthen our organization so that we not only defy it, but defeat it . . . the emphasis should be on defying the bill rather than complying with it" (IWA 1947b, 28-38).

Many of the conservatives expressed reservations about the blatantly anti-labor nature of the act. But the temptation to use it for their own political interests could not be resisted. Rationalizing their opportunism as mere acquiescence to the status quo, the White Bloc members of the board supported compliance. "The law has been passed. We have it now," argued Vice-President Bill Botkin. With the three left-wing members of the council voting nay, the council voted for compliance with the Taft-Hartley Act (IWA 1947a, 28-38).

On August 21, 1947, the Taft-Hartley issue went before the IWA's International Convention in St. Louis. The Canadian delegates to the convention were stopped at the border and, according to Jack Greenall, "all known communists were refused entry" (IWA 1947c, 109-28). Greenall, who was already in the United States on other business, was the only known Canadian communist at the convention. How the outcome of the vote on Taft-Hartley would have been different had the Canadian delegation been allowed to attend cannot be known, of course, but as it was, the convention voted to comply with the anticommunist provisions of the Taft-Hartley Act.

The anticommunist faction on the international executive board quickly took advantage of the Taft-Hartley Act. Larsen was asked to resign on September 18, 1947 by International President James Fadling. Fadling wrote to Larsen and Ed Laux, the international's communist secretary treasurer elected with Larsen, asking them to sign the necessary affidavits, or "tender your resignations immediately." Larsen and Laux refused to sign the anticommunist affidavits saying they did not want to become "a legal party with Taft-Hartley and the Labor Management Board in destroying industrial unionism in the lumbering industry" (IWA 1947d). Larsen was the first CPUSA member to resign under Taft-Hartley, giving his case added national and international significance (Starobin 1975, 169).

The IWA anticommunists extended their use of Taft-Hartley into Canada. On October 8, 1947 Jack Greenall, an international trustee from British Columbia, was sent the appropriate affidavits (NLRB Form 1081) and asked to sign them. He refused on October 20 on the grounds that he was a Canadian citizen. On October 22, Fadling wired Robert N. Denham, general counsel of the NLRB, asking for an interpretation of the act with regard to Canadians and was informed by Denham on October 23 that a "Canadian citizen serving as trustee is required to sign affidavit in order to complete compliance with Section 9(h) Labor Management Relations Act." On October 25 Greenall was asked by President Fadling to resign (see Appendix).

The invocation of Taft-Hartley on an international scale set the stage for a new round of maneuvers by union leftists and the state. Mine-Mill made the first move. On October 23, 1947 the union announced that because of the "organizational difficulties [in the United States] imposed by the Taft-Hartley Act, it seems logical that we shift our organization concentration to Canada." The Kirkland Lake, Ontario local invited Reid Robinson to "come and take charge of an organizing drive in the gold industry" (Abella 1973, 94). On November 16 Robinson announced he would "take up residence" at Kirkland Lake. While Robinson (Robinson 1948) later denied that the move was an attempt to evade the Taft-Hartley Act, the circumstances surrounding it make it very difficult to conclude that the unprecedented step was not a de facto move of the international headquarters out of the United States for exactly that purpose. By early 1948, according to Abella (p. 95), "it appeared that . . . the entire Communist apparatus in Mine-Mill had been sent north across the border to escape the restrictions of the Taft-Hartley Act in the United States."

Ultimately, the internationalist strategy of the left-wing CIO unions would prove inadequate. Key sectors of the Canadian movement turned against the IWA and Mine-Mill. While that turn of events has conventionally been understood to have resulted from the nationalist proclivities of the Canadians, the following section points out the difficulties of such an analysis and suggests that the period is better understood within a class framework.

PROLETARIANIZATION AND INTERNATIONALISM

As in the previous chapters, the relationship between class formation (proletarianization) and organizational (unions) forms has to be considered on two levels. One level is that of the actual social characteristics of the rank-and-file union members. Theoretically, we would expect to find that the unions in the most proletarianized industries and the most proletarianized fractions of particular industries would spawn the most internationalized forms of organization.

An attempt to survey union constitutions for provisions related to Canada and make that data comparable to the proletarianization data in Chapter 2 was only partially successful. Using a combination of primary and secondary sources, it was found that 13 of the 27 unions claimed some Canadian presence. Of those 13, only 6 had constitutional clauses that formalized the relationship with Canadian affiliates. The reliability of the data is questionable, however, because at least one of the 13 unions, the IWA, had numerous Canadian locals and a founding president who was Canadian, yet its constitution made no mention of its Canadian affiliates.

Content analysis of union constitutions is thus an insufficient method of data collection in this case. Nevertheless, it raised some interesting questions about the formal relationships between U.S.-based internationals and Canadian affiliates. The International Ladies Garment Workers Union (ILGWU) and the International Typographical Union (ITU), both former AFL unions, collected a per-capita tax from Canadian members and then remitted a portion of that tax to the Canadian Trades and Labour Congress. According to Jack Scott (1978, 44), this was a standard practice of AFL unions stemming from the late 1880s and it was a practice that became a symbol of Canadian subordination to U.S. international unions. In Mine-Mill, the Canadian District could elect its own executive board member. Curiously, however, Ontario and Quebec constituted an autonomous district, while British Columbia was lumped into District 1 with Montana and other western states. The UE constitution granted Canada its own district, allowed it to elect its own general vice-president who sat on the executive board, and granted it the power to adopt rules and by-laws. Mine-Mill, UE, and the IWA are generally regarded as having a high level of Canadian autonomy (J. Scott 1978, 44; ILGWU 1937, 6; Mine-Mill 1937, 8; UE 1939a; Crispo 1967, 55; Lembcke 1980).

Although the incompleteness of the quantifiable data—even supplemented with the conclusions of historians—is inadequate for drawing conclusions, the fact that the three unions with the highest levels of Canadian autonomy were also among those with the most proletarianized members and highest levels of rank-and-file control (see Chapter 2) indicates the validity of the theory put forth here.

A second level of analysis examines the relationship between rank-and-file union members and the union organization itself. Theoretically, we would expect those unions with the highest levels of rank-and-file control (i.e., the most democratic unions) to exhibit the greatest internationalism. We would also expect to find in the historical record evidence of the struggle between factions that, on the one hand, had a social base outside basic industry and the communities of rank-and-file workers, and those, on the other hand, whose social base and source of power was in the rank and file. By locating the social roots of the contending factions and tracing the history of their involvement in U.S.-Canadian relations we can identify the pattern of certain recurring political tendencies and attain a deeper understanding of their objective roles.

Except for minor differences, the development of unions in the United States and Canada followed similar paths prior to the 1860s. In both countries it was craft unions of printers and carpenters that were among the first to organize. Beginning in the 1860s, unions based in the United States began acquiring Canadian membership and renamed themselves "internationals." Among these were the Iron Molders, the Locomotive Engineers, and the Cigar Makers.

In 1886 the Trades and Labour Congress of Canada was established as a Canadian counterpart of the American Federation of Labor (AFL) in the United States. Ware (1937, 20-31) noted significant differences between the structure and authority of the two, however. All power to charter national and international unions remained in the hands of the AFL, and unlike the AFL, the Trades and Labour Congress (TLC) had no authority in jurisdictional disputes. Although subordinate to the AFL by virtue of these structural arrangements, the TLC was also more democratic and more responsive to rank-and-file sentiment. It kept the Knights of Labor and other independent organizations (organizations not affiliated with internationals) within its ranks until 1902 while the AFL had been organized in reaction to the Knights of Labor on the other side of the border. In 1902 the second-class status of the Canadian affiliates provoked a dispute that ended with all but the Canadian international affiliates being expelled from the Trades and Labour Congress.

Immediately after being expelled, the Knights of Labor organized the National Trades and Labour Congress on the principle of "national autonomy" (Ware 1937, 28). Its strongest support came from French-speaking Canada where the Roman Catholic church's stand against internationalism (especially Anglo-Saxon internationalism) sometimes took the form of Canadian nationalism. The church's position was supported by employers and government. In 1908 the National Trades and Labour Congress changed its name to the Canadian Federation of Labour. The new organization sought legislation barring "foreign" labor officials, that is, representatives of internationals, and the dues check-off practice of the United Mine Workers. By 1927 the Canadian Federation of Labour was a "dying concern" (Ware 1937, 29-38). Seeking organizational survival, it joined with the One Big Union (the OBU, a one-time sibling of the IWW) and several independent organizations (building and printing trades, motion picture operators, electrical workers, etc.) to form the All-Canadian Congress of Labour. The All-Canadian Congress united elements of the anarcho-syndicalist movement (the OBU), which had broken with the Communist Party's Worker Unity League, with conservative Canadian counterparts of AFL craft unions. Two of its larger and more progressive would-be affiliates—Lumber Workers' Industrial Union, Mine Workers' Union of Canada, and Vancouver Waterfront Workers' Association—abandoned the All-Canadian Congress for the Communist Workers' Unity League. It was a loss that accelerated the hardening of the Congress's anticommunism (Ware 1937, 41, 49).

According to Ware (1937, 38), the All-Canadian Congress was a manifestly conservative organization. The social base of its anarchosyndicalist splinter was petty bourgeois and ideologically disposed to a libertarian frontier individualism (Lembcke and Tattam 1984, 13-17, 80-81). Most of the All-Canadian Congress affiliates were craft unions, which made the Congress an alternative to the Trades and Labour Congress but not an industrial union. In 1935 its president, A. R. Mosher, stated its explicitly social democratic agenda: to open "a channel of communication between the workers and the government." Ware's (1937, 38, 41-42) assessment was that All-Canadian leaders were not motivated chiefly by nationalist sentiment, but rather a "desire to replace the Trades and Labour Congress officers in the affections of the party in power." Ware also found little evidence that rank-and-file workers supported the antiinternationalist expressions of Congress leaders and concluded that the Congress was virtually devoid of radicalism.

Two things are evident from this sketch of pre-CIO history. One is that any notion of working-class international solidarity against capitalism was foreign to AFL leaders; the AFL's "internationalism" was really labor imperialism. The Canadian affiliates to U.S.-based international unions were second-class citizens, wanted solely for their financial contributions. Second, we see the emergence of a stratum of opportunistic labor leaders who were willing to sacrifice the principle of labor internationalism in order to advance themselves. The "nationalism" of the All-Canadian Congress leadership was not an expression of progressive anticolonialism but rather a demagogic device with which to bait both AFL international unions and communists who held the principle of internationalism very high. What appears in the Canadian case as a general working-class nationalism was really the tactical rhetoric employed by a narrow class fraction motivated by ambitions for leadership rather than an interest in socialist unionism. It is that fraction of the Canadian movement that gained control of the Canadian Congress of Labour soon after the CIO began to organize in Canada. The emergence of very similar fractions within CIO unions on the U.S. side is immediately apparent in the context of the union histories examined below.

At the time the CIO began to show major interest in its Canadian affiliates, numerous rank-and-file organizing movements were already underway in Canada (Abella 1973, 5). Most of the movements were led by the Communist Party's Workers' Unity League. A social democratic formation, the Cooperative Commonwealth Federation (CCF), had shown some interest in the union movement but it was primarily based in the agrarian population of the western provinces and had little experience in the unions. The "arrival" of the CIO heightened the CCF's interest in trade union work, however, and hardened its competitive stance toward the Communist Party.

The CCF saw the CIO's arrival as a "magnificent opportunity," one the CCF "must not mess up" (Horowitz 1968, 67). Many CCFers became CIO organizers. Pat Conroy, who would become secretary treasurer of the Canadian Congress of Labour during the 1940s, "regarded the young CCFers who had helped to organize the new CIO unions as 'trade union illiterates' . . . whose primary motivation was not to build a labour movement but capture it for the CCF" (Horowitz 1968, 87). Even so, Conroy and other anticommunists in the Canadian labor movement "valued the CCF's strength in the CCL as a bulwark against the communist 'menace' " (Horowitz 1968, 17). The anticommunist agenda of the CCF fit well with the late 1930s agenda of CIO leaders to begin containing the influence of communists within its U.S. affiliates. As a result of their distorted priorities, however, the coalition between the CCF and CIO resulted in neither a well-balanced internationalism nor Canadian self-determination within the movement. The UAW case illustrates the point.

The sit-down strikes that swept the Detroit automobile industry in 1936 spread labor militancy to General Motors' operations in Oshawa, Ontario in April 1937 where an independent communist "Unity Group" had been organizing for about a year. As recounted previously in this chapter, CCF member Allen Griffiths, an opponent of the Unity Group, invited the Detroit office of the UAW into the strike. Hugh Thompson, the UAW representative from Detroit, set up Local 222. Another CCF member, Charlie Millard, was elected president of the local and on March 26 was appointed a full-time CIO organizer (Abella 1973, 9-10). In this way, the CCF's working relationship with the UAW was solidified, Canadian autonomy within the industrial union movement was compromised, and the communist leadership of the movement in the Canadian auto plants was broken.

Negotiations began, and just when it appeared a settlement was imminent, Premier Mitchell Hepburn asked for the deportation of

Hugh Thompson. The Canadian immigration officials, citing insufficient grounds, refused but Hepburn, who by this time was playing a central role in the negotiations, continued to resist any settlement with a "foreign" union. On April 3, 1937 the local struck (Abella 1973, 12-13). Six days later, Homer Martin, UAW international president, agreed the strike "should be settled on a Canadian basis without recognition of the CIO" (Abella 1973, 17). Local 222 President Millard signed a statement drawn up by the company denying any connection with the CIO and the strike was settled. Although Local 222 was clearly a UAW local, "nowhere in the contract was there any mention of the CIO, nor even of Local 222 of the UAW" (Abella 1973, 18, 21). The only way to interpret this strange sequence of events is that the settlement had been a contract at any costs for the CCF, which was trying desperately to capture the growing industrial union movement from the communists (Abella 1973, 24-25). The absence of any recognizable formal relationship between Local 222 and the UAW in Detroit, moreover, meant that there was no accountability for the activities between the local's leaders and the UAW and CIO. This left CCFers a clear path to create their own opportunities within the international. Millard was soon accused of spending more time in Detroit than on organizing in Canada. In 1939 he was ousted by the local only to be hired by the CIO as its representative in Canada (Abella 1973, 33, 37). On October 4, 1939, the CIO established the Canadian Committee for Industrial Organization and on August 18, 1940 the committee merged with the All-Canadian Congress of Labour to become the Canadian Congress of Labour (CIO-CCL). Millard and A. R. Mosher, head of the All-Canadian Congress, became CCL executives.

The marriage of the Canadian CIO and All-Canadian Congress, while appearing bizarre on the surface, served the interests of both Millard and Mosher. Millard, having by now been repudiated by his own local, had no real political base of his own save his ties with the CIO and the UAW across the border. Mosher's rabid anticommunism and pretentious nationalism, on the other hand, had rendered the ACCL marginal to sentiments of workers in mass industry and irrelevant to the emergent trends of the industrial union movement. What this unlikely pair had in common was a disdain for communism—a disdain they also shared with the CIO leaders in the United States.

The events in the UAW, coupled with those in the Steelworkers (see above), left a major sector of the CIO-CCL movement in the hands of the Canadian social democratic leaders and under the domination of international unions based in the United States. There are several ironies in the episode that are understandable only if analyzed within a class framework. That the ultranationalist All-Canadian Congress would deliver itself into the hands of U.S.-based international unions is, of course, a major irony. But the CCF's rejection of communism as an alien influence was also a form of nationalism that resonated with the prairie populism of its social base; that the CCF would lead the collaboration with U.S. internationals is, thus, equally ironic. Finally, that the All-Canadian Congress, the roots and rhetoric of which were in most respects those of ultra-left, anarcho-syndicalist traditions, and the CCF, which would have to be placed at the opposite end of a working-class political continuum, should make common cause to sell out Canadian self-determination within the industrial union movement is perhaps the greatest irony.

If one tries to understand the period in class terms rather than nationalist or ideological terms, however, the ironies dissolve. The leaders of neither the All-Canadian Congress nor the CCF shared wide-spread political support among rank-and-file industrial workers. Thus, they both had to seek political bases outside the working class and they found them in the burgeoning bureaucracy of the CIO. The nationalism of both Mosher and Millard was a form of opportunism: Feeling more threatened by the mass movement of industrial workers led by communists, they chose subordination to Washington. Still, as CCL leaders during the 1940s, Mosher and Millard would play the Canadian nationalism card whenever it was convenient—a tactic that would obscure the real political issues and confound later attempts to understand what transpired during those years.

In the late 1940s the CCL launched an attack against the very unions in which the Canadian affiliates had the most autonomy. While the IWA and Mine-Mill were both nearly destroyed in the campaign, the Mine-Mill case best reveals the opportunism of the CCL leadership. When Mine-Mill's leadership attempted to escape the clutches of Taft-Hartley by moving its operations center to Kirkland Lake, CCF leaders urged the CCL to "use its influence with Minister of Immigration to prohibit Robinson from entering Canada" (Abella 1973, 94). Abella (p. 97) summarizes the warning issued by Mosher at the CCL executive board meeting on March 3, 1948:

> Mosher warned that [Canada] "must not become a playground for communism" and stated that the Congress would not ask the government to protect these men or even permit them stay in Canada. "Communists camouflaged as labour organizers," he said, would not be brought into Canada.

Similarly, [CCL Secretary-Treasurer Pat] Conroy condemned the "stupidity" of Mine-Mill importing Communist organizers. This action, he argued, not only alienated the mine owners, the government, and the public, but it also brought "under suspicion all labour organizers sent from the United States."

What is notable about the incident is that the erstwhile ultranationalist Mosher was now rejecting the possibility of a major international union headquarters relocating to Canada. Moreover, he used virtually the same rhetoric about "Communists camouflaged as labour organizers" as that wielded by U.S. nationalists against the Canadian IWA president, Harold Pritchett, ten years earlier. The incident made clear that anticommunism and solidarity with the CIO bureaucracy in the United States, not Canadian nationalism, was the prime motivation of the CCF-CCL bloc. For at the very time (1948) when they were enlisting the support of the Canadian government to deport Robinson, they were collaborating with IWA officials in Portland, Oregon to smash the IWA's District Council in British Columbia.

"Taking its cue from the Congress position," (Abella 1973, 98) the Canadian government arrested Robinson in March and held him until May 5 when he was deported (Mine-Mill, *The Union*, 1948:18). During the summer months of 1948, other Mine-Mill organizers were arrested and deported to the States (Mine-Mill 1948, 3).

The experiences of the IWA and Mine-Mill were not exceptional for left-wing unions during the CIO-CCL period. By August 1948 Canadian members of the Rubber Workers, United Auto Workers, United Packing House Workers, and United Electrical Workers had all been denied entry. The March 19, 1948 edition of the UE's Canadian paper reported that the Canadian government was using the Taft-Hartley Act "as the basis for determining whether or not U.S. trade unionists will be permitted entry into Canada" (UE 1948a, 6). Like the other unions with communist leadership, UE's internal structure was very democratic; of all the CIO unions, the UE Canadian affiliates were the most autonomous. But, "since both the international and the Canadian leadership were suspected of being linked to the Communist Party, Canadian members could not attend union conventions in the United States nor could international representatives cross the border to meet their Canadian counterparts" (Abella 1973, 148). In 1948 the Canadian delegation to the UE convention in New York was denied entry to the United States. C. S. Jackson, Canadian director of the UE who had flown to New York, was taken into custody and forced to return to Canada (UE 1948b.8).

SUMMARY AND CONCLUSIONS

In retrospect, it is clear that the CCL unions came out of the period examined with neither autonomy nor an authentic and militant inter-nationalism—both had been traded for a short-term alliance against the Left.

It is equally clear that the best interests of the U.S.-Canadian work-ing class was in a strong, balanced international organization. It was the unions with communist leadership that represented the most serious attempt actually to build such organizations. Thus, by attack-ing and breaking the communist presence in the CIO-CCL movement, capital was, in effect, breaking working-class internationalism. Union-ists who aligned themselves with those efforts unwittingly helped prepare the way for a new era of U.S. economic imperialism.

The essential lines of struggle were, then, formed by class lines rather than national or ideological identities, per se. The leadership blocs opposing the unions with the most well-balanced international organizations were also quite estranged from rank-and-file bases. This fact makes plausible the assertion that there was a class or class frac-tional dimension to the struggles. In other words, the fractions that opposed internationalism (or vacillated opportunistically between internationalism and nationalism) were composed of leadership groups whose aspirations for power aligned them with small pockets of rank-and-file conservatism, corporate interests, and state power.

Although it is difficult to prove that the destruction of interna-tionalism in North American unionism was a necessary precondition for the expansion of U.S. capital in the post-war period, the relation-ship is suggested by the sequence of the two developments and by the involvement of employers in the actions taken against the Left. Clearly, the best interests of capital were served by the fragmenting of the labor movement. Capital was moving toward an increasingly internationalized mode of production in the post-war years, and by breaking international union ties it was able to prevent labor from defending itself on the same plane.

I would argue that their triumph testifies not to the nationalist proclivities of the U.S.-Canadian working class but to the ability of capital to penetrate, disrupt, and control certain portions of the trade union movement.

5

There Was a Difference: Communist and Noncommunist Leadership in CIO Unions

> We believe in democratic unions, organizations in which the member-
> ship determines policy, and we work for a broad leadership thorough-
> ly representative of and responsive to the wishes of the rank and
> file. Communists fight against all clique control and dictatorial ten-
> dencies among union leaders, no matter from what direction it comes.
> As for ourselves, we ask no rights beyond those accorded all other
> workers. We accept the same responsibilities and duties that non-
> Communists do.
> —William Z. Foster, general secretary of the CPUSA (1947)

> Communists' rule within the U.S. unions they control is dictatorial:
> although they talk the language of democracy, they do not believe
> or practice democratic principles.
> —C. Wright Mills, sociologist (1948)

INTRODUCTION

The above epigrams underscore the disparity between the organizational behavior of communists as perceived by their own leaders and
the portrayal of that behavior by the leading social theorist of the
New Left.

This chapter examines the organizational practices of communists
in CIO unions. Using primary documents, such as union constitutions
and convention proceedings, the chapter attempts to assemble the
kind of evidence needed to answer the question posed by its title.
The variable "union democracy" is approached two ways in this chapter. The first approach is consistent with that of liberal, pluralist
sociology. Although I have argued in preceding chapters that the lack
of class specificity in this notion of democracy has obscured the strategical dimensions of organizational problems, the work of communists in the CIO unions has conventionally been assessed solely by
this criteria. Thus, it is important to examine the evidence bearing on

the pluralist contention that communists were not democratic. Contrary to the conventional wisdom, the evidence shows that communists were vastly *more* democratic, by pluralist standards, than their opponents. The second approach is to see if communists were more or less likely than noncommunists to adopt organizational forms consistent with what I have called "associational" or working-class organizational forms. The evidence is mixed on this point. When communist union factions were based in the most proletarianized working-class fractions, they advocated associational organizational forms. But in cases like the UAW, where many of the communists came out of former AFL craft locals, they sometimes supported pecuniary forms of organization.

OLIGARCHY VERSUS DEMOCRACY IN CIO UNIONS

This section surveys a small sample of CIO unions. The sample was chosen by the criteria of size, industrial distribution, and the centrality of the respective unions to the history of the CIO. Five noncommunist and five communist unions are surveyed. The sample of noncommunist unions includes the three largest CIO affiliates as of 1937: the United Mine Workers of America, the United Steelworkers of America, and the United Auto Workers. The Amalgamated Clothing Workers Union (ACWU)—sixth largest—is included because it represented an important industry and because its president, Sidney Hillman, was very central to the formation of the CIO. The International Union of Electrical Workers (IUE) was selected because of its unique status as the only CIO union specifically established for the purpose of raiding another affiliate, the United Electrical Workers (UE). The comparison between the IUE and the UE, which was a communist-led union, is important because the struggle between them was so sharp and because for many people the UE remains nearly synonymous with communist unionism.

The sample of communist unions includes the UE, which was the largest of the left-wing unions and one of nine unions driven out of the CIO in 1949 for being communist dominated. The National Maritime Union was one of the most controversial of all the CIO unions on the question of democracy because its president, Joe Curran, switched political loyalties as the Cold War set in. The International Longshoremen's and Warehousemen's Union (ILWU), also one of the unions expelled in 1949, was the home union of Harry Bridges, West Coast CIO director and, like the UE, a union that is linked in the minds of many people with communist influence in the unions. The IWA was the largest CIO affiliate on the West Coast and the union that experienced the sharpest internal splits along political lines. The International Woodworkers of America (IWA) and the International Union of Mine, Mill and Smelter Workers have been characterized by Harvey Levenstein as "the most obvious examples of the persistence of an indigenous radical tradition" (1981, 64).

In this examination, union democracy is defined in a relational sense as a matter of control. "Control" is operationalized in this chapter in the same way as in Chapter 2. This chapter uses the right of rank and file to directly elect and recall officers and restrict the power of elected leaders to appoint or hire staff as indicators of membership control. A longer discussion of the validity of these indicators can be found in Chapter 2. A summary of the data is presented in Table 5.1.

Factional Struggles over Organizational Questions

The most direct control union members can have over leadership is through the election process. The basic principle is that each union member should have voice and vote in that process and should be able to exercise that right directly rather than through a representative

Table 5.1
Direct Rank-and File Control of Leadership

	Referendum Election of Officers			Provisions for Direct Recall Referendum			Power of Officers to Appoint Other Officers and Staff		
	Yes	Qualified	No	Yes	Qualified	No	None	Limited	Extensive
Communist-									
led Unions									
UE			x	x			x		
ILWU	x			x				x	
IWA	x			x			x		
Mine-Mill	x			x				x[a]	
NMU	x					x	x		
Noncommunist									
Unions									
UAW			x			x	x[b]		
Steel		x[c]				x			x[d]
UMWA		x[e]				x			x
IUE		x[f]			x[g]			x	
ACWU		x[h]				x			x[i]

Table 5.1 continued

Notes:

a. President's powers of appointment are limited to organizers but the elected executive board members from each district are also staff organizers.

b. The international president "shall fill by appointment all vacancies occurring in the International office except as otherwise provided for in this constitution . . . may appoint a member whose duties shall be to collect and compile statistics . . . may appoint such organizers, field and office workers as may be necessary . . . shall appoint subject to the approval of the International Executive Board one or more competent traveling auditors who shall examine the accounts of all subordinate bodies at least once a year. All appointments or suspensions from office done by the President shall be subject to the approval of the International Executive Board.

c. " . . . no person shall be notified or be a candidate who has not been nominated by 15 or more local unions. . . . The International tellers shall decide the legality of the votes of any local union . . . and all contests growing out of the report shall be filed with the International Executive Board which body shall have the power to decide the contest" (p. 27). The complexity of the United Steelworkers' election procedure is indicated by the length of its constitutional specifications, 12 pages. By comparison, the ILWU specifications of officer elections are one page long.

d. "The International President shall have the authority to appoint, direct, suspend, or remove, such organizers, representatives, agents and employees as he may deem necessary." There is no mention of any need for executive board approval for these presidential actions.

e. The UMWA provisions for elections, recalls, and powers of appointments are almost exactly the same as those for the United Steelworkers.

f. "A candidate shall be eligible for election only if he has been nominated in Convention by a delegate from each of 10 or more local unions from 3 or more districts, the combined per capita representations of which locals at the convention is no less than fifteen per cent (15%) of the total per capita representation." Only the president and secretary-treasurer are elected in this manner. Other officers, such as trustees, are elected in convention (p. 43). The IUE election procedure is encumbered with legal technicalities to a degree comparable to those of the United Steelworkers and United Mine Workers.

g. To initiate a recall a local "must first receive official endorsements from not less than ten (10) other locals from at least three different districts, comprising twenty-five (25%) percent of the total membership of the Union, as determined by the paid per capita on the average of the three previous months, before submitting the petition to the International trustees" (p. 15).

h. "No person shall be eligible for nomination of election . . . unless, for not less than five years immediately preceeding the date of the convention which nominates him he has been a member of the Amalgamated . . . employed by it, or in a trade or industry within its jurisdiction."

i. The Amalgamated president can appoint representatives, organizers, administrative, technical, and other employees without executive board approval.

Source: Reprinted from *Recapturing Marxism: An Appraisal of Recent Trends in Sociological Theory*, Rhonda F. Levine and Jerry Lembcke, eds., 1987, with permission of Praeger.

or delegate. Of the five communist-led CIO unions examined here, four provided for direct rank-and-file referendum elections of their top leadership. The exception, United Electrical Workers, elected leaders in convention.

There were similar differences between communist and noncommunist unions on provisions for recall elections. Four of the five communist unions examined provided for a direct rank-and-file recall referendum. Among the noncommunist unions, only the IUE provided for referendum recalls. But, as was pointed out in Chapter 2, the complexity of the IUE recall provisions seriously compromised it.

Two of the five communist unions, the UE and the IWA, gave no power to elected officers to appoint, hire, or dismiss staff. The other three limited officers to staff decisions approved by the executive board. Among the noncommunist unions the ACWU, Steelworkers, and UMWA granted almost total autonomy to officers to appoint, hire, and fire. The powers of UMWA presidents, and their abuses of that power, are legendary. Two of the noncommunist unions, the UAW and the IUE, allowed limited powers to officers in matters of staffing.

A narrative account of the struggles between communist and noncommunist factions over organizational questions is useful for highlighting the strategical and tactical dimensions of the issues. We can see, in other words, that the factions differed not just on some kind of quantitative scale of formal democracy but also in their perceptions of class relations under capitalism. Those differences are revealed in the expressions of workers speaking in support of, or opposition to, specific organizational forms.

Unions were selected for the narrative on methodological grounds. The method is historical-comparative: We want to see if the democratic character of unions varies with the ideological identity of its leadership. Following Smelser (1976), the kind of static picture that emerges from the data in Table 5.1 is only part of the picture. We also need *internal* comparisons so we can see the changes in organizational form that occur as changes in leadership factions take place within particular unions; only by seeing the *emergence* of organizational forms in historical context can the logic of organizational forms be revealed. We need, in other words, to see the relationship between the variables as dynamic, not static.

The narrative begins with a brief account of how eligibility for election was circumscribed in CIO unions. The excerpt from the IWA's history at the beginning is intended to set the strategical issues in relief from the purely formal issues. With the IWA case as a backdrop, the cases of the National Maritime Union (NMU) and UE-IUE are examined at greater length. The NMU and UE cases are used precisely because their organizational forms under communist leadership were less than fully democratic by pluralist standards. The struggles over organizational forms in these unions were thus all the more interesting because they add weight to the thesis that the real issues in the context of the times were not about formal democracy but strategy. These issues, it becomes apparent, really had less to do with ideological factionalism than with the class-fractional nature of the organizations themselves.

Respectability Versus Solidarity

The disqualification of members for political reasons was by far the most serious means by which democracy in CIO unions was circumscribed. The only political reason that anyone was ever disqualified for was for Communist Party affiliation, which means, of course, that this was a watershed issue between the communist and noncommunist unions and between internal factions. Constitutional clauses that forbade discrimination on the basis of political affiliation became a virtual hallmark of communist unionism by the late 1940s, while it was common for noncommunist unions to forbid discrimination on all grounds (e.g., race, nationality, sex, religion) except political; many noncommunist unions specifically excluded communists from eligibility for office and even membership.

A typical anticommunist clause adopted by the noncommunist unions was worded: "Any member accepting membership in the Communist Party shall be expelled from the International Woodworkers of America and is permanently debarred from holding office" (IWA 1941, 4). The United Mine Workers adopted a clause similar to this in 1928, the UAW in 1941, and the IUE adopted one at its founding convention in 1949. Although the Clothing Workers never had such a clause, Harvey Levenstein (1981, 89) notes that ACWU President Sidney Hillman "marched from union convention to convention, calling for anti-communist purges" during 1940 and 1941. Hillman was instrumental in bringing about the UAW's adoption of constitutional exclusion of communists.

The IWA

Battles over the inclusion of the anticommunist clauses were intensely fought. Lengthy accounts of those struggles have been presented elsewhere (Levenstein 1981; Keeran 1980; Lembcke and Tattam 1984), making it necessary to briefly review only one here. The fight in the IWA was typical. For three consecutive years, from 1938 to 1940, the anticommunist bloc sought the constitutional disbarment of communists. Each time their resolutions were defeated. During 1941 the CIO national office seized control of the IWA's organizing program (see Chapter 3) and shifted the balance of forces within the international. This enabled the anticommunist faction to pass their amendment and subsequently unseat the union's left-wing leadership. Throughout the 1940s the provision was invoked numerous times to bar elected delegates from convention and to unseat officers at various levels of the organization. There appear to have been attempts to pass such provisions in virtually all CIO unions at one time or another, but they were not always successful.

Convention debates over the anticommunist clauses are useful for highlighting tactical divergences between communist and noncommunist factions. While both wrapped their arguments in rhetoric about freedoms of speech, assembly, and beliefs, the anticommunist factions could only do that by maintaining that communists suppressed such freedoms elsewhere (namely the Soviet Union); from that, it followed that freedom and democracy were best served by suppressing communists' rights here. Contentions like the following were common:

> We do have, to some extent at least in this country, the right of free assemblage, the right of free speech, the right of free press. [But] the people presented by the Communist, Nazi and Fascist movements do not have these rights, as indicated by the governments established in Russia, Germany and Italy. . . . If we are Americans and Canadians that want democracy, then let's eliminate from membership inside the IWA those people who work like snakes to destroy the foundation of democracy [IWA 1940, 168].

Other lines of argument had a more direct bearing on questions of strategy and tactics for organizing the unorganized. The communists would typically argue that working-class unity was the highest priority and that anticommunist clauses constituted the thin edge of a wedge that employers could drive more deeply. Frances Murnane's statement at the IWA's 1940 convention reflected this reasoning: "Division in our ranks only benefits the bosses and the only way to safeguard against [it] is to see to it that we don't have any jokers in our Constitution that will enable the boss's agents to single out [individuals] who are outstandingly active in the affairs of the organization" (IWA 1940, 175).

In 1941 Ilmar Koivunen, a communist leader in the IWA, reiterated this position when debate on the clause resumed: "I appeal to you in all fairness to vote this thing down so our ranks will not be split, so that we will not be fighting the issue of Communism instead of fighting the issue of organizing those 200,000 workers" (IWA 1941, 158).

Implicit in these statements are (1) a strategy: working-class unity against a common enemy, the employer, and (2) two tactics: protecting the unity of the whole by protecting any individual or political minority from attack, and concentrating energy and resources on organizing the unorganized.

The anticommunist factions took very different positions when debating the effects the exclusionary clauses would have. Essentially they were willing to acquiesce to a political status quo shaped by other class forces. Consider the following, a typical statement made in support of excluding communists:

> I will tell you one thing, as a person working in the Willamette Valley, to organize workers in that area where organization has been unknown, I know that the . . . denying of membership of the Communist [s] . . . will rally those workers to sign cards inside the IWA. But as long as the employers and the lumber barons are able to say that when you join the IWA you are joining a Communist-Fascist subsidiary, those people say they don't want any of it (IWA, 1940:169).

The strategy that can be discerned in this statement is one consistent with traditional business unionism and some strands of parliamentary socialism: seek an appearance of respectability and legitimacy, as measured by the standards of the employers, in the eyes of the workers. The tactic toward that objective is to sacrifice those elements of the movement that jeopardize that appearance of respectability.

A class analysis of the IWA struggle presented in Chapter 3 interpreted the factional differences in class-fraction terms. It argued that the communist and noncommunist factions in the IWA were manifestations of materially different historical conditions. It identified in the uneven development of the wood products industry the historical forces that had fractured a cluster of cultural and economic determinants and given rise to the schism in the industry's work force. Briefly, it was argued that uneven industrial development (an early decentralized, craft-dominated form of production and unionism in Oregon and a later, monopolized, mass-production form of industry in Washington and British Columbia) were the conditions that produced a conservative form of trade unionism in Oregon and a more radical, industrial form of unionism in Washington and British Columbia. The correspondence between these two poles of the union and certain eligibility requirements for union officers suggests the usefulness of a class-based interpretation of union democracy questions.

The NMU

Attempts were made on many other grounds to narrow the pool of members eligible for office. Citizenship was one of those, and its use in the National Maritime Union (NMU) had a distinct political bias to it. Its examination provides additional support for the thesis that there were organizational rationales to the factional issues, and that one can identify in them a class-based logic.

Like the IWA, the NMU grew out of organizing efforts conducted outside the established AFL unions. In 1930 the Communist Party organized the Marine Worker's Industrial Union (MWIU), an affiliate of the TUUL. The MWIU revived union activity in the East Coast maritime industry, and shortly after the passage of Section 7(a) of the NIRA, the party approached the AFL's International Seaman's Union (ISU) about a merger but was rebuffed. The MWIU decided to carry out a "merger from below in spite of ISU officialdom," and dissolved the MWIU in 1935 (Galenson 1960, 433). Between 1935 and 1937 communists built a rank-and-file movement against the conservative leadership of the ISU. Joseph Curran had emerged as the leader of the insurgent movement by the time the rebels announced the formation of a new union, the National Maritime Union, on May 5, 1937 (Galenson 1960, 433-36).

The Communist Party played a major role in the NMU until the mid-1940s. As president of the union, Joe Curran "followed the party assiduously, though he has denied ever being an actual member" (Galenson 1960, 443). From its inception the NMU had elected its officers by rank-and-file referendum and until the mid-1940s there had been no conflict over eligibility requirements. By 1945 Joe Curran had broken with the Communist Party and a struggle for control of the union ensued. As part of that struggle, Curran and his followers began a campaign to change the constitutional provisions on elections and recall.

At the 1945 convention Curran submitted a resolution that would have required a candidate for NMU office to have "first papers," that is, that foreign-born union members were required to have taken steps toward attaining citizenship. Speaking in favor of the resolution, Curran argued that it was necessary to preempt employer and governmental attacks on that issue. According to Curran, by limiting the eligibility of foreign-born workers itself, the union would make itself less vulnerable to external attack. Curran's motion may have been motivated by other considerations, however. Curran's pending break with the communists made it necessary for him to neutralize their power and influence within the NMU. Ferdinand Smith, a foreign-born communist and secretary of the NMU, would have been immediately affected by the change. Smith spoke on the proposal when it reached the convention floor, saying he hoped Curran "would discuss it objectively [but it had become] a personal issue" (NMU 1947, 329).

Curran's ambitions, moreover, were by no means limited to the NMU, and within a few years he would be contending for national recognition within the CIO. Curran needed to distance himself from the communists, and by attacking the vulnerability of foreign-born unionists Curran was, in effect, attacking the symbol of the Communist party's presence in the CIO—Harry Bridges. Bridges, an Australian citizen, was the leader of the West Coast Longshoremen's Union, the former West Coast CIO director, and had been fighting deportation since 1938. According to Levenstein (1981, 256), Curran feared Bridges' extension of power eastward through the communists' Committee for Maritime Unity, which the NMU and ILWU had formed in 1946. References to Bridges' deportation case were sprinkled throughout the debate of Curran's resolution, indicating that both he and his opponents were aware of its significance for the larger issue.

Curran's career ambitions aside, the strategical and tactical implications of Curran's move are very similar to those pursued by the IWA's anticommunist bloc: under attack from capital, they were willing to sacrifice the more vulnerable sections of the union. The communists' emphasis on the strategy of unity, by contrast, comes through in a statement made by Howard McKenzie, a communist NMU delegate, who pointed out that the foreign-born issue only masked the attack on left-wing unionists:

> With respect to the vulnerability of officials, whether you filed your first intentions technically or not . . . you are going to get a blast as far as reaction is concerned. There are many examples. There was the case of Ferdinand Smith. The case of Bridges. . . . If they can't get you on the technicality that you were born in another country . . . then you will be framed in other ways as long as you work for the people [NMU 1945, 335].

Cases like the NMU invite voluntarist explanations: Curran simply decided to place his personal priorities over those of the union and opportunely switched allegiances. But it would be a mistake to abstract Curran's action from the historical context in which it was taken. However ambitious he was and whatever contempt he may have had for rank-and-file democracy, Curran could not disregard the membership as a political factor in his own future. Thus, he could risk an attack on the status of foreign-born members and the communists only if the future of the union could be secured through the same course of action. The situation provided tactical choices: Curran could ingratiate himself with the employers and conservative political leaders by distancing himself from the Left in the hope that the union would be spared the wrath of intolerance that was sweeping the country. On the other hand, he could cast his lot (and the union's) with the tactics of rank-and-file mobilization in the hope that a fight against reaction could be won.

The tactical choices implied questions about the viability of working-class independence and the effects of alliances with class strata lying outside the working class. For our purposes, the questions revolve around matters of organizational democracy and, as will be contended in the concluding portions of this chapter, the course that Curran chose was decidedly detrimental to union democracy.

Curran's efforts to use constitutional reforms to disqualify his communist opposition, unsuccessful at the 1945 convention, were resumed at the 1947 convention. The 1947 NMU convention was a marathon event, lasting 24 days. Nearly a week was taken up before disagreements over the seating of delegates were settled. Much of the remaining time was spent on constitutional revisions; the issue of a rank-and-file recall referendum was one of the most hostly debated questions.

By 1947 Curran had publicly broken with the communists. He and several followers (some of whom were former communists) now formed the main anticommunist bloc with the NMU. Their efforts to introduce recall referendum provisions at the 1947 convention have been interpreted by Spira (1972, 53) as an attempt to "democratize the NMU constitution and give control back to the membership." Inconsistencies in their proposed referendum suggest, however, that tactical considerations about the consolidation of their own power within the NMU weighed more heavily in its formulation than did matters of democratic principle or tactics vis-a-vis employers. Moreover, in light of the fact that the Curran faction abolished most of the NMU's democracy after it defeated the communists suggests that disruption, rather than democracy, was the objective of the reforms proposed in 1947.

Prior to 1947 charges made against an NMU officer were acted upon through a complex hearing, trial, and appeal process that involved the national office, subcommittees of the national office, and the membership meeting of the headquarters port, New York. The final appeal was to the national convention. Insofar as this procedure involved the rank and file of at least one local and ended with the convention having the final say, it was more democratic than the procedures of many other unions. Still, it was a very cumbersome procedure, fraught with opportunities for abuse.

The procedure proposed by the Curran bloc in 1947 was only a slight improvement, if that. The proposal would have had the accused tried by the headquarters local. If the officer was found innocent, the procedure ended there; if found guilty, the officer could appeal through a referendum (NMU 1947, 1191). Although the proposed amendment streamlined the procedure and decreased the role played by the national office, the referendum seemed more designed to *protect* an accused officer than to facilitate rank-and-file initiative in recalling the officer. Moreover, the Curran faction immediately undercut its position even more by amending the resolution so that if an officer was found guilty by the referendum vote, he could appeal to the convention. Delegate John DeNiff hastened to note that to make the procedure more democratic by adding the rank-and-file referendum and then to neutralize the effect of the referendum by allowing an appeal to the convention "doesn't seem to me to be too consistent" (NMU 1947, 1228-29). A second constitutional amendment called for a recall provision for local level officers. It too was inconsistent in that it excluded "patrolmen" from coverage by referendum recall. Patrolmen in the NMU were the counterparts of business agents in most unions. In the NMU, according to Spira (1972, 49) "patrolmen have been the direct link between working seamen and the union." Prior to 1947 patrolmen were elected, but when charges were brought against them they were tried by the national council. A motion to amend the amendment to make patrolmen subject to referendum recall was ignored by Curran who was chairing the debate. With communists apparently voting against it, the main amendment failed to get the two-thirds majority it needed to pass. Howard McKenzie explained that the exclusion of the patrolmen was the major reason for the communists' opposition to the measure:

There was an amendment offered on the floor which was not recognized by the Chair, and was not recognized by the committee, and that is when patrolmen are brought on charges and found guilty, they should also have the right to have that question submitted to a [referendum] . . . . That's the beef, and not, as [Charles] Keith and Curran are trying to say, that we are trying to keep a set-up to have officials try officials. That is not so. That is a distortion (NMU 1947, 1234).

There was a disturbing ambiguity in the communist's advocacy of recall referendum inasmuch as McKenzie's argument was couched in terms of protection of officers rather than the need to facilitate rank-and-file decision making but, as previously noted, the same ambiguity can be found in the statements of the other faction. It is also important to keep in mind the context in which the struggle over NMU's constitutional reforms was taking place. The United States was entering a period of unprecedented anti-unionism and anticommunism. Both communist and anticommunist factions in the NMU were undoubtedly reaching for an extra bit of leverage for the coming struggle, and it may have been the case that the Communist Party thought its elected trade union leaders would fare better in the court of rank-and-file opinion than they would in the trial procedure. If that were the case, the communist bloc probably should have preempted their opponents by initiating the call for recall referendums before the crisis of the late 1940s began unfolding. Whether or not the communists were trying to "protect" some of their incumbent patrolmen by submitting their recall to referendum, it is hard to construe their behavior in this instance as undemocratic.

It is even more difficult to sustain Preis' (1972, 325) characterization of the communist presence in the NMU as a "Stalinist stranglehold." During their years in power the communists maintained rank-and-file election referendums and fought the 1945 attempt by their opposition to narrow the eligibility requirements for nomination. The allowance for election of patrolmen or business agents during the period of communist leadership was a democratic provision enjoyed in very few unions.

From the record of debate and Curran's record of leadership after the communists were expelled from the NMU, it is very difficult to accept the conclusion that the intent of the 1947 proposals coming from the Curran/anticommunist bloc was the democratization of the union. If, as Spira (1972) and Preis (1972) charge, the communists were the main obstacles to union democracy in the NMU, then one would expect to find democracy flourishing with the communists out of the way. But, by their own account, that did not happen:

Since [the purge] Curran has bureaucratized the union even further. In 1959 he turned the strike fund over to the financing of buildings named for himself; in 1960 he forced a constitutional amendment giving him the power to appoint convention committees; in 1963, he forced through amendments giving him the power to appoint patrolmen, depriving the membership of the right to a secret referendum on major policy decisions and constitutional amendments, and barring from running for national office any member who has not served a full term as a salaried official [Spira 1972, 55].

In retrospect, the attempts of the anticommunist bloc to "democratize" the NMU in 1947 appear to be better understood as the tactical maneuvers of a faction that ultimately proved to be less democratic than the communists.

The UE

The UE began in March 1936. It was formed by the merger of the National Radio and Allied Trades (NRAT), which had broken away from the AFL, and a group of independent electrical locals. The NRAT was led by James Carey who became president of the UE, and the independent locals were led by Julius Emspak, a communist who became secretary treasurer. The UE affiliated with the CIO in September, which meant that technically it was an "independent" union at the time. But the UE's genesis had been within the AFL, and at the time the UE was formed Carey's bloc of former AFL locals constituted a political majority. Based on an analysis of the resolutions presented at the early UE conventions, Galenson (1960, 256) was led to doubt the claim that "the UE, from the very beginning of its organization within the CIO, was dominated by an organized Communist minority." NRAT, moreover, claimed 30,000 of the UE's 33,000 founding members. Thus, when one looks at the UE as a "Communist union," the organizational structure one sees probably more accurately reflects the influence of the conservative NRAT bloc. By the time the communists gained majority political power after 1936, the UE's organizational structure was already in place.

At its founding convention the UE adopted procedures for electing union leadership at international conventions and the referendum recall procedures described in Chapter 2. There was no attempt to challenge the convention election procedure until Carey was defeated for reelection in 1941.

By 1941, there was no question that the Communist Party was a majority force in the UE. The party bloc defeated Carey's attempt to bar communists from local offices and then elected its candidate, Albert J. Fitzgerald from Local 201, Lynn, Massachusetts. Fitzgerald received 653 delegate votes to Carey's 539 (Matles and Higgins 1974, 134). The convention reelected Carey to his position as secretary of the CIO.

At the 1944 convention Philadelphia Local 101, Carey's home local, introduced a resolution reading: "locals throughout the International Union shall vote on officers by referendum in the same manner as they vote on constitutional amendments." The wording of the resolution resulted in considerable confusion. Constitutional amendments were voted on in local union meetings and not through a referendum, per se. Moreover, in the event an amendment failed, the constitutional status quo remained in effect. Given the wording of the proposed change of election procedure, it was not clear whether its objective was elections by referendums or by unit vote of the locals, nor was it clear who was in office if the rank and file failed to ratify the convention's choice of officers.

When asked if he thought the proposal was democratic, President Fitzgerald, who was chairing the convention, replied, "I don't know whether it is democratic or whether it is conniving. I can't tell" (UE 1944, 135). The communist opposition to the change was based on a suspicion that the Carey bloc was less interested in expanding democracy than in finding an alternative route back to office. Calling it a "phony issue," delegate Joseph Kres observed, "It seems very strange, nine conventions—and suddenly today we have to have a referendum vote. . . . Suddenly, at this convention, the tenth convention, we become undemocratic" (UE 1944, 140).

Supporters of the change, including James Carey, charged that the left-wing opposition was based on technicalities and that the real issue was the right of the rank and file directly to select officers. The resolution failed, however. There was no convention in 1945 but at the 1946 convention Local 101 again introduced the election issue and again it was defeated (UE 1946, 260).

The question of the UE's election procedure was never raised again but when UE officers refused to sign the anticommunist affidavits required by the Taft-Hartley Act, the CIO allowed other unions to raid UE locals. In response, the UE ceased paying dues to the CIO and in November 1949 the CIO declared the UE "expelled." The CIO then established another union, the International Union of Electrical Radio and Machine Workers (IUE) and put James Carey at its head. The

IUE proceeded to carry out a massive campaign that threatened to destroy the UE.

The kind of organization set up by Carey allows us to compare contemporary communist and noncommunist unions in the same industry. As noted in Table 5.1, the UE had convention election of officers, a "qualified" form of referendum recall, and gave virtually no power to officers to appoint other officers and staff. The IUE had referendum elections but negated the democratic character of that provision with a nomination process that was unique to CIO unions: "A candidate shall be eligible for election only if he has been nominated in Convention by a delegate from each of 10 or more local unions from 3 or more districts, the combined per capita representations of which locals . . . is no less than fifteen per cent of the total per capita representation" (IUE 1955, 40-43).

The uniqueness (there was no other CIO union that had a procedure resembling it) of this procedure and the sheer awkwardness of it lead one to search for an explanation for the logic behind it. The political bias in the procedure is difficult to discern because membership figures are not obtainable. On the face of it, however, large locals were clearly favored: The ten largest locals easily constituted 15 percent of the membership and were distributed in more than three districts. Based on an analysis of the delegate strength at the 1949 IUE convention, moreover, it appears the nomination procedure also favored James Carey. Of the eight locals having the maximum ten delegates to the convention, three were in Carey's home District No. 1 and two of those three were in Philadelphia, his home town. One was his local, Local 101.

Based on the assumption that the large Philadelphia locals controlled District No. 1 and that Carey's influence was sufficient to control the Philadelphia locals, it is reasonable to conclude that effective opposition to Carey would have had to come from the other districts. But District No. 1 was almost 30 percent larger than the next largest district. Moreover, the combined strength of the four smallest districts (totalling 20 locals) would have been insufficient to satisfy the criteria requiring 15 percent of the total per-capita strength to nominate a candidate. It would have been necessary to unite the 50 smallest of the IUE's 126 locals for them to place a candidate's name in nomination.

The IUE nomination procedure gave an enormous advantage to James Carey because of his base in the union's largest district and one of the largest locals. The advantage he gained from this gerrymandered nomination procedure was amplified by the recall provisions. To initiate a recall it was necessary to have 25 percent of the total membership, from no less than ten locals from at least three districts. Based on the data available, it appears that no ten locals were in fact large enough to satisfy the 25 percent criterion. This meant that a minimum of 11 or 12 locals would have had to have been enlisted in the recall effort to even call a vote. If one uses the reasoning employed in the analysis (above) of the election procedure to eliminate Carey's own district as an initiator of a recall against him, it would have been extremely difficult to mount a recall challenge of incumbent leadership.

Incumbency, finally, is exactly what was assured Carey from the outset. The following resolution was passed at the founding convention of the IUE:

> Whereas the organizational problems now confronting the IUE-CIO are of such a pressing nature that . . . the election of officers, establishment of a Board and the execution of mass details incident thereto may impede the achievement of the immediate objective of the IUE-CIO, therefore be it resolved that the present officers and members of the administrative Committee . . . conduct the affairs of the IUE [IUE 1949, 78].

That clause, coupled with the nomination provisions that made it very difficult for nonincumbents to campaign for nomination in subsequent elections, virtually ensured the tenure of IUE President James Carey.

The case of the UE-IUE strongly resembles that of the National Maritime Union. In both unions communist leaders abided less than fully democratic provisions until anticommunist opponents appropriated the democracy issue and wielded it against the Left. The important difference between the two is that the NMU was a communist organization from the outset, thus allowing us to attribute more directly its characteristics to that political tendency. The UE, on the other hand, was formed as an AFL union by noncommunists. By the time the UE communist bloc came to power, the constitutional provisions were already in place.

In retrospect, it appears that the substance of communist opposition to the "democracy" represented by Curran and Carey was objectively democratic. What remains unanswered is why the Left leadership in both unions waited until a crisis and then found themselves embarrassingly opposed to what on the surface were movements for democracy. Why, in other words, did they not seize the initiative earlier and thereby preempt the opposition on this issue?

While a definitive answer to the question will probably never be known, the following section suggests that Communist Party members probably did not have a "line" on organizational questions and no a priori notion of what was "democratic" or otherwise desireable as an organizational form. Their position on organizational questions appears to have been situationally defined with strategical (i.e., the union's capacity versus the employer, the state or what they perceived as reactionary elements within the union itself) as the primary consideration. The party, in other words, was inconsistent; it seldom transcended the organizational logic of the class fraction in which it was located. Thus, if its political base was in a craft fraction of a union, it would be more likely to follow pecuniary forms of representation than associational. An examination of the Communist party's relationship to the organizational questions discussed in this book supports the contention that class, rather than ideological preferences, was the strongest determinant of organizational form.

CLASS CAPACITIES: A "COMMIE" APPROACH TO THE UNION ORGANIZATIONAL PROBLEM

In Chapter 3 an incident was recounted whereupon Adolph Germer, one of John L. Lewis' troubleshooters, was dispatched by the CIO national office to help rid the International Woodworkers of America (IWA) of communist influence. In an April 10, 1941 letter to Allan Haywood, Germer made reference to a "commie organizational structure" that he claimed increased the power of the IWA's communist faction. Is there, in fact, an identifiable form of organization that has a history of being associated with communists? Did the Communist Party have a "line" on organizational questions that would have mandated party members to push for certain forms of organization in all CIO unions?

A review of party literature on organizational questions as they have been discussed in this book casts doubt on the assertion that the Communist Party had a "line" on how unions should be organized internally. Indeed, one finds remarkably few statements in the party's documents about union organizational forms. What is clear, however, is that organizational questions were perceived to be *strategical*, rather than formal, problems. Moreover, where forms of representation were concerned, it appears that the representation of *units*, rather than individuals, was the key consideration. This can be seen in the party's discussions of both its own structure and the structure of the mass organizations (such as unions) in which it worked.

The basic building blocks of the party were its shop and street, or community, "units." Unit leaders were elected by unit members, presumably (because the documents do not specify any other rules for election) on a one person, one vote basis. Units in a common geographic area made up a "section." Sections made up "districts," of which there were nine in 1934 (Peter 1934, 2). The district "committee," elected by the delegates of the sections at the district convention, was responsible for carrying out the decisions of the convention. District convention delegates elected delegates to the national convention which, in turn, elected the party's central committee.

J. Peter explained in the June 1935 *Party Organizer* how units and sections were represented at the higher levels of decision making:

> The number of delegates to the Convention are not fixed in the Constitution of the Party. It depends on the conditions in a given situation besides the numerical strength of the given units, Sections and Districts.
>
> The *strategic importance* of a shop unit, or concentration Section, or of a District, *is the governing factor* in deciding number of delegates to the Conventions. The Party Committee, for example, can decide whether a shop unit from a big factory sends proportionately more delegates to the Section Convention than a street unit with the same or less number of members [emphasis added] [Peter 1934].

Peter went on to note that as a general rule units elect one delegate for each five members to the section convention, section conventions elect one delegate for each 15 members to the district convention, and districts elect one delegate for each 100 members to the national convention.

Representation in the Communist International, or Comintern, was very similar, according to Peter (1934, 23). The World Congress was composed of delegates from all parties affiliated to the Comintern, and the number of delegates was "decided upon by the Executive Committee of the Communist International (ECCI). But the number of votes allocated to each Party at the World Congress is decided upon by special decision of the Congress itself in accordance with the membership of the given Party, and the political importance of the given country."

From the description offered by Peter, it is clear that the party mixed numerical and strategical criteria in determining representation. In the absence of additional records it is hard to know how those two criteria were weighted in instances of competing logics. The CPUSA districts ranged in size from 5,272 (District 2) to 449 (District 4) in 1934, a disparity that translated into a 13 to 1 voting differential.

How, when, and by whose initiative that power imbalance could be redressed by the criteria of strategical importance is not clear. Given that the party was heavily concentrated in the east and, therefore, in industrial sectors that were more heavily craft dominated, the question of numerical versus strategical forms of representation is very important. The question will be addressed again in Chapter 6.

Was party organizational structure simply reproduced by party members working in mass organizations, or were mass organizations perceived to be a different case, requiring separate consideration? We have very little documentation on the forms of organization the party preferred for its mass organizations. Generally, party documents speak of the necessity for membership participation in elections and policy decisions (e.g., Lozovsky [1921] 1978). Beyond that, we can only infer from the historical record what the party's preferences seem to have been.

The party's first major experience with mass organization work came with the unemployed councils, organized during the early 1930s. The preface to the Constitution of the National Unemployed Council noted, "Our movement depends upon the united strength of the masses and not upon the 'genius' of some 'great' individual or isolated group. . . . Collective leadership and mass action are the keystone of our organization" (National Unemployed Council 1934, 3). The Constitution requires a national executive board with 50 members and does not specify any distribution of voting power on a per-capita basis (National Unemployed Council 1934, 9).

During the miners' strike of 1931 the *Party Organizer* (1931, 7) discussed the form that strike committee organization should take: "In the miners strike the strike committee should take the following forms: elected local mine strike committees with representation from the women; section strike committees composed of a minimum of 3 delegates (2 men, 1 woman) from each struck mine in a given territory; central committee composed of three delegates, one a woman, from every mine in the strike area." The article went on to note:

> It is impossible to give proper leadership to a strike of more than 40,000 strikers, totalling with women and children, probably 150,000, covering a strike front of 70 miles, with only a handful of organizers and strike committee chairmen who assume the responsibility for all tasks and if arrested or become sick have not trained others to step into their plans. So it becomes absolutely necessary to draw as many strikers and their families into group activity [as possible].

From this article we can infer two things that are important to the thesis of this chapter. First, the communist leadership sought the broadest possible base of participation and support for strike activities. They saw strikes as occasions for the mobilization of entire families and communities and they advocated structures that empowered all members of the communities, not just the striking workers. Second, the workers of each mine constituted a unit of organization and each unit had the same representation on the central strike committee (two men and one woman). There is no indication that the largest units had more power than the small mines. From this instance we could conclude that in strike situations, at least, the strategical priority of uniting the largest number of workers and supporters prevailed over the formal democratic priority of ensuring representation on a one worker, one vote basis. Associational logic, in other words, prevailed over pecuniary logic.

SUMMARY

In the CIO histories we find general support for the proposition that communists advocated organizational forms that maximized the unity of the largest numbers of workers in an industry or geographic region. Evidence for that is presented above. There does not, however, appear to have been a communist "line" on the form that representation in centralized bodies should take. The associational logic that Adolph Germer referred to as a "commie structure" was generally preferred by party activists. In the UAW case, for example, it was communist Nat Ganely who led the opposition to the "dollar democracy" of the Reuthers (see Chapter 3).

The exceptional cases where communists, like Reid Robinson in Mine, Mill and Smelter Workers, did support pecuniary forms of representation are revealing in two ways. First, they are cases where communist power (like Robinson's) was based in craft fractions with an organizational form inherited from the AFL. For historical reasons these cases are the exceptions to the rule that communists were based in the unskilled, industrial worker fractions of the CIO unions. But it appears that communists adopted the organizational forms organic to the fractions in which they were based rather than imposing a form that was theoretically conceived. What Germer called a "commie structure" was, in other words, a proletarian (or associational) organizational form that the IWA communists had adopted because their political base was in the most proletarian fraction of the industry. Second, the consequences for Mine-Mill of Robinson tailing the craft-based leadership from Butte on the organizational question were serious. Had Mine-Mill organized Arizona (possibly *instead of* Brass Valley in Connecticut, which brought still more craft workers into the union) its future may have been altered. As it was, Reid Robinson, who by all accounts was a great organizer, was unable to overcome the organizational deformities created by Mine-Mill's representation structure. The superiority of communist leadership in organizing campaigns was based not just on their commitment and zeal, but also on their sense of which organizational forms would most efficaciously advance their effort. When their judgement was clouded, or when for political reasons they had to go with an organizational form that was less than ideal, the difference in effectiveness between them and noncommunist leaders was diminished.

6

Uneven Development, Class Formation, and Organization Theory: New Departures for Understanding Current Struggles

INTRODUCTION

The first five chapters of this book have found support for the thesis that organizational forms are class specific. This support has been found by adopting the "two logics of collective action" model of Offe and Wiesenthal (1980) to a study of 27 CIO unions. It has been established that unions composed of the most proletarianized workers are more likely to have "associational" forms of collective action, while the least proletarianized workers are more likely to favor "pecuniary" or capitalist organizational forms.

While this study has established level of class formation as the primary independent variable determining organizational form, it has also revealed interesting organizational variation along temporal and spatial lines. It has been noted, for example, that organizations that favored pecuniary organizational forms tended to be the older organizations (i.e., those originally founded as AFL organizations) with memberships based in the eastern United States, while those favoring associational forms tended to be industrial unions formed later in the western region.

These features first may appear to be spurious by-products of more fundamental forces but, in fact, they provide the links between organization theory and the broader problem of theorizing the historical experience of the U.S. labor movement. The organizational variability identified in the previous chapters is, in other words, only one dimension of uneven working-class formation in the United States. It is the purpose of this chapter to make those links explicit and thereby suggest a new point of departure for studies of the larger issues.

TOWARD A STRUCTURAL ANALYSIS OF U.S. LABOR

Organizations can be visualized as a kind of elbow-joint through which inherited social characteristics can be transferred to a different space. The fractions of the U.S. working class formed in the late 1800s spawned strongly protectionist forms of organization. This was consistent with the needs of the class at that time. This organizational form was reproduced intergenerationally well beyond the time when it benefited the majority of workers. Moreover, it transmitted the power relationship it represented between craft and skilled workers, on the one hand, and unskilled industrial workers, on the other. At another level of abstraction, it also transmitted the power relationship between the working class as a whole and the capitalist class. Given that the nature of pecuniary organizational forms translated size into power vis-a-vis other class fractions (see Chapter 2), it was an historical impossibility for associational organizational forms to take root and supplant the pecuniary forms within the same industrial and geographic space. Space unoccupied by previous organizational forms would have to be created by the class struggle, and working-class advances (organizational and other) would not proceed until that occurred. In the meantime, the pecuniary forms of union organization intergenerationally transmitted the dominance of the craft/skilled fraction of the working class.

It was not until the 1930s, when the contradictions described in Chapter 2 came to fruition, that the pace of organizational developments would quicken. The organizational situation extant at that time had two features significant for this discussion. One was that the business unionists like John L. Lewis of the United Mine Workers were moved by their own pecuniary orientation to pursue the organization of millions of unskilled workers. In short, the potential gain in dues dollars collected outweighed the political problems created and the status loss incurred. Second, the accumulated power of monopoly capital could be challenged by industrial workers only with the cooperation and material assistance of the already existing unions. Moreover, the passage of the Wagner Act that provided a stimulant for union organizing in mass industry was to some extent dependent on the political effort that came out of the more progressive wing of the AFL. Before the pecuniary needs of the business unionists like Lewis and the organizing needs of industrial workers could be joined, however, a split in the AFL had to occur. This happened when several unions left the AFL in 1936 and joined with independent organizing efforts to form the CIO.

The historical promise of the industrial union movement was that it would be able to harness the class capacities generated by capitalism's contradictions and move them in a potentially revolutionary direction. The CIO formed the organizational elbow between the accumulated capacity of the U.S. working class and the potential that lay in a different sectoral and geographic space. The power of the working class could no longer be simply accumulated in a linear fashion; rather, the class formation process had to momentarily shift laterally in order to resume its forward motion. The lateral shift, however, had to occur in such a way that the accumulated resources of the union movement were not abandoned but brought on line for a struggle in a different space, with a different logic. The transformation called not for destruction of the past (the advances made under the AFL), but rather for a kind of negation of one level of organization in order that a higher level could be achieved.

The mobilization and dispensation of those accumulated resources was the key link between the past and the future of the union movement and, as was seen in Chapters 2 and 3, the struggle to make that link manifested itself in conflicts over organizational forms. The unorganized working-class capacity lay, first, in the numbers of workers. The large numbers were important because of their location in the industries most critical to the functioning of the nation's economy. The more politicized nature of the class struggle by the 1930s also necessitated an electoral strategy that, without the concerted involvement of millions of industrial workers, was doomed. Second, as has been consistently argued throughout this book, the more proletarianized conditions of workers in the industrial sector encouraged collective action. Brought into the union movement, these workers thus stimulated a kind of unionism that went beyond the workplace and spoke to the needs of the working *class*. The CIO unions took up issues of national politics, foreign policy, civil rights, environmental control, and the welfare of the unemployed. They also brought more collectivist cultural forms, such as theater and group singing, into union institutions. Theoretically speaking, these more collectivist orientations were expressions of a key contradiction within advanced capitalism: that with proletarianization, individualism would break down, workers would begin to think and act as a class and in so doing lay the groundwork for a socialist movement. They represented, in other words, a transition from individualized struggle aimed at preserving precapitalist individual autonomy to collective struggle aimed at class control of economic and social life. A corollary of the shift to industrial unionism was that communists who had been purged from AFL unions were solidly entrenched as leaders of the independent organizing efforts that had been going on throughout the early 1930s. Bringing industrial workers into the union movement meant bringing communist leaders into the mainstream. Their influence, like the cultural influence of the industrial workers themselves, would extend beyond the boundaries of their own organizations and become a general influence on the unions.

Organizational form was the mechanism linking the accumulated capacity of the working class and the *potential* for increasing the class's capacity. It was only through organization that the unevenness created by the development process, which capital could endlessly manipulate to its advantage (by fostering competition between fractions of the working class and geographic regions), could be offset or counterbalanced by the unions. The key, in other words, was to mobilize the sectors of the working-class movement that were regionally, sectorally, and politically *over*-developed in such a way that those sectors underdeveloped at the time could advance, sling-shot fashion, beyond the presently more advanced sectors.

This is, in effect, what happened during the growth years of the CIO and, as we have seen, the organizational form that was responsible was one consistent with what we have called an "associational" logic of collective action. But the movement stalled and it is important to understand why.

First, struggles ensued over organizational forms. As recounted in Chapter 3, those struggles pitted the powerful conservative factions of the formerly AFL unions and the craft fractions within the industrial union sector against the emergent masses of industrial workers. In the organizational terms employed in this study, it pitted the pecuniary logic of the business unionists against the collectivist or associational logic of the industrial workers and their left-wing leaders. The contested terrain of the intra-class struggle became the rules by which the respective power of the two fractions would translate into power over organizing resources and strategies. As seen clearly in the cases of the International Woodworkers of America and the United Auto Workers (Chapter 3), the organizational struggles were most often won by the conservatives. Thus, the articulation of organizational development from one period of history with that of another was broken.

Second, the conflicts over organizational forms articulated with the attacks on the left-wing unions by the CIO national office, corporate, and state powers. Had the struggle over representation forms been left for the forces indigenous to the IWA to resolve on their own, there probably would have never been rule changes. The organizational sophistication that channeled the factional dispute into a struggle over organizational form came not from rank and file woodworkers but from CIO leaders Adolph Germer and Allan Haywood. Moreover, it is unlikely that efforts to change the rules, which came down to a convention floor fight in 1941, would have been successful if Harold Pritchett had not already been deported. Pritchett's deportation and the U.S. government's subsequent refusal to allow Canadian communists into the country on union business diminished the leadership capacity of the union and impaired its ability to exploit the limitations of nation-state power through labor union internationalism. Finally, the full significance of the organizational struggles was realized only through capital's mobility in the post-World War II years. The move of the wood products industry from Washington to Oregon and then to the South, the growth of the auto industry out of the Detroit area, and the shift of metal mining to the southwest all strengthen capital's hand vis-a-vis the working class *only because the unions' ability to follow and check capital's moves had been curtailed.* Capital mobility, as a strategy in the class struggle, was viable, in other words, only to the extent that working-class capacities to follow suit were blocked.

Third, the leadership of the left-wing forces within the unions appears to have been oblivious to the significance of the organizational questions. It is an axiom of Marxist theory that objective social conditions—for example, the contradictions inherent in capitalist development—become "real" only if they are given expression through the conscious actions of the working class. In other words, a contradiction is an abstraction if it is not identified as such and used as the basis for strategizing the class struggle. In the case of the organizational struggles in the CIO, the left-wing leaders appear to have been unaware of the full significance of the issues. As we saw in Chapter 5, there appears to have been no Communist Party "line" on organizational questions. Thus, party members proceeded on the basis of personal experience and instinct. Because they were often indigenous members of the working class, their instincts usually led them toward collectivist, or what we have called "associational," forms of organization. But the party's composition was itself a product of uneven historical development, and in the absence of a conscious recognition of that fact it never overcame its limitations. The party grew out of the old Socialist Party, which itself was rooted in the communities of craft and skilled workers. Although the Communist Party came into being as the historical agent of an expanding sector of industrial workers, it emerged out of an earlier period of development. Thus, the party, like the unions, carried with it certain characteristics inherited from the past. The oldest sections, and therefore the sections that were in many ways the most influential, were those based in the craft and skilled fractions of industry like the Mechanics Educational Society of America (MESA) and the Auto Workers Union (AWU) in the auto industry. The organizational expressions of those party fractions were influenced by the value systems characteristic of their social base. More important, with the power of party union fractions based on the size and political power of the craft and skilled fractions, strategies to advance party influence (and, thus, on a more general level, the progressive union movement) were sometimes at odds with strategies to advance the influence of the industrial worker fractions. This was clearly the case of the communist faction of Mine, Mill and Smelter Workers, which was led by Reid Robinson whose original political base was the anticommunist local in Butte, Montana.

Finally, the political unevenness within the Communist Party had interesting geographic implications. Within the party itself it has been noted (Richmond 1972) that the West Coast sections of the party were often at odds with the East Coast leadership. Sometimes those differences were over style of leadership. But they often entailed organizational differences such as the appropriate degree of centralism within the party and relations with the Communist Party of the Soviet Union. In studying the role of the Communist Party in the CIO unions, one is often struck by the difference between eastern-based party fractions and those based on the Pacific Coast, the latter being more decentralist in orientation, more directed by local conditions, and definitely more rooted in the traditions of the unskilled industrial working-class communities. Indeed, the conventional portrait of communists and their organizations as authoritarian and undemocratic appears as a Cold War caricature against the backdrop of West Coast party experience. As a result, the party was not always united on strategical questions, a fact that became more apparent during the Cold War years (Lembcke and Tattam 1984, 145-47).

The uneven development within the left-wing political community combined with the unevenness of the class formation process spelled double trouble for the CIO on the West Coast. One of the important untold stories of CIO history is just how important it was for the CIO national office to break the Communist Party tie with the West

Coast unions like the IWA and the ILWU and to prevent a CP leadership from consolidating within the West Coast UAW. While there were many strategical turning points in the CIO's history, the struggle for the West Coast affiliates was as important as any. In geographic terms, the future of the union movement lay outside the traditional industrial centers of the northeast. The growth regions of the country during the post-World War II years were west of the Rockies, and the CIO unions in that region were solidly in the hands of communists prior to 1940. The IWA was the largest West Coast affiliate and the ties between Harold Pritchett and ILWU leader Harry Bridges were very tight. Bridges, as we saw in Chapter 4, could plausibly have used the ILWU as a stepping stone to the leadership of unionism in the entire maritime industry. Moreover, Bridges' position as West Coast CIO director in the late 1930s resonated with the presence of communists like Wyndam Mortimer in the UAW's organizing drive in the West Coast defense industries: If the West Coast aircraft industry had come under CP-led UAW locals, and if Bridges had retained hold of the CIO regional directorship and extended his leadership within the maritime industry, CIO history may have come out very differently. Finally, the nation's precious metals, located overwhelmingly in the western states, were being mined by miners under CP leadership in the Mine, Mill and Smelter Workers Union.

In summary, it appears that the unevenness of development within the party resulted in some ambivalence on organizational questions and, generally, in a lack of a consciously articulated position that was strategically informed. As a result, party activists in the CIO were not only unable to make objective contradictions work in their favor, but in many cases found themselves reacting to situations and making organizational choices on a case-by-case basis. The opposition, led by more organizationally astute people like Adolph Germer, were able to deploy organizational tactics in ways that articulated with the deeper, more basic social forces, which proved decisive.

It is clear from this sketch that the geographic dimensions of the struggle for control of the CIO were critical. It has been argued (Lembcke and Tattam 1984, 93) that when Adolph Germer was sent west to take control of the IWA's organizing program (Chapter 3), his real mission was nothing less than securing a staging area from which an assault on the CP's dominating presence in the CIO's West Coast empire could be launched. The contradictions in the uneven class formation of the wood products work force was a reality upon which Germer based his immediate strategy.

Whether Germer and other national CIO leaders were fully aware of the historical forces they were harnessing cannot be known. What is clear in retrospect is that there were strategical choices embedded in the organizational choices they made. Formal organizational structures were the lynch pins connecting economic, cultural, and political developments that had occurred in different time frames, and they were the conveyance by which interregional levels of development were bridged. This study has been an attempt to "read" the record of organizational struggle left behind by CIO activists as a kind of sediment on which the history of class formation is etched.

ORGANIZATIONAL STRATEGY FOR LABOR IN LATE TWENTIETH CENTURY AMERICA

As noted in Chapter 1, current studies of class formation and class capacities generally emphasize the fragmented and divided nature of the U.S. working class. Finding no contradictions in those conditions, these studies are generally pessimistic about the capacity of the working class to make social change. Subsequent chapters employed the framework of uneven development and recent developments in organization theory to reinterpret the U.S. working-class experience in a way that makes the contradictory properties of its development more evident. This section extends the analysis in an attempt to understand current conditions as a continuation of that same dialectical motion.

This section argues that the process of uneven development has continued to out-flank the organized capacity of the working class through the creation of new (and non-union) sectors of the economy and new fractions of the working class, isolating the political Left from the trade union movement. The key to a successful working-class strategy during this period is the recognition that each of these developments has a dialectical underside with the potential to enhance class capacity.

There are both major and minor ways in which the pattern of capitalist crises creating opportunities for the working class is being repeated. While the parallels between the 1930s and today are imperfect, similarities exist. Just as the Palmer Raids and AFL reactionism had isolated the Left from the union movement by the late 1920s, so has the legacy of McCarthyism inside and outside the labor establishment isolated the Left in the current period. The contradictions in that course of events are also similar: As the system's crisis pushes larger numbers of workers to the social and economic margin, it also pushes them to, and beyond, the margin of the established labor movement and into the influence of the organized Left. Thus, we see in situations like the Hormel strike in Austin, Minnesota or the cannery workers in Watsonville, California, where workers struggling against capital's crisis-resolution tactics have gained support mainly from left-wing organizations, that the dynamics of the capitalist political economy have produced conditions favorable to overdetermination.

A second minor contradiction can be seen in the relationship between the left wing of the union movement and the racial and ethnic composition of the working class. Just as capital partially resolved its crisis of the late nineteenth century by using large numbers of immigrant workers to redivide the working class, it is true that nonwhite, especially immigrant, Spanish-speaking workers are an important part of capital's vision of a reindustrialized America. And just as immigrant workers were shunned by the labor establishment during the monopoly phase of capitalist development, so today few unions make the attempt to reach these workers. In part, the incapacity of the labor movement in this regard is a logical extension of its collaboration with imperialism during the post-World War II years. Through its CIA conduits like AIFLD, the AFL-CIO has contributed to the economic hardship and political repression that has driven millions of Third World workers into the domestic U.S. economy.

The major dynamic being repeated, however, is that capitalism is once again resolving a crisis through the creation of an entirely new sector. Thus, the crisis of mid-nineteenth century commercial capitalism was resolved through the emergence of industrial capitalism, the late nineteenth century crisis through the emergence of monopoly capitalism, and the crisis of the 1930s through the emergence of full-blown imperialism. With national liberation movements having limited the international options of U.S. capital for the closing decades of the twentieth century, the capitalist class must create social space within the domestic economy through the creation of new sectoral options. Left strategies and tactics for the remainder of the century must be premised on the dialectical qualities of capitalism's own crisis solutions—in this case, the expansion of the public sector.

NEW SECTORAL DEVELOPMENT: AN ENTREPRENEURIAL ROLE FOR THE STATE

"Reindustrialization" will be at the heart of capital's attempt to restructure the economy.[1] Based on an analysis of the needs, logic, and trajectory of monopoly capitalism, reindustrialization must achieve two major objectives: to rebuild economic infrastructure, and to co-ordinate and guide private investment and industrial activity. These will be accomplished by allowing the state vastly increased responsibilities and power to manage the economy. The contention that an expanded state sector will be the historical sequel to dominance of the monopoly sector in the U.S. political economy is based on a logical argument plus the testimony of current policymakers and planners and a certain amount of already available empirical evidence.

Rebuilding Infrastructure

There is little doubt that the U.S. economy will be unable to compete effectively on a world level without a rebuilt infrastructure. Countless studies show that bridges, roads, sewers, ports, and the like—in the snowbelt as well as the sunbelt—are in desperate need of upgrading and expansion, and that their current condition is a major obstacle to any economic recovery. *Business Week* (1981, 136-89) called attention to the "growing numbers of bursting water mains, flooding basements, creaking bridges, collapsing roads and stalling buses [that] have awakened the public and elected officials alike to the problem of deteriorating infrastructure." *Business Week* estimated that it would take $600 billion in the next 15 years just to maintain existing infrastructure and warned that the amount was equal to total state and local investments for the previous 20 years.

For reindustrialization to succeed, then, state and local governments are going to have to greatly increase their spending and employment to ensure an infrastructure that can support private growth. Financing such an undertaking, according to *Business Week*, will require new state and local government spending practices, as well as new federal initiatives. Specifically, *Business Week* recommended federal subsidization of state and city borrowing, "a national capital budget" to rationalize public works spending, and a "new agency—perhaps on the lines of Herbert Hoover's Reconstruction Finance Corporation . . . to provide capital for the revitalization of . . . the nation's deteriorating infrastructure of roads, bridges, and other public plant" (1981, 180).

Investment in Industrial Activity

A number of key U.S. industries are in great need of modernization to restore their competitiveness: steel, auto, rubber, wood products—

the list is long. The economy as a whole is suffering from insufficient and misguided (short-term, speculative rather than long-term, productive) investment. As a result, there appears to be significant support for entrepreneurial state activity that can channel investment funds, through stock purchases, into enterprises and industries that are in need and/or are considered of national importance. Felix Rohatyn, Lester Thurow, and many Democratic party "neo-liberals," among others, have all expressed recognition of such a role for the government.

Large-scale state intervention in equity and loan markets will require the development of an industrial policy to guide state actions. While there is, as of yet, no agreement on the specific content of such a policy, the need to develop one is now taken seriously.

Says Lester C. Thurow of the Massachusetts Institute of Technology, "Suddenly everyone is willing to talk seriously about a national industrial policy, and the reason is a four-letter word called fear. We all fear we may be going down for the count as an industrial power if we don't counter Japanese and European growth strategies built around industrial policies." Robert B. Reich of Harvard University's Kennedy School of Government agrees with Thurow that it is getting late to argue over the propriety of the industrial policy in terms of having more or less government. "Foreigners may argue," say Reich, "over which IP [Industrial Policy] option is best but never over the appropriateness of IP itself. For them, it's the third leg on the policy stool, as critical as monetary and fiscal policies for economic growth and stabilization" [*Business Week* 1983, 55].

Regardless of how the industrial policy debate turns out, reindustrialization will greatly increase state power to shape the economy. Corporations, for example, are likely to receive state support only if management is willing to follow specified state production and investment criteria. As Felix Rohatyn puts it, "The RFC [Reconstruction Finance Corporation], like any other equity investor, should have the right to insist on management changes and changes in the board of directors if it deems them appropriate" (Watkins 1981, 46).

While not currently advocated, at least in public, it is nevertheless likely that limited equity participation through some kind of RFC would evolve into complete state ownership of certain enterprises. Moreover, as the state exercises increasing influence over private investment and production decisions, some type of state-capital-labor tripartite planning body will have to be created to ensure that future industrial policy meets capital's long-term needs and will not be opposed by organized labor. Calls for a social contract to build support for a capitalist reindustrialization drive have already begun in earnest (*Business Week* 1980, 146).

The cue in this analysis for left-labor organizing is derived from the historical pattern, of which the current developments are a continuation. Capitalism's own logic produced the monopoly form that succeeded the competitive form and an imperialist form that succeeded the monopoly form. Where and when fractions of the working class premised their organizational strategies on capitalism's own momentum (e.g., the superior capacity of industrial working-class fractions over the craft fractions, and the superior capacity of Third World liberation movements over labor movements in advanced capitalist countries), the working-class movement, as a global phenomenon, advanced. Likewise, it is today imperative that organizers recognize that the creation of a new political economic sector—the public sector—creates new opportunities for organizing. The key to that logic lies largely in the nature of the working-class fraction that is being brought into being by capitalism's own logic of crisis resolution.

THE STRATEGIC IMPORTANCE OF THE PUBLIC SECTOR WORK FORCE

For reasons of size alone, public sector workers—over 90 percent of whom work for state and local governments—must be considered important. At present, these workers total approximately 18 percent of the U.S. labor force, and, based on the analysis of future economic restructuring and already observable long-term trends, their numbers are bound to grow. Between 1940 and 1980 the percentage of the work force in the public sector rose from 8 to 18 percent. While that increase appears at first glance to be spread fairly evenly over the period, a comparative analysis shows that it grows fastest during times of economic recession and fastest in occupations mostly closely associated with the state's accumulation functions (Hart-Landsberg, Lembcke, and Marotto 1981, 247; U.S. Department of Commerce, Bureau of the Census 1983).

The location of public sector workers in the political economy also argues for their importance to a working-class organizing strategy. Legitimation workers, such as teachers and social workers, remain essential to the continued reproduction of capitalist ideology. Yet, because of budgetary pressure and future "reindustrialization" priorities, they can expect little from the system but austerity. Meanwhile, the numbers of state and local government workers engaged in accumulation activities will grow in number and in importance.

The location of public sector workers is significant in yet another sense. Through work relations that link, for example, social service workers with the poor, aged, unemployed; health care workers with the sick; and teachers with students; public sector workers tie together, in a unique way, trade union and nontrade union constituencies and issues. This offers a natural basis for connecting economic to political issues and the trade union movement to the broader political movement.

Finally, the racial, sexual, and class composition of the public sector work force provides additional support for the position that organizing in the public sector deserves a high priority. In the largest urban areas almost twice as many blacks are employed in the public sector as in the private sector. The figures are not as dramatic in terms of female and Hispanic employment, since participation rates for both groups of workers in the public sector are now almost identical to those in the private sector. The heavy concentration of nonwhite workers and the substantial percentage of women workers in the state sector means that organizing efforts among state sector workers will be likely to confront racism and sexism directly.

The occupational composition of the public sector work force is also significant. Over half of state and local government employees are employed in service-maintenance, skilled crafts, clerical, or paraprofessional jobs, and if fire fighters and teachers (most of whom are in elementary and secondary schools) are added, we find that nearly two-thirds of this work force is proletarian. This is obviously important, since it encourages greater class consciousness and solidarity with other workers. In addition, because the public sector work force is comprised of a wide variety of occupational and trade union categories, public sector unions can, in local labor councils and state AFL-CIO organizations, help advance working-class unity on a broad level.

Control of Pension Funds

Public-employee pension funds, which serve as a mechanism of capital accumulation, give added weight to the political importance of public sector workers.

As Rifkin and Barber (1978, 10) point out,

Pension funds are a new form of wealth that has emerged over the past thirty years to become the largest single pool of private capital in the world. They are now worth over $500 billion and represent the deferred savings of millions and millions and millions of American workers. Pension funds at present own 20-25 percent of the equity in American corporations and hold

40 percent of the bonds. Pension funds are now the largest source of investment capital for the American capitalist system.

Approximately $78.4 billion in pension funds belong to state and local government retirement systems; 92 percent of these funds are invested in nongovernment (private) securities. Government workers are thus a major source of private investment capital and strategically positioned in the capital accumulation process to affect its political direction.

Until very recently, however, public-employee pension fund management has been carried out by professional and private investment institutions. As a consequence, public funds have been used to bankroll the expansion of private corporate enterprises, which in turn have wielded this economic leverage in their own interest, not the public's. Rifkin and Barber point to the flight of capital from the northeast as a case in point. Pension funds of public employees in northeastern cities have been invested in companies that have closed their operations in that region and opened new operations elsewhere, thereby eroding the economic base upon which the jobs of northeastern state and local workers are dependent.

To date, the exercise of pension-fund control by unions has been mainly of a protest or defensive nature. An offensive program entailing union control over pension-fund investment has yet to be developed. Rifkin and Barber suggest that social and political (as well as economic) criteria need to be applied to investment decisions. The social impact of an investment in low-cost housing, for example, may be more desirable in the long run than an investment in corporate stock that, while paying a higher immediate return, underwrites runaway shops.

The most significant aspect of the pension fund issue is, however, that capital's need for the pension funds of public sector workers as a source of equity for a reindustrialization strategy means that the processes of equity formation, heretofore privatized, are now becoming intertwined with the processes and institutions of popular democracy. The politicization of the accumulation process in this way represents a qualititative new development in the level of state intervention in the private economy.

The Left and the Public Sector

Heretofore the Left has generally dismissed public sector workers as part of a labor aristocracy that benefits directly from a welfare state built upon imperialism, or as a nonrevolutionary fraction of the "new working class." Instead, the Left has focused on private sector manual workers; national, racial, and sexual minorities; and lumpenproletarian fractions.

There is no doubt that these fractions of the working class are important for any strategy for transformation; it is also doubtful that revolutionary change is possible without the mobilization of public sector workers. Given their increasing involvement in accumulation and their continuing importance for legitimation (e.g., the capacity of public sector workers such as teachers to influence the political consciousness of the working class in general), it appears that the Left can no longer ignore 12 million state and local workers.

The Left's greatest day in unionism was the 1930s. Excluded from the union movement until 1935 by a combination of its own dual unionist strategies and political repression (see Chapters 2, 3, and 5), the Left reentered the movement on the crest of its own wave of organizing in the late 1930s. The CIO broke into new industrial areas. Organizing, which the Left did better than anyone, was the order of the day; leadership was earned, not bought. The Left in the 1930s did not gain control of existing unions or wrest leadership from the reactionary AFL leaders; it built its own unions as part of the CIO drive in the new industrial sector and consequently found itself organically linked with these unions.

The public sector offers special opportunities for "organizing the unorganized" and "unionizing the associationized." In 1970 only 26 percent of state and local workers were "organized" but only 9 percent were in unions. The remainder were in "associations." In 1974 there were 1,492,000 (out of 11,754,000) state and local workers in AFL-CIO unions across the country, or 12.7 percent of the total.

Public employees, as did the noncraft industrial workers in the 1930s, threaten the labor establishment. If 12 million state workers are to enter the "house of labor," Lane Kirkland and the building trades unions want them under their wing or not at all. Consequently, a new bureaucratic structure is developing. Each level of the AFL-CIO—international, state, and local labor councils—will have new structures to accommodate public employee unions. New structures mean new, unfilled positions open to the Left.

In addition, each new union organized creates new positions in the union structure: local officers, and delegates to AFL-CIO central labor councils and state and national conventions. Positions within these unions are likely to be filled by people who have proven their mettle in organizing; in unions organized by the Left, they will be filled with leftists.

Fortunately, the ability to forge militant and progressive unions is greatly advanced by the fact that historical forces have concentrated much of the Left in the public sector. The Cold War drove the Left from the industrial union movement during the 1950s. During the 1960s and much of the 1970s left-wing politics survived on college campuses. The New Left movement primarily energized people who were headed for academic, paraprofessional, or other jobs found most often in the state sector. While some New Left organizing strategies have taken people into private industry and some communist groups still have strong roots in basic industries, most radicals of 1960s' vintage are in, or on the fringe of, the public sector. Organizing unions where they are and using these unions as vehicles to legitimately enter the labor movement is a most expedient way to accomplish links with other segments of the working class. In this manner, the same dialectical process that linked the communist organizers driven out of the unions during the 1920s with the unorganized industrial workers during the 1930s is repeated.

The Strategical Significance of Organizational Forms

No less than in the 1930s, key questions facing the left wing of the labor movement include not only who, when, and how to organize, but also who controls the decision-making process that decides the answers to those questions, and how that control is exercised. No less than in the previous period, the answers to those questions are largely determined by organizational realities. In other words, the struggles over organizational forms such as have been described in this book will largely determine the answer to the more practical questions.

Throughout the book I have alluded to the continuing significance of organizational structures that bear on determination of strategies for organizing. Power at the top levels of the AFL-CIO, representation in decision making is on a per-capita basis. Convention roll call votes are on a straight per-capita basis—one vote for every dues-paying member. Votes on the general board, the governing body between conventions, are taken the same way. This structure has ensured the building trades' domination of the federation since its formation (AFL-CIO 1985, 18, 31). In face of capital's hyper-mobility during the 1970s and 1980s, the AFL-CIO's structure has skewed priorities toward the oldest and richest union bodies, while the needs of workers in the

South and the inter-mountain states, nonwhite and immigrant workers, and public sector workers have been inadequately addressed.

The legacy of organizational imbalance can be observed within specific unions as well. The concentration of the UAW's power in the Detroit region (Chapter 3) is undoubtedly related to the current leadership's pursuit of collaborationist tactics to keep pace with an industry that has largely left Detroit. It is important to recognize, moreover, that struggles over organizational forms continue and their resolution becomes the groundwork for future struggles, just as the struggles in the UAW during the 1940s continue to shape our present.

One such example occurred recently within the Oregon Federation of Teachers (OFT), an affiliate of the American Federation of Teachers (AFT).[2] In 1976 the OFT was a small organization struggling to survive in face of competition from the state affiliate of the National Education Association. In the spring of that year 700 teaching and research assistants at the University of Oregon formed an AFT local (the Graduate Teaching Fellows Federation, or GTFF) and won a collective bargaining election. The victory was a huge shot in the arm for OFT fortunes. Besides the additional revenue that the new local brought into the organization, the GTFF became the source of progressive leadership with a high level of energy for organizing. Within a few years the OFT Executive Council had several GTFFs and former GTFFs on it.

The graduate students who organized the GTFF in 1976 had chosen to affiliate with the OFT (rather than AFSCME or other unions) primarily because of its representation structure. The OFT Executive Council was composed of officers representing occupational areas within education. There were officers for K-12 teachers, college and university faculty, classified workers, community college faculty, and so on. If a local did not have one of its members on the council by virtue of the occupational representation system, it could elect its own representative. Thus, each local had a representative on the council and no local had more than one representative. Most important, each council member had one vote, regardless of the size of his/her local or occupational constituency.

The latter point was key for the GTFF. At the time it affiliated it had about 25 members. It needed money to organize, it needed a certain amount of service in the form of advice on collective bargaining law and procedure, and yet, it needed to maintain its autonomy. The OFT structure gave the GTFF representation equal to the largest of the affiliates even though it was the smallest.

Following the GTFF 1977 election victory, its influence began to be felt within the OFT. Convention resolutions coming from the GTFF brought issues of foreign policy, national economic planning, and civil rights to the floor and GTFF members initiated a program for OFT internal education. Most important, the GTFF brought its own energy and visions for an organizing program into the OFT. It was disagreements about the priorities of the organizing program that led to major internal confrontations by the early 1980s.

The first confrontation of organizing strategy came in the spring of 1978. The GTFF leadership active within the OFT sought to put organizing energy into organizing the unorganized, low status, and least skilled educational workers first. Among these were other teaching and research assistants at Oregon State University and Portland State University (PSU), part-time faculty at PSU, and paraprofessional workers in the Portland public schools. This strategy was in keeping with the theory that these workers with the greatest *need* were also most likely to bring additional progressive politics and energy into the organization. But it was also a strategy that ran counter to a major political trend and organizing program of the Shanker administration of the AFT.

Shanker's organizing priorities in the late 1970s consisted of raiding the locals of the National Educational Association and of the Nurses Association. Shanker loyalists within the OFT opposed GTFF strategies with AFT ones and invoked the authority of the national leadership to support their arguments. The issue of nurses was most central. The large Kaiser health facilities in the Portland area were a target of AFT's national leadership. AFT was prepared to put money and organizers into the campaign to raid the nurses, with most of the organizers being former Nurses Association staff people.

In strategical terms, the campaign for the nurses ran counter to the GTFF plan in several ways: It would bring a large number of high-status, professional-type workers with conservative leanings into the OFT; it would create an organizational seam between educational workers and health care workers, between workers in the public sector and those in the private sector; it would bring staff workers with a strongly bureaucratized history into a democratic organization; and it would be an open invitation to the influence of the reactionary Shanker administration.

As long as debate over organizing priorities was conducted at the council level, the GTFF and other progressive forces were able to stem the tide. But as a tactical maneuver, the conservative forces took the issue to the annual convention, which was a somewhat more complex political setting.

At the spring convention in 1978 the resolution to raid the nurses produced a tie vote and the OFT president broke the tie in favor of the raiding program. Within days all the OFT's organizational resources went into the nurses project. The other organizing efforts were abandoned. A year later OFT won a representation election for the nurses.

By 1981 the conservativism of the nurses had manifested itself in strong opposition to progressive forces within the OFT. That opposition took the form of constitutional changes that revised the representation structure at the executive council level. Led by the nurses, a proposal was made to abolish representation by constituency and by local. Instead, council members would be elected in convention on an at-large basis. Although the one person, one vote system on the council was retained for the time being, the at-large elections made it possible for the largest and most conservative bloc, the nurses, to dominate the selection of the entire council.

The stated rationale for the change was that the nurses wanted a more professional, service-oriented union. They wanted an end to the political resolutions that had become a hallmark of OFT conventions and they were tired of the internal education programs. Servicing the existing locals, not organizing the unorganized, was to be the new priority. The old form of the council was said to be too large and unwieldy; a smaller, task-oriented council would provide more efficient service. With that change made, the conservative future of the OFT was virtually assured.

Most of the features of the struggles described in detail in Chapters 2 and 3 were present in the OFT struggle. Most important, the association between class (or class fractions) and organizational preferences is consistent with those found in the CIO cases. The logic or rationale for those preferences is also similar. The union organization became the bridge linking a previous era of organization (i.e., the private sector nurses who, as professionals, had traditionally been "associationized" but not unionized) and the newer, higher level of organizational development in the public sector. Whether the more recently formed and more progressive fractions of the public sector would be dominant within the union or the least advanced fraction—the nurses—would dominate was essentially a question of organizational form. Finally, the consequences of the changes in terms of future organizing priorities follows the pattern of past experience.

The OFT case is but one example of the type of struggles, parallel to those described in greater detail in previous chapters, that continue to go on in union organizations. On the surface they appear to be fairly technical issues concerning organizational formalities. But they are driven by class forces that need to be recognized. In turn, organizational forms become part of parameters within which future struggles take place.

SUMMARY

The theme reiterated throughout this book has been that the working-class capacity is enhanced by the process of proletarianization endemic to capitalism. Proletarianization has several stages. The initial separation of labor from capital occurs during the stage of competitive capitalism, the homogenization of labor occurs during the stage of monopoly capitalism, and the internationalization of labor takes place during the imperialist stage. The boundaries between the successive stages of capitalist development and phases of class formation are formed by crises; each crisis is solved by restructuring the political economy.

There are certain constants running throughout the history of development and class formation in the United States. One of those is the increasing homogeneity of the working class. Most recent working-class history has emphasized the segmentation and fragmentation, in skill and cultural terms, of the U.S. working class. But class formation is a dialectical process. Division at one point in history is the precondition for a greater level of unity at a later point. As long as workers of different nations remained separated by distance, their potential for unity was low and their potential for exploitation by capital was high. As colonialism and imperialism dissolved the spatial boundaries and brought workers of different races and cultures together, the appearance was one of greater competition within the class, greater division, and so on. In fact, the ground was thereby laid for greater unity. To paraphrase Engels on the effects of capitalist centralization during the nineteenth century, the conditions of exploitation that lay chronic at the earlier stage are made acute by the development process, which also brings into existence the means of curing the illness, that is, the empowerment of the working class.

A second constant is the increasing role of the state. Progressing from a laissez-faire role during the early stages to a mainly repressive role during the competitive stage, a regulatory role during the monopoly stage, and a militarist role during the imperialist stage, the state now emerges as an economic actor in a full sense. Each stage of the process has increasingly politicized the terms of the class struggle.

Most historical and sociological accounts of the capitalist state have emphasized the negative: The power of the state has been used by the capitalist class to smash strikes and coopt social movements. These accounts generally have only examined the role of the state in the affairs of the private sector while ignoring the contradictions accruing within the state or public sector itself. Those contradictions are manifested in the formation of a public sector work force as described above.

The strategical implications of this analysis is that each sectoral stage in the development process has brought into being a work force that, for structural reasons, is qualitatively different and superior in terms of its capacity as an agent of social transformation. In other words, the structural location of job positions in the most advanced sector constitute the cutting edge of the historical process. Social movements historically have proven to be progressive when they have based themselves on the population occupying those advanced job positions.

It is unfortunately the case that petty bourgeois conceptualizations of class capacities found in the "work process" literature (see Chapter 1) have continued to dominate the radical thinking on working-class capacities. The analyses flowing out of that literature speak to developments that were central to the transition from competitive to monopoly capitalism, but they are tangential, at best, to the organizational needs of the working class in late 20th-century United States. As a result, much of this work simply has been largely ignored, leaving practical organizational developments (e.g., unions) to be influenced by bourgeois theory, thinking they can fight capital with capital, pursue bigger treasuries, purchase professional expertise, and seek high-tech solutions for their problems. Where New Left-vintage theory has had an effect, it has resulted in a kind of "yuppification" of union strategies that feature high-tech (and highly-paid) media consultants trying to give the labor movement a new look.

This last chapter has argued that the public sector is the latest sectoral advance in the U.S. political economy. Thus it is this sector that imparts to the jobholders a greater class capacity than do job positions in the private economy—either in the monopoly or competitive sectors. The chief reason for this is that public sector jobs make a break with market logic. Because the determination of work life in the public sector is overtly political and not mystified by market logic, workers in the public sector are more likely than their private sector counterparts to see the unity of political and economic realities and thus to become politicized. It is thus no accident that public sector unionists emerged as the most progressive elements in labor councils and the labor movement in general during the 1970s.

Left strategies and tactics for coming decades must be premised on the dialectical qualities of capitalism's own crisis solutions—in this case, the motion created by the reindustrialization process. That strategy must simultaneously solve basic needs for massive numbers of suffering people, yet advance the capacities of the working class to struggle for socialism. The public sector strategy advanced in the last section of this chapter recognizes that social ownership of productive capital is a prerequisite to economic planning and further advances in social and political democracy.

NOTES

1. The public sector analysis presented here is more fully developed in Lembcke and Hart-Landsberg (1985); Landsberg, Lembcke, and Marotto (1981); and Landsberg, Lembcke, and Marotto (1978).

2. During the mid- to late 1970s I was an executive board member of the Oregon Federation of Teachers (OFT). While I consulted Martin Hart-Landsberg and Jeff Edmundsen, both of whom were OFT activists at the time, I have mainly relied on my own recollections for some details of the following account.

Appendix

Supplement No. 2

October 8, 1947

<u>Copy</u>

Mr. Jack Greenall
International Trustee, IWA
503 Holden Building
Vancouver, B.C.

Dear Sir and Brother:

In compliance with the decision reached by the delegates at the Eleventh Annual Convention of the International Woodworkers of America held in St. Louis, Missouri; which decision was that the IWA would comply with that section of the Taft-Hartley Law dealing with the use of the NLRB. The four present International Officers have filed the necessary affidavits and material designated under this section of the Taft-Hartley Law.

However, we have been informed by the NLRB that in accordance with our International Constitution, Article 3, Section 1 which states: "Section 1: The named officers of the Union shall be an International President, an International First Vice President, an International Second Vice President, and International Secretary-Treasurer and three Trustees who shall be nominated at the Convention and elected by referendum vote of the membership..."; that it will therefore be necessary for the three Trustees to file from 1081 inasmuch as they are named officers of the International Union in the International Convention.

You will find enclosed one of the NLRB forms 1081 which I am requesting you to sign before a notary public and immediately return to the International Office so that we may complete the instructions of the delegates of the Convention. The NLRB has extended the time in which to file the necessary forms to October 31, 1947.

It is necessary that we have these forms properly signed by you as soon as possible because your delay beyond October 31, 1947 would cause the NLRB to dismiss 75 petitions for election and 18 Unfair Labor Practices charges now pending before the Board.

I hereby feel obligated to formally request you to comply with decision of the delegates at the Eleventh Annual Convention or to tender your resignation immediately so as to make it possible for the compliance to the wishes of the membership as expressed in Convention.

Fraternally yours,

William Botkin
International Vice President

2305 - Trinity Street
Vancouver, B.C.
October 20, 1947

James Fadling, President
International Woodworkers of America, CIO
314 S.W. 9th Avenue
Portland 5, Oregon

Dear Sir and Brother:

Please excuse the delay in replying to Brother Botkin's letter wherein I am asked to choose between signing a document prepared by the United States Government, or renouncing my right as a Canadian to hold office in the I.W. of A.

The principle involved is very simple and boils down to the fact that a government to which I owe no allegiance, in a country where I haven't a vote, has no right to tell me or any other Canadian what political principles must be endorsed or rejected. When an international union of workers allows itself to be used as an instrument for such a purpose, then one of the basic principles on which unions are termed has been violated.

On the other hand, for me to resign would be to betray, in my opinion, the majority of workers in the IWA who voted confidence in me to years ago.

It is difficult for me to understand the line of reasoning that permitted yourself and the others responsible to lead the IWA into the pr4esent position. It should be obvious that once labor begins capitulating to reaction, that new and greater concessions will be demanded. The first capitulation weakens the structure and the road backward is graded up as the gains of reaction are consolidated.

Frankly, I wouldn't care to be in your shoes at the present moment and feel myself responsible for the steps already taken and the steps you will now be forced to take in a frantic effort to avoid disintegration of the IWA. Even a moron can see that the gains you hope to make as a result of capitulating to the N.L.R.B. will be more than off set by weakened morale within the union.

You have my sympathy in your predicament, Brother Fadling, but not my endorsation.

Fraternally yours,
/s/ Jack Greenall
Jack Greenall,
International Trustee
IWA-CIO

cc: B.C. Lumber Worker

Supplement No. 8

WIRES

NITE WIRE   OCTOBER 22, 1947
ROBERT N DENHAM, GENERAL COUNSEL
NATIONAL LABOR RELATIONS BOARD
815 CONNECTICUT AVENUE NW
WASHINGTON 25 D.C.

REURLET DATED OCTOBER 17, 1947, IN THE MATTER OF TRUSTEES OF
INTERNATIONAL WOODWORKERS OF AMERICA SIGNING AFFIDAVITS IN
COMPLIANCE SECTION 9(H) LABOR MANAGEMENT RELATIONS ACT, TWO
TRUSTEES HAVE SIGNED AFFIDAVITS. THIRD TRUSTEE IS CANADIAN
CITIZEN RESIDING IN VANCOUVER B.C. HE IS PROTESTING SIGNING
AFFIDAVIT AS A CANADIAN CITIZEN NOT UNDER AUTHORITY OF UNITED
STATES LAWS. INTERNATIONAL OFFICERS LIKEWISE PROTEST THIS
TRUSTEE SIGNING AFFIDAVIT. YOUR INTERPRETATION Regarding THIS
MATTER DESIRED IMMEDIATELY. PLEASE ADVISE BY WIRE.

                           J.E. FADLING, INTERNATIONAL PRESIDENT
                           INTERNATIONAL WOODWORKERS OF AMERICA
                           314 SW NINTH AVENUE PORTLAND, OREGON

                    * * * * * * * * *

GOVT PD PORTLAND ORG 23   12 P

JE FADLING   INTL PRES
INTERNATIONAL WOODWORKERS OF AMERICA

REURTEL CANADIAN CITIZEN SERVING AS TRUSTEE IS REQUIRED TO SIGN
AFFIDAVIT IN ORDER TO COMPLETE COMPLIANCE WITH SECTION 9/H/
LABOR MANAGEMENT RELATIONS ACT. THIS INTERPRETATION IS BASED ON
THE FACT THAT TRUSTEE IS AN OFFICER OF THE INTERNATIONAL AND THE
LAW REQUIRES ALL OFFICERS TO COMPLY. CANADIAN CITIZENSHIP DOES
NOT ELIMINATE HIM FROM COMPLIANCE WITH LAW APPLICABLE TO YOUR
INTERNATIONAL.

                           ROBERT N DENHAM   GEN COUN
                           NATIONAL LABOR RELATIONS BOARD WASHDC

October 25, 1947

<u>Copy</u>

Mr. Jack Greenall
International Trustee, IWA
403 Holden Building
Vancouver, B.C.

Dear Sir and Brother:

I have received your communication dated October 20, 1947, which was in reply to a communication dated October 8, addressed to you by Vice President Botkin, as acting President during my absence.

In your communication you refuse to abide by the decision of the majority of the delegates at the Eleventh International Convention held in St. Louis, Missouri, in regard to compliance with the Taft-Hartley Law in connection with the use of the National Labor Relations Board.

You likewise refuse to resign as International Trustee so that the International Officers may comply in line with the instructions of the International Convention.

Since receiving your letter. I have addressed a telegram to Attorney Denham of the National Labor Relations Board requesting an interpretation as to whether or not you must comply as a Canadian citizen. I likewise protested the forcing of you, as a Canadian citizen, to sign the affidavits.

I have received a reply from Attorney Denham in which his decision is that all International officers named in the International constitution must sign the necessary documents. These telegrams are a matter of record in the International Office.

I sincerely regret that your decision of refusing to sign the necessary affidavits and of refusing to resign so that the instructions of the Convention may be carried out, makes it necessary for me to take definite action in line with my duties as prescribed in the International Constitution. I quote from Article III, Section 12, as follows:

Jack Greenall   -2-   October 25, 1947

"The International President shall devote all his time to the affairs of the Union <u>executing the instructions of the convention</u> and of the Board and exercising general supervision over the field and office work of the Union."

Whereas, the International Convention has instructed me, as International President, to see that compliance is made with the Taft-Hartley Law, in order that the facilities of the National Labor Relations Board will be available to the membership of the IWA, and

Whereas, you have refused to comply with the instructions of the Convention, using your office as trustee to obstruct the carrying out of the mandates of the International Convention,

Therefore, because of the time limit of compliance, which is October 31, 1947, at which time all the IWA cases before the NLRB may be dismissed, and by the authority as granted me in the above-quoted section of the International Constitution, I do hereby declare you suspended from office as International Trustee.

You will be notified of the next International Executive Board meeting in ample time so that you may appeal to the Executive Board if you so desire.

Sincerely and fraternally yours,

J.E. Fadling
International President

References

Abella, Irving. 1973. *Nationalism, Communism, and Canadian Labor*. Toronto: Univ. of Toronto Press.

AFL-CIO. 1985. Constitution of the American Federation of Labor and Congress of Industrial Organizations. Washington, DC: AFL-CIO.

Allen, V. L. 1954. *Power in Trade Unions*. New York: Longmans, Green.

Amalgamated Clothing Workers Union (ACWU). 1940. Constitution. New York: Amalgamated Clothing Workers of America.

Aminzade, Ronald. 1984. "Capitalist Industrialization and Patterns of Industrial Protest." *American Sociological Review*, 49, 4 (August).

Aronowitz, Stanley. 1973. *False Promises*. New York: McGraw Hill.

————. 1983. *Working Class Hero*. New York: Pilgrim.

Benenson, Harold. 1985. "The Community and Family Bases of U.S. Working Class Protest, 1880-1920: A Critique of the 'Skill Degradation' and 'Ecological' Perspectives." In Louis Kriesberg, ed. *Research in Social Movement, Conflicts and Change*. Greenwich, CT: JAI.

Bergren, Myrtle. 1966. *Tough Timber*. Toronto: Progress.

Bernstein, Irving. 1970. *Turbulent Years*. Boston: Houghton Mifflin.

Blee, K, and Al Gedicks. 1980. "The Emergence of Socialist Political Culture among Finnish Immigrants in Minnesota Mining Communities." In Maurice Zeitlin, ed. *Classes, Class Conflict and the State*. Cambridge, MA: Winthrop.

Braverman, Harry. 1974. *Labor and Monopoly Capital*. New York: Monthly Review Press.

Bridges, Amy. 1986. "Becoming American: The Working Classes in the United States before the Civil War." In Ira Katznelson and A. Zolberg, eds. *Working-class Formation: Nineteenth-century Patterns in Western Europe and the United States*. Princeton: Princeton Univ. Press.

Brody, David. 1960. *Steelworkers in America: The Non-union Era*. New York: Harper & Row.

————. 1975. "Radical Labor History and Rank-and-File Militancy." *Labor History* (winter).

Business Week. 1980. "The Reindustrialization of America," (June 30).

————. (1981). "State and Local Governments in Trouble." Special Issue (October 26).

————. (1983). "Industrial Policy: Is It the Answer?" (July 4).

Cary, Lorin Lee. 1968. "Adolph Germer: From Labor Agitator to Labor Professional." Ph.D. dissertation, Univ. of Wisconsin.

Chamber of Commerce of the United States. 1947. *Communists within the Labor Movement*. Washington, DC: U.S. Chamber of Commerce.

Chandler, A. 1962. *Strategy and Structure: Chapters in the History of the Industrial Enterprise*. Cambridge, MA: MIT Press.

Child, John. 1972. "Organizational Structure, Environment and Performance: The Role of Strategic Choice." *Sociology* 6.

Christie, Robert. 1956. *Empire in Wood*. Ithaca, NY: New York State School of Industrial and Labor Relations.

Cornfield, Daniel B. 1986. "Declining Union Membership in the Post-World War II Era: The United Furniture Workers of America, 1939-82." *American Journal of Sociology* 91, 5: 1112-53.

Cox, Thomas. 1974. *Mills and Markets: A History of the Pacific Coast Lumber Industry to 1900*. Seattle: Univ. of Washington Press.

Crispo, John. 1967. *International Unionism: A Study in Canadian-American Relations*. Toronto: McGraw Hill.

Davis, Mike. 1980. "Why the U.S. Working Class is Different." *New Left Review* 123 (Sept.-Oct.):3-44.

de Janvry, Alain. 1981. *The Agrarian Question and Reformism in Latin America*. Baltimore: Johns Hopkins Univ. Press.

"Dick." 1941. Letter to Adolph Germer, March 15. Adolph Germer papers, State Historical Society, Madison, Wisconsin.

Dubofsky, Melvyn. 1966. "The Origins of Working Class Radicalism, 1890-1905." *Labor History* (spring).

———. 1969. *We Shall Be All*. New York: Quadrangle.

Dubofsky, Melvyn, and Warren Van Tine. 1977. *John L. Lewis*. New York; Quadrangle.

Dunn, Marvin. 1977. "Kinship and Class: A Study of the Weyerhaeuser Family." Ph.D. dissertation, Univ. of Oregon.

Edel, Candace K., et al. 1978. "Uneven Regional Development." *Review of Radical Political Economics* 10, 3:1-14.

Edelstein, J. David, and Malcolm Warner. 1976. *Comparative Union Democracy*. New York: John Wiley.

Edwards, Richard. 1978. *Contested Terrain: The Transformation of the American Workplace*. New York: Basic Books.

Ehrenreich, John, and B. Ehrenreich. 1976. "Work and Consciousness." *Monthly Review* (July-August).

Elster, Jon. 1985. *Making Sense of Marx*. Cambridge: Cambridge University Press.

Engels, Frederick. 1975. *The Condition of the Working Class in England*. Collected Works of Marx and Engels IV. New York: International Publishers.

Faunce, William. 1967. "Size of Locals and Union Democracy." In William Faunce, ed. *Readings in Industrial Sociology*. New York: Appleton-Century-Crofts.

Foner, Philip. 1975. *History of the Labor Movement in the United States*, Vol. 2. New York: International.

Foster, William Z. 1947. *American Trade Unionism*. New York: International.

Friedman, Samuel. 1982. *Teamster Rank and File: Power, Bureaucracy, and Rebellion at Work and in a Union*. New York: Columbia Univ. Press.

Galenson, Walter. 1960. *The CIO Challenge to the AFL*. Cambridge, MA: Harvard Univ. Press.

———. 1981. *The International Labor Organization: An American View*. Madison, WI: Univ. of Wisconsin Press.

Gedicks, Al. 1976. "The Social Origins of Radicalism among Finnish Immigrants in Midwest Mining Communities." *Review of Radical Political Economics* 8, 3 (fall).

Germer, Adolph. 1940. Office memo, August 9. Adolph Germer papers, State Historical Society, Madison, Wisconsin.

———. 1941a. Letter to Allan Haywood, April 1. Adolph Germer papers, State Historical Society, Madison, Wisconsin.

———. 1941b. Letter to Allan Haywood, April 10. Adolph Germer papers, State Historical Society, Madison, Wisconsin.

———. 1941c. Diary, October 8, 1941. Adolph Germer papers.

Geschwender, James. 1977. *Class, Race & Worker Insurgency: The League of Revolutionary Black Workers*. New York: Cambridge Univ. Press.

Gordon, David, R. Edwards, and M. Reich. 1982. *Segmented Work, Divided Workers*. Cambridge: Cambridge Univ. Press.

Gorz, André. 1982. *Farewell to the Working Class*. Boston: South End.

Greer, Edward. 1979. *Big Steel*. New York: Monthly Review Press.

Griffin, Larry, M. Wallace, and B. Rubin. 1986. "Capitalist Resistance to the Organization of Labor Before the New Deal: Why? How? Success?" *American Sociological Review* (April).

Hamilton, Richard F. 1972. *Class and Politics in The United States*. New York: John Wiley.

Hart-Landsberg, M., J. Lembcke, and B. Marotto. 1981. "Public Sector Workers and the Crisis of Capitalism." In URPE editors, *Crisis in the Public Sector*. New York: Monthly Review Press.

———. 1984. "Class Struggle and Economic Transformation." *Review of Radical Political Economics* 16, 4 (winter).

Horowitz, Gad. 1968. *Canadian Labour in Politics*. Toronto: Univ. of Toronto Press.

Howe, Carolyn. 1985. "The 'Americanization' of Women vs. the Finnish Family: A Struggle for Cultural Hegemony." Paper delivered at the annual meeting of the Society for the Study of Social Problems, Washington, DC.

Howe, Irving, and B. J. Widick. 1949. *The UAW and Walter Reuther*. New York: Random House.

International Ladies Garment Workers Union (ILGWU). 1937. Constitution. New York.

International Longshoremen's and Warehousemen's Union (ILWU). 1941. Constitution. San Francisco.

International Union of Electrical Workers (IUE). 1949. Proceedings of Annual Convention.
_____. 1955. Proceedings of Annual Convention.
International Woodworkers of America (IWA). 1940. Proceedings of the Fourth Annual Convention. Portland.
_____. 1941. Proceedings of the Fifth Annual Convention. Portland.
_____. 1947a. Proceedings of the Tenth Annual Constitutional Convention. Portland.
_____. 1947b. International Executive Board Minutes, July 22-23.
_____. 1947c. Proceedings of the Eleventh Constitutional Convention, St. Louis.
_____. 1947d. *B.C. Lumber Worker*, September 22.
_____. 1948. International Executive Board Proceedings, March 9-10.
_____. 1958. Proceedings of the Special Convention, March 24-28. Portland.
Jensen, Vernon. 1945. *Lumber and Labor*. New York: Farrar & Rinehart.
_____. 1950. *Heritage of Conflict: Labor Relations in the Non-ferrous Metal Industry up to 1930*. Ithaca, NY: Cornell Univ. Press.
_____. 1954. *Nonferrous Metals Industry Unionism, 1932-1954: A Story of Leadership Controversy*. Ithaca, NY: Cornell Univ. Press.
Kampelman, Max. 1957. *The Communist Party vs. the CIO: A Study in Power Politics*. New York: Praeger.
Keeran, Roger. 1980. *The Communist Party and the Auto Workers Unions*. Bloomington, IN: Indiana Univ. Press.
Kerr, Clark, and Abraham Siegel. 1954. "The Interindustry Propensity to Strike —An International Comparison." In A. W. Kornhauser, R. Dubin, and A. M. Ross, eds. *Industrial Conflict*. New York: Arno.
Kuczyniski, Jurgen. 1967. *The Rise of the Working Class*. New York: World Univ. Library.
Landsberg, Martin J. Lembcke, and B. Marotto. 1978. "Public Employees: Digging Graves for the System?" In URPE editors, *U.S. Capitalism in Crisis*. New York: Union of Radical Political Economics.
Laxer, Robert. 1976. *Canada's Unions*. Toronto: James Lorimer.
Leab, Daniel. 1967. "United We Eat: The Creation and Organization of Unemployed Councils in 1930." *Labor History* (fall).
Lembcke, Jerry. 1978. "International Woodworkers of America: A Comparative Study of Two Regions." Ph.D. dissertation, Univ. of Oregon.
_____. 1980. "The International Woodworkers of America in British Columbia." *Labour/La Travailleur* (fall).
_____. 1984a. "Uneven Development, Class Formation, and Industrial Unionism in the Wood Products Industry." In M. Zeitlin, ed. *Political Power and Social Theory*. Vol. 4. Greenwich, CT: JAI.
_____. 1984b. "Labor and Education: Portland Labor College, 1921-29." *Oregon Historical Quarterly* (summer).
_____. 1987. "Class and Class Capacities: A Problem of Organizational Efficacy." In Rhonda F. Levine and Jerry Lembcke, eds. *Recapturing Marxism: An Appraisal of Recent Trends in Sociological Theory*. New York: Praeger.

Lembcke, Jerry, and M. Hart-Landsberg. 1985. "Reindustrialization and the Logic of Class Politics in Late 20th Century America." *The Insurgent Sociologist* 13, 1-2 (summer-fall).

Lembcke, Jerry, and Carolyn Howe. 1986. "Organizational Structure and the Logic of Collective Action in Unions." In Scott McNall, *Current Perspectives in Social Theory*. Vol. 7. Greenwich, CT: JAI.

Lembcke, Jerry, and William Tattam. 1984. *One Union in Wood: A Political History of the International Woodworkers*. New York: International.

Levenstein, Harvey. 1981. *Communism, Anticommunism, and the CIO*. Westport, CT: Greenwood.

Levins, Richard, and R. Lewontin. 1985. *The Dialectical Biologist*. Cambridge, MA: Harvard Univ. Press.

Lichtenstein, Nelson. 1982. *Labor's War at Home: The CIO in World War II*. Cambridge Univ. Press.

Lindberg, John. 1930. *Background of Swedish Emigration in the United States*. Minneapolis: Univ. of Minnesota Press.

Lipset, S. M. 1952. "Democracy in Private Government." *The British Journal of Sociology* 3:47-63.

Lipset, S. M., M. A. Trow, and J. S. Coleman. 1956. *Union Democracy*. New York: Anchor.

Lockwood, David. 1975. "Sources in Variation in Working-class Images of Society." In Martin Blumer, ed. *Working-class Images of Society*. London: Routledge & Kegan Paul.

Lorwin, Lewis. 1929. *Labor and Internationalism*. New York: Macmillan.

Lowy, Michael. 1981. *The Politics of Combined and Uneven Development: The Theory of Permanent Revolution*. London: Verso.

Lozovsky, A. [1921] 1978. *Program of Action of the Red International of Labour Unions*. Montreal: Red Flag.

_____. 1935. *Marx and The Trade Unions*. New York: International.

Mandel, Ernest. 1978. *Late Capitalism*. London: Verso.

Marable, Manning. 1985. *Black American Politics*. London: Verso.

Marglin, Stephen. 1974. "What Do Bosses Do?" *Review of Radical Political Economy* 6, 3 (summer).

Marx, Karl. 1967. *Capital*, vol. 1. New York: International.

Marx, Karl, and F. Engels. 1972. *Selected Works in One Volume*. New York: International.

Matles, James, and J. Higgins. 1974. *Them and Us*. New York: Prentice-Hall.

Meiksins, Peter. 1987. "New Classes and Old Theories: The Impasse of Contemporary Class Analysis." In R. Levine and J. Lembcke, eds. *Recapturing Marxism: An Appraisal of Recent Trends in Sociological Theory*. New York: Praeger.

Michels, Robert. 1959. *Political Parties*. New York: Dover.

Mills, C. Wright. 1948. *The New Men of Power*. New York: Harcourt, Brace.

_____. 1959. *The Sociological Imagination*. New York: Oxford Univ. Press.

Mine, Mill and Smelter Workers, International Union of (Mine-Mill). 1933. Convention Proceedings, August 7-11. Butte, Montana.

_____. 1934. Convention Proceedings, August 6-11. Salt Lake City, UT.

_____. 1936. Convention Proceedings, August 3-11. Denver, CO.

_____. 1937. 3-11. Constitution. Butte, Mont.

_____. 1939a. Constitution. Butte, Montana.

_____. 1939b. "The CIO News: Mine-Mill Edition." November 6.

_____. 1939c. "The CIO News: Mine-Mill Edition." December 4.

_____. 1939d. "The CIO News: Mine-Mill Edition." October 16.

_____. 1940a. Convention Proceedings, August 5-10. Denver, CO.

_____. 1940b. "The CIO News: Mine-Mill Edition." January 22.

_____. 1940c. "The CIO News: Mine-Mill Edition." April 20.

_____. 1943. Convention Proceedings, September 13-18. Butte, Montana.

_____. 1948. *The Union* (a newspaper of the International Union of Mine, Mill, and Smelter Workers).

Morgan, Murray. 1955. *The Last Wilderness*. Seattle: Univ. of Washington Press.

Mortimer, Wyndam. 1971. *Organize*. Boston: Beacon.

National Maritime Union (NMU). 1947. Proceedings, Annual Convention.

National Unemployment Council of the United States. 1934. *Constitution and Regulations of the National Unemployment Councils of the U.S.A.* New York: Workers Library Publishers.

New York Times. 1984. "U.S. Experts Cite Unesco Benefits." December 28, section 6Y.

_____. 1985. "Free Trade and the Canadian Psyche." December 29, section 3E.

Noble, David. 1977. *America by Design: Science, Technology, and the Rise of Corporate Capitalism*. New York: Knopf.

Nyden, Philip. 1984. *Steelworkers Rank-and-File*. New York: Praeger.

Offe, Claus, and Helmut Wiesenthal. 1980. "Two Logics of Collective Action: Theoretical Notes on Social Class and Organizational Form." In M. Zeitlin, ed. *Political Power and Social Theory*, Vol. 1, pp. 67-115. Greenwich: JAI.

Olson, Mancur. 1980. *The Logic of Collective Action*. Cambridge: Harvard Univ. Press.

Party Organizer. 1931. "The Miners Strike." (May).

Perlman, Selig. 1947. *A Theory of the Labor Movement*. New York: A. M. Kelly.

Peter, J. 1934. "On Party Organization." *Party Organizer*.

_____. 1935. "The Organizational Structure of the Party." *Party Organizer*.

Phillips, Paul. 1967. *No Power Greater*. Vancouver: British Columbia Federation of Labour.

Pike, Robert. 1967. *Tall Trees, Tough Men*. New York: W. W. Norton.

Piven, Frances Fox, and Richard A. Cloward. 1977. *Poor People's Movements*. New York: Pantheon.

_____. 1982. *The New Class War*. New York: Pantheon.

Preis, Art. 1972. *Labor's Giant Step*. New York: Pathfinder.

Prickett, James. 1981. "Communist Conspiracy or Wage Dispute? The 1941 Strike at North American Aviation." *Pacific Historical Review* 50 (May): 215-33.

Radosh, Ronald. 1969. *American Labor and U.S. Foreign Policy*. New York: Random House.

Richmond, Al. 1972. *A Long View from the Left*. New York: Dell.

Rifkin, Jeremy, and R. Barber. 1978. *The North Will Rise Again*. Boston: Beacon.

Robinson, Reid. 1948. "Development of Deportation Conspiracy." Unpublished manuscript in author's possession.

Roemer, John. 1982. *A General Theory of Exploitation and Class*. Cambridge, MA: Harvard Univ. Press.

Roley, Ron. 1977. Interview with Jerry Lembcke.

Rosenzweig, Roy. 1975. "Radicals and the Jobless: The Musteites and the Unemployed Leagues, 1932-1936." *Labor History* 16 (Winter).

Schwantes, Carlos. 1979. *Radical Heritage: Labor, Socialism and Reform in Washington and British Columbia*. Seattle: Univ. of Washington Press.

Scott, Denny. 1973. "Technological Change in the British Columbia Forest Products Industry." In W. T. Stanbury and M. Thompson, eds. *People, Productivity and Technological Change*. Vancouver: Versatile Publications.

Scott, Jack. 1978. *Canadian Workers, American Unions*. Vancouver: New Star Books.

Seidman, Joel. 1953. *American Labor from Defense to Reconversion*. Chicago: Univ. of Chicago.

Sewell, William H. 1986. "Artisans, Factory Workers, and the Formation of the French Working Class, 1789-1848." In Ira Katznelson and A. Zolberg, eds. *Working Class Formation: Nineteenth Century Patterns in Western Europe and the United States*. Princeton: Princeton Univ. Press.

Smelser, Neil. 1976. *Comparative Methods in the Social Sciences*. Englewood Cliffs, NJ: Prentice Hall.

Smith, Neil. 1984. *Uneven Development*. New York: Basil Blackwell.

Sparks, N. 1935. "The Northwest General Lumber Strike." *The Communist* (September).

Spira, Henry. 1972. "The Unambiguity of Labor History." In Burton Hall, ed. *Autocracy and Insurgency in Organized Labor*. New Brunswick, NJ: Transaction Books.

Starobin, Joseph. 1975. *American Communism in Crisis*. Berkeley: Univ. of California Press.

Steelworkers (United Steelworkers of America). 1944. Constitution. Washington, DC: United Steelworkers of America.

Stephenson, Isaac. 1915. "Recollections of a Long Life, 1829-1915." Chicago: published by the author.

Stolberg, Benjamin. 1938. *The Story of the CIO*. New York: Viking.

Stone, Katherine. 1975. "The Origins of Job Structures in the Steel Industry." In Richard Edwards, M. Reich, and D. Gordon, eds. *Labor Market Segmentation*. Lexington, MA: Lexington Books.

Szymanski, Al. 1978. *The Capitalist State and the Politics of Class*. Cambridge, MA: Winthrop.

Tabb, William, and Larry Sawyers. 1978. *Marxism and the Metropolis.* New York: Oxford Univ. Press.

Therborn, Goran. 1983. "Why Some Classes Are More Successful Than Others." *New Left Review* 138 (March-April):37-55.

Todes, Charlotte. 1931. *Labor and Lumber.* New York: International.

Trotsky, Leon. 1959. *The Russian Revolution.* Garden City, NY: Anchor.

Trotter, Joe. 1985. *Black Milwaukee.* Urbana: Univ. of Illinois Press.

Tyler, Robert. 1967. *Rebels of the Woods: The IWW in the Pacific Northwest.* Eugene: Univ. of Oregon Press.

United Auto Workers of America, International Union of (UAW). 1935. Proceedings of the First Constitutional Convention. Detroit.

_____. 1937. Proceedings of the Third Annual Convention of the International Union United Auto Workers of America. Milwaukee.

_____. 1939. Proceedings of the Special Convention. Cleveland.

_____. 1940. Proceedings of the Fifth Annual Convention. Cleveland.

_____. 1941. Proceedings of the Sixth Annual Convention. Cleveland.

United Electrical, Radio and Machine Workers of America (UE). 1939a. Constitution. New York.

_____. 1939b. Proceedings of the Fifth Annual Convention. Springfield.

_____. 1944. Proceedings of Annual Convention.

_____. 1946. Proceedings of Annual Convention.

_____. 1948a. *UE Canadian News.* March 19.

_____. 1948b. *UE Canadian News.* August 12.

United Mine Workers of America (UMWA). 1938. Constitution. Washington, DC.

United States Congress. 1939. "Investigations of Un-American Propaganda Activities in the U.S." Hearings before the Special Committee on Un-American Activities, House of Representatives, 76th Congress, First Session.

United States Department of Commerce. 1940. Sixteenth Census of the United States. Mineral Industries 1939, Volume 1.

United States Department of Commerce, Bureau of the Census. 1977. Historical Statistics of the United States Colonial Times to 1970, Bicentennial Edition, September.

_____. 1983. 1980 Census of Population, General Social and Economic Characteristics, Part 1, United States Summary.

United States Department of the Interior, Census Office. 1890. Eleventh Census of the United States. Mineral Industries Census.

Valentine, Cynthia E. 1978. "Internal Union Democracy—Does it Help or Hinder the Movement for Industrial Democracy?" *The Insurgent Sociologist* (fall).

Wall Street Journal. 1984. "ITU Votes Teamster Merge" March 23, p. 5.

Wardell, Mark, and Robert Johnson. 1985. "Limitations to Collective Action." Paper presented at the annual meetings of the Midwest Sociological Society, St. Louis, April 1985.

Ware, Norman. 1937. *Labor in Canadian-American Relations.* Toronto: Ryerson Press.

Watkins, Alfred J. 1981. "Felix Rohatyn's Biggest Deal." *Working Papers*. (September-October):44-52.

Widman, Michael. 1940. Letter to Adolph Germer. Adolph Germer papers.

Wood, Ellen Meiksins. 1986. *The Retreat From Class.* London: Verso.

Wright, Eric. 1979. *Class Structure and Income Determination*. London: New Left Books.

———. 1985. *Classes*. London: Verso/New Left Books.

Zieger, Robert. 1983. *Rebuilding the Pulp and Paper Workers' Union, 1933-41*. Madison: Univ. of Wisconsin Press.

Index

About the Author

JERRY LEMBCKE is a member of the Department of Sociology at The College of Holy Cross, Worcester, Massachusetts. His earlier books include *One Union in Wood: A Political History of the International Woodworkers of America* (with William Tattam), *Recapturing Marxism: An Appraisal of Recent Trends in Sociological Theory* (with Rhonda Levine, Praeger Publishers, 1987), and *Race, Class, and Urban Social Change*.

DATE DUE

JAN 0 7 1992			